The Ultimate New Travel Guide

(20+ Years of New Zealand Travel Experience)
by Ron Laughlin

On the Road (Moke Lake – near Queenstown)

Mackenzie Country – South Island

ISBN-13:
978-1500194789

ISBN-10:
1500194786

My Personal Introduction to You

After my own personal discovery of New Zealand in 1989 when myself with good friend and photographer, Howard Sweet, spent six weeks in a camper van from Cape Reinga to Bluff I decided this was <u>the</u> place in the world I wished to settle. I had done quite a bit of travelling from my home port of the Florida Keys in search of the final place to enjoy my life. I would like to dedicate this book to Howard who has gone on to the final adventure.

The natural world of scenic wonders coupled with the closeness of the sea and the myriad of animal life was exactly what I loved. In addition the lack of people and the fabulous seafood, lamb and venison coupled with an unending supply of fresh fruits and vegetables made it pure nirvana for my lifestyle.

I spent over five years on my bus/home/office going down every road I could in discovery mode and visiting as many of the variety of places I could. I wrote and photographed for magazines. I was always in pursuit of the best in coffee (one of my many weaknesses) visiting as many cafes/restaurants as possible all over New Zealand not to mention the personal research of all the wine regions.

The most satisfying though, in effort, to me has been creating personal itineraries for hundreds of visitors to these shores. Providing my personal knowledge and insight from the years of local travel experience and dedication to discovery of everything to see and do in my adopted heaven on earth of New Zealand.

Thus I felt it necessary to convey this personal knowledge and insight to as many people as I can who are looking to visit New Zealand on a holiday so they will be able to know what they can see and do from an insider's understanding. One who has actually travelled the country on a purposeful agenda and wanting to share this knowledge with everyone.

I don't want you to come this far and miss anything that will make the adventure anything but spectacular.

Ron

website – www.ronlaughlin.net

Brunch at Marfell's Beach south of Blenheim

Haere Mai – a Maori welcome to you from New Zealand.

So let's introduce the natural world of New Zealand - a fabulous natural place to explore by the most ardent outdoor pursuit or the easy casual drive through fantastic vistas. New Zealand lies about 6500 miles south of San Francisco and about 1200 miles southeast of Sydney, Australia. The country consists of the North, South, Stewart, Antipodes Islands, Auckland Islands, Bounty Islands, Campbell Island, Chatham Islands, and Kermadec Islands.

Origins of the New Zealand Landscape –

550 million years in the creation of New Zealand. The country of New Zealand was the result of upheaval and collision along two of the earth's major tectonic plates – the Pacific and the Indian-Australia plate. It is a part o f a mass of continental crust. The area that is down the middle of the South Island where the Southern Alps have been thrust up is known as the Alpine Fault. In the south-west the Indian-Australian plate s being dragged along under the Pacific

plate. Rocks from Fiordland have slid over 500kms north to as far as Nelson. In the north-east the Pacific plate is being drawn under the Indian-Australian plate. Deep down in the crust under the country the rock material melts and in areas of New Zealand this rises to the surface. The Taupo volcanic zone from Mt Ruepehu to White Island is a good example. New Zealand is a part of the Pacific Ring of Fire.

The distribution of fossil plants and animals and detailed comparisons of rock show the country of New Zealand was once a part of the massive continent of Godwanaland that was made up Australia, Antarctica, India, Africa and South America. New Zealand is very young. New Zealand parted ways around 70 million years ago.

The scenery of Fiordland is the most dramatic where granite upheavals have been carved by natural forces such as glaciers and the remaining steep fiords have been drowned by the rising sea. The flat agricultural plains of Canterbury were created by intense glacial erosion and the extreme frost of the ice age.

When the first Polynesian settlers came to New Zealand around 1000 years ago there was no other human population and the only land mammals were small bats. There were a number of birds such as the giant flightless Moa. There still is a population the Tuatara a direct descendent of dinosaurs.

For a thousand years the early Polynesian settlers with the use of uncontrolled fire for clearing decimated the majority of the lowland forest. They completely destroyed the Moa population and seemingly many others. They also introduced the rat.

The arrival of Europeans took a heavy total on the environment with the introduction of pigs, goats and fowl by Capt James Cook. Near extinction of seals and whales can be attributed to the over hunting.

The arrival in the first part of the 19th century of early settlers brought a host of animals they required to hunt and fish for. With no natural predator and abundant natural food supply they exploded in numbers then the predators were introduced for their control.

The two main islands, North Island and South Island, extend about 1600kms/1000 miles along a diagonal fault line. The impressive alpine mountain chain of the Southern Alps extends 650kms/400miles along the western side of South Island from the Marlborough Sounds in the far north of the island clear through to the fiords in the far south. Its highest peak is Mount Cook, also known as Aoraki in the Maori language, at 12,349 ft (3,764 m). It is a land mostly shaped by volcanic action in the north and glaciers in the south. This natural world of lakes, streams and mountains dominates life in New Zealand and what draws visitors from all over the world.

The size of the country is only 268,680 square kilometres (104,000 sq miles approx – about the size of Colorado) but the scenery found in very short distances to one another represents almost every type of landscape found in the world. It is but a short distance (68 miles) to the sea anywhere you are with a coastline of 15,134kms (9,404 miles) more than the entire USA.

Don't take it for granted you can drive around and see the entire country in a few days. The extreme least you would want to do is two weeks but 4-6 weeks is more like it.

The South Island is of breath-taking beauty with vista after vista of nature's best from snow capped peaks to black beech forests plus the magical rain forests of the South Island West Coast. Great portions of much of this untamed land are uninhabited. There are over twenty mountains that reach over 3000metres (9843 feet) with many mountains rising, it seems, directly from the sea.

The landscape is dotted with volcanoes some still active. There are bubbling mud pools and geysers of steam. The many shorelines range from vast amounts of golden sand with others of grey volcanic sand or scenic rocky shorelines with crashing sea. The vegetation of New Zealand is striking with giant tree ferns that appear primeval like having stepped into Jurassic Park or in other areas high country desert. Vast forests of native black beech with some remaining giants of the forest, the Kauri. Most is called bush that is formed with heavy underbrush.

Much of the flora and fauna is unique and found in no other land. The New Zealand hardwood forests are left over from before the ice ages. 84% of New Zealand's flowering plants are found nowhere else.
Remember seasons are reversed in the Southern Hemisphere very important when you plan your visit. I will describe more in detail further along on the best times to visit.

The southerly winds from the Antarctic affects the trees a bit in the South

Here is a quick overview -

Location - New Zealand is southeast of Australia between latitudes 34 degrees south and 47 degrees south.
Area. New Zealand is 1600 kilometres north to south with an area of 268,680 sq km. It comprises two major islands: the North Island (115,000 sq km) and the South Island (151,000 sq km), separated by Cook Strait and a number of small islands. One third of New Zealand is protected park land and reserves.

Climate - New Zealand is a maritime climate meaning it has its weather governed by the surrounding sea. The weather conditions around New Zealand can cause real climatic volatility. I will add more later on this subject.
The South Island receives the brunt of the Antarctic chill making it great for winter activities plus the rains are here as noted by the rain forests but what magic waterfalls!
Major cities - Auckland and Wellington in the North Island are the largest cities with Christchurch and Dunedin in the South Island. Wellington is the nation's capital.
Queenstown in the South Island is known as the Adventure Capital of the World.

Population - New Zealand has a population of around 4.36 million, of whom 10 per cent are Maori. An influx of people from the Polynesian Islands and also many from Asia are diversifying the overall population. Every person you will meet in New Zealand is either an immigrant or a descendant of one.
Official languages: English, Maori.
80% of the population lives in cities.

Government - New Zealand is a constitutional monarchy with the Queen of England as head of state. The New Zealand Parliament is a unicameral body without an Upper House It is divided into 12 regions and 74 districts, both of which have elected councils, as well as several community boards and special-purpose bodies. It is considered an independent part of the Commonwealth of Nations. It has no formal written constitution and was formally declared a dominion in 1907.

Political conditions - Political parties: Labour, National, Progressive Party, New Zealand Green Party, New Zealand First, ACT, United Future New Zealand, Maori Party, and several smaller parties.
The traditionally conservative National Party and left-leaning Labour Party have dominated New Zealand political life since a Labour government came to power in 1935. The 2008 general election on November 8 was comfortably won by the John Key-led National Party. Voting is at 18.

Travel Requirements - You need a valid passport to visit New Zealand but may not need a visa. Check the section I have provided more information in.

Money - The monetary unit is the New Zealand dollar equal to 100 New Zealand cents. Currently the New Zealand dollar has a lower value than the US dollar but hovers around 80 US cents but note that the exchange rate fluctuates.

European exploration - Dutch explorer Abel van Tasman in 1642 sailed up the west coast of what he named Nieuw Zeeland, after the province of Zeeland in the Netherlands.

Cook's voyages - The number one explorer was without a doubt Captain James Cook. He sailed around New Zealand on three separate voyages, the first in 1769. Captain Cook named many of New Zealand places.

First inhabitants - New Zealand's first inhabitants 1000 years before Europeans are known as the Moa Hunters. Arriving around 800 AD were the Moriori. The Chatham Islands still have the remaining people with Moriori blood lines. Whatever there was no indigenous population prior to the arrival of Polynesians from islands to the north.

First settlers – After the Maori settlement from around the world came the settlers who were sealers and whalers then the usual missionaries followed. In the early 19th century an influx of early pioneers began coming in numbers with greater numbers arriving when gold was discovered in the Coromandel in 1852 by whalers. The real gold rush began in 1861 when Gabriel Read discovered gold in the Otago region.

Treaty of Waitangi - This treaty signed in 1840 ceded sovereignty over New Zealand to the Queen of England with the English colonists and the Maori chiefs signing. British heritage joins with Maori culture in this land of scenic wonders.

There is a constant battle with Maori asking for redress over land and rights claimed taken by incoming settlers to this day.

Culture - Cultural activities and café society are as good as anywhere in the world. Outside of venues that top entertainers in the world come to play. We also have our own world class musicians, singers, writers and painters and available in small venues easily accessed by the public.

Trade and investment - New Zealand's top six trading partners (total trade) as of November 2009 included Australia, the United States, the People's Republic of China, Japan, the United Kingdom, and the Republic of Korea.

New Zealand welcomes and encourages foreign investment without discrimination. The Overseas Investment Office (OIO) must give consent to foreign investments that would control 25% or more of businesses or property worth more than NZ $100 million. Restrictions and approval requirements also apply to certain investments in land and in the commercial fishing industry. Foreign buyers of land can be required to report periodically on their compliance with the terms of the government's consent to their purchase. The American Chamber of Commerce is active in New Zealand, with its main office in Auckland.

Other interesting information for the traveller –

Some important concepts:

- New Zealand gave women the right to vote in 1893, a quarter century before Britain or the US.
- It was the first sovereign state with free public health and minimum wage.
- New Zealand has been declared a nuclear free zone
- In 2004 same sex couples were given the right to marry
- Ranked the 2nd least corrupt country in the world.
- Doesn't have pollution, congestion, health issues and cramped city living as in so many places
- People are not judged on their gender or how they sound or what colour they are, how they vote, or where – or if – they go to church.
- 76% of New Zealanders (known as Kiwis) live on the North Island with 32% living in the Auckland region.
- 15% of New Zealand's energy comes from renewable sources
- There are no snakes in New Zealand
- Sheep farming and dairy farms are the major farming activities
- Tourism ranks right up there for economic returns and eco-tourism is high on the agenda
- Major oil reserves off the coast with wells mostly off the Taranaki coast
- The sport of rugby is king in New Zealand
- Fabulous sailors having won the America's Cup and always on top in any sailing world regattas

- New Zealand is one of the world's main exporters of wool, cheese, butter and meat and a large producer of kiwi fruit, apples and grapes.
- Maritime claims: continental shelf: 200 nm or to the edge of the continental margin
- Exclusive economic zone: 200 nm
  International disputes: territorial claim in Antarctica (Ross Dependency)
- Natural resources: natural gas, iron ore, sand, coal, timber, hydropower, gold, limestone
- Environmental current issues: deforestation; soil erosion; native flora and fauna hard-hit by species introduced from outside.
- Internet savvy - As of March 2008 New Zealand had 1,506,000 Internet subscribers, amounting to approximately 65% of New Zealand households, ranking above Australia, the U.K., and the U.S.

The people of New Zealand known as Kiwis

So what is a Kiwi? A flightless, nocturnal bird and a New Zealand Kiwiana icon – New Zealanders take their nickname from the little fellow! They are seldom seen in the wild coming out at night mostly not exactly like the people known as Kiwi.(but they do enjoy nightlife)

I have briefly written a few comments above but let's go a little further since I feel it is very important to know what kind of people live, work and play in New Zealand. What makes them tick?
From a personal basis I have found they have great honesty and integrity and are hard working down to earth folks with big hearts. As a visitor you are welcome to share their world as long as you treat it with respect as they do. They are very sports minded and spend a great deal of time involved in sport and outdoor pursuits and as a result are generally a healthy lot but I am afraid in the cities they

have taken up the fast food sport and are showing it. They are adventuresome represented by Edmund Hillary and Peter Blake for instance and the bungy jump along with other adrenalin rush concepts. They are a very intelligent and inventive lot with great discoveries to their credit and very quick to pick up on new ideas and usually improving them. It is a privilege and great fun to stop by a pub and get to know the local Kiwis. If you know and enjoy sport and especially rugby you may be there awhile.

You can just be yourself here as the Kiwi are generally tolerant and accept different ideas and views. It is a very modern society with no class system being secular and democratic.

But when it comes to understanding the words they speak even though it is English you may find some phrases difficult to interpret.

Don't be too frustrated when you hear Maori. After twenty years here I still can't get my tongue around the majority of the words but then I never was any good at language differences. They are very forgiving people when you slaughter their words so just smile and hope for the best as they do.

Kiwi speak – You are bound to hear the following in your travels

Cheers - thanks
Mate – a good friend
Shout a drink – to buy a drink for someone
Bach – the vacation cabin
Tramp – hike
Bush – the woods or forest
Holiday – vacation
Bloke – a fellow

Pommie – English person (POM - stands for prisoner of her majesty)
Pakeha – a New Zealander of European descent or non-Maori person
Paddocks – fields
Smoko – coffee break
Torch – flashlight
Jersey - sweater
Biscuit - cookies
Ablution block – toilet/shower block at camp grounds
Don't worry it will come right – (it will be okay)

And while driving:

Boot – trunk of the car
Windscreen – windshield
Petrol – fuel
Bonnet – hood
Panel beater – car body repairman
Caravan - mobile home that you tow behind your car
Ute - small pickup truck
Torch – flashlight

Greetings sound different such as 'Kia Ora' a Maori form of greeting or 'Gidday' that has a farming background. You may be called a 'bro' or a 'cobber' or a 'mate' all friendly greetings.

Ordering a beer at the pub (bar or hotel that serves liquor) is a bit different. You are asked if you want a handle or a jug or a glass all dependent upon size. Then there is the tinnie (a can of beer) or a Steinie (bottle of Steinlager) or maybe you would want spirits – (liquor) by the way they are not big on ice!

Other words you will hear at a pub (bar) or at a piss up (party, social gathering):
Ta – thanks
Shout - to treat, to buy something for someone
Pisshead - someone who drinks a lot of alcohol, heavy drinker
Scull - consume, drink quickly

Food and drink on offer:
Banger - sausage, as in bangers and mash
Snarler - sausage
Barbie - barbecue
Cuppa - cup of tea, as in cuppa tea
Entree - appetizer, hors d'oeurve
Fizzy drink - soda pop
L&P - Fizzy soda water made in NZ
Lolly - candy
Pav - pavlova, a NZ dessert topped with kiwifruit and cream
Pikelet - small pancake usually had with jam and whipped cream
Plonk - cheap liquor, cheap wine
Pudding - dessert
Serviette - paper napkin
Shandy - drink made with lemonade and beer
Shark and taties - fish and chips
Spud – potato
Veges - vegetables
Take-aways - food to be taken away and eaten, fast food outlet
Chook – chicken.
Tea - evening meal, dinner

When you go to the supermarket or are buying food some very Kiwi products are hokey-pokey ice cream (one of my favourites) and marmite or vegemite (not one of my favourites). Watties or tomato sauce is what we call ketchup.

For other words that are different how about their foot wear such as gummies (gum boots the black ones worn on the farm and the white ones worn by commercial fishermen) and the most popular summer foot wear in New Zealand the jandals we know as thongs. Togs are what the call their swim suits.

Other words and terminology you may hear:

Good on ya, mate! - congratulations
Chippy - builder, carpenter
Cockie - farmer
Crib - bach
Footie – rugby game
Arvo – afternoon
Bugger - damn!
Rattle your dags - hurry up, get moving
Rellies - relatives, family
Ring - to telephone somebody
Rubbish - garbage, trash
Dole - unemployment benefit
Scroggin - trampers high energy food including dried fruits, chocolate
Sheila - slang for woman/female
Shoot through - to leave suddenly
Dunny - toilet, bathroom, lavatory
Sickie - to take a day off work or school because you are sick
Skite - to boast, boasting, bragging
Sook - cry baby, wimp
Fizz Boat - small power boat
Flannel - wash cloth, face cloth

Sparkie - electrician
Wally - clown, silly person
Lift - elevator
Loo - bathroom, toilet
Wobbly - to have a tantrum
Wop-wops - situated off the beaten track, out of the way location
Yack - to have a conversation with a friend, to talk
And remember the last letter of the alphabet is called a zed....

And here is one for you when it comes to pronouncing some of the Maori names of communities:
The "wh" are pronounced as an "f" such as Whangarei is pronounced "F"ongara (with a long a for ei) "

Special New Zealand Kiwiana to look out for -
The silver fern emblem – made famous by the world famous rugby players known as the All Blacks copied from the silver fern plant found everywhere in the country.
Rugby – New Zealand's national sport probably closer to their religion. The world famous All Blacks.
Netball – second most popular sport. Played by women - top team the Silver Ferns. Much like basketball.
Bungy Jumping - AJ Hackett turned jumping off high places with rubber bands on your legs into a world wide attraction..
Sheep - The fields are full of them with 10 sheep for every one New Zealander – over 40 million
Gum boots – What is known in the US as Wellingtons and worn by every farmer and commercial fisherman.

Buzzy Bee - Since the 1940's this has been the Kiwi child's top toy and has to be real Kiwiana.

Pohutukawa tree – Scarlet red flowers bursting out during Christmas time.

Jandals – The flip-flops of the Kiwi's in the summer the footwear of choice.

Paua – A beautiful blue green shell known as abalone in the US. Used here by artists to create beautiful jewellery.

Fish & Chips – Every town has the local fish and chip shop. Shark and taties are what most people ask for.

L&P - This is a soft drink originally made in the town of Paeroa where today stands the giant bottle in the city square.

Marmite/Vegemite – A strong taste that must be acquired but most Kiwis find it delicious.

Kiwi fruit – Originally from China now known as the fruit of New Zealand. Great eating.

Pavlova - Arguments that this is an Australian dish but not so! Definitely a fabulous Kiwi dessert.

Meat Pies – You have to try this great Kiwi tradition. Some of the best eating in the country.

Hokey Pokey Ice Cream – Crunchy toffee Yum! Don't miss this Kiwi favourite on your trip

A & P Shows – Rural New Zealand on show like our county fairs. Worth a stop on your travels.

New Zealand Maori Culture

Maori are from Polynesia having migrated to New Zealand over 1000 years ago according to the experts. They make up around 10% of the total population of New Zealand with the culture, language and customs alive and well.

Maori Art & Performance
Weaving and carving are used to visually convey important myths, legends and history.
Many people will be familiar with the Maori haka used at the beginning of the All Black rugby games and other events.
I am a big fan of the poi dances that are performed.

Maori Carving
Maori use bone, wood and greenstone for their carvings. When you visit a marae or a meeting house pay close attention to the carvings throughout the meeting house. They are made by the best carvers who are knowledgeable about tribal history and traditions and are conveyed in the carvings.

Bone carving is another very important Maori art form that is usually worn as a necklace.

Specific shapes are symbols such as the fish hook or hei matau that represents the power of their ancestors and brings good luck and protection on a trip especially over water.

The koru design represents the fern fond unfurling and symbolises new life and regeneration.

The tiki is based upon mythical figures.

Greenstone or Pounamu is extremely hard to carve, therefore are highly treasured. Pounamu carvings have and create their own history over time, and are many are deemed Taonga (treasured possessions) by the Maori.

Marae Protocol

Perhaps you may want to take photos of a Maori marae you come across as you travel. The Maori are very particular about that and I suggest you receive permission from an elder or someone there in charge. Some Maori sites are considered sacred (*Tapu*) especially any burial grounds.

Here are some rules to remember when invited to a meeting house (and you must be invited first)

The Maori marae or meeting ground is not tourist attraction - they are sacred part of Maori life. Always ask permission before entering a marae. If invited you will experience a traditional welcome (*powhiri*) and learn about Maori culture and mythology.

Always remove footwear before entering a meeting house. Food cannot be eaten inside a meeting house (*Wharenui*). Do not sit on surfaces used for eating or food preparation such as an edge of a table.

If you go onto a marae you will experience:

The formal welcome (Powhiri) begins with a *wero* (challenge). During the *wero* a host warrior will challenge the guests (*manuhiri*). Carrying a spear (*taiaha*), the warrior will lay down a token for the guests to pick up - indicating they come in peace.

A group of host *kuia* (women) then perform a *karanga* (chant) of welcome. Women from the group of guests in turn respond as they move onto the *marae*.

Whaikorero (Speeches of Welcome)

Once inside the *wharenui* (meeting house), *mihimihi* (greetings) and *whaikorero* (speeches) are made. *Waiata* (songs) may also be sung.

After greeting the hosts with a *hongi* (traditional touching of noses) the guests will then present a *koha* (gift) to the hosts.

After the formal greetings *kai* (food) is shared

Myths and Legends

Maori is an oral culture, consisting of many oral myths and legends. It covers everything from creation myths to migration.

It is also used to recite Maori genealogy (Whakapapa), and tribal affiliation.

Creation Story

The Maori creation story follows the concept of the formation of the world through the separation of Ranginui (the Sky Father), and Papatuanuku (the Earth Mother) by their children. The children of Ranginui and Papatuanuku forced the two apart, Tane (God of the Forest) successfully holding the two forever apart. This action transformed the world from a state of darkness (Te Po) to a world of light (Te Ao-Marama).

Maui

The legend of Maui is about the creation of New Zealand (Aotearoa). Maui fished up the North Island from his waka (the South Island). The tail of the fish is Cape Reinga, and the mouth is Wellington Harbour. Stewart Island is known as the punga (anchor) of Maui's canoe.

Notes:

A quick explanation of several questions to help you understand a bit:

Question: What Is a Hongi?
Answer: The hongi is the Maori welcome expressed by the rubbing or touching of noses, something akin to the Western custom of kissing someone by way of greeting. The literal meaning of "hongi" is the "sharing of breath."

Question: What Is a Hangi?
Answer: Hopefully you get to experience a hangi while here....
Hangi is a method of cooking in the ground with hot stones. It is a feast of Maori food cooked in the manner described. Various types of meats and vegetables, such as kumara or sweet potato, are wrapped in leaves or aluminium foil. These items of wrapped food are then placed in a hole in the ground and cooked with hot stones. Hangi is also known by the term *umu*. Rotorua has a number of hotels that offer a hangi, accompanied by Maori music and folk dancing.
This is a real "taste" of Maori culture. Don't miss it!

Question: What Is Matariki?
Answer: Matariki is the constellation of stars known as the Pleiades. Matariki is also known as the Seven Sisters. Matariki's appearance in New Zealand skies marks the start of the Maori New Year. Matariki rises on New Zealand's northeast horizon in May or June. The constellation was a key navigation tool for the early ocean voyagers.
The Maori New Year celebrations begin on the sighting of the new moon after the appearance of Matariki.

Visiting New Zealand

Who visits New Zealand?

Overseas visitor arrivals numbered 2.5 million in the year ended June 2009. This was a 2.5% decrease from the June 2008 year. The largest sources of visitors to New Zealand in the year ended June 2009 were Australia, the United Kingdom, the United States, China, and Japan.

All in all it is a fabulous lifestyle in one of the most beautiful places in the world. (my personal opinion) So that should provide a good basis to begin on understanding a little bit about the country of New Zealand. I just wanted to touch base and not get too carried away as the most important to you is what does it all mean to you and your visit here. What you can see and experience. That is the pure essence of this book, your enjoyment while here, so let's get started...

New Zealand, one of the southernmost countries in the world, is for many tourists a place they'd like to visit.
The question that arises is: How easy is it to visit New Zealand?
If you're a tourist, and qualify as a tourist, the answer is: Easy.
If you hold a passport from one of a number of specified countries, the answer is: More than easy (such as the USA)

Follow the rules on visas

In a country where unemployment is relatively high, New Zealand, like many other nations, is wary of visitors who arrive in the guise of tourists and then work or otherwise overstay their visas. So it is important for some intending visitors to be able to indicate in some way that they will neither work (unless they apply for and secure a work permit) nor overstay their visas.

It is unfortunate that some really genuine intending tourists get knocked back and fail to get visas because of a perceived chance that they may violate the terms of their visas. No worries from US citizens so come on down! I made it so I am sure you can. I have been a New Zealand citizen since 1997 with a duel US citizen.

The subject of New Zealand visas concerns many travellers to New Zealand, particularly those visiting for the first time

New Zealand Visa Requirements:

To enter New Zealand you must have a passport valid for 3 months after the date of your intended departure.

You must also be carrying an onward/return ticket to a country you have permission to enter.

British Citizens and passport holders are entitled to enter New Zealand for up to 6 months and do not require a visa or visitor's permit.

Citizens of Australia are also exempt from having to obtain visitor permits when holidaying in New Zealand.

Passport holders from the USA do not need to apply for visitor visas or permits, and may visit New Zealand for up to 3 months including nationals of the USA.

Health Requirements

Anyone intending a stay in New Zealand of more than 12 months will need to complete health certificates. When applying online, an applicant will automatically receive a request for the appropriate medical documents, based on the length of stay permitted by the scheme for which the applicant is applying.

For further information on visas, immigration and visitor permits contact the New Zealand Immigration Service.

If you are from a visa-free country, you will not need a Visitor's Visa prior to arriving in New Zealand.

Before you leave home!

You have been through the book many times, checked out all the information provided, been on the internet going through all the websites I have pointed out, sent me an email full of questions and now feel comfortable in preparing for your travel arrangements to get here.

I won't begin to provide any direction there with airlines as it is easier for you to decide the one you wish to travel on and book.

Here are some suggestions that will make your flights less stressful:

Airfare, accommodations and rental vehicles -- these are your primary concern, but nailing down these aspects of your vacation is only a portion of the trip planning process. What about getting your cash in order and taking care of your home while you're away? There are plenty of things you will want to take care of that have nothing to do with airlines, hotels or rental cars.

REGISTER YOUR TRIP: I think this is very important in today's environment wherever you travel

The U.S. Department of State encourages all American travellers to register with their local Embassy or Consulate when arriving in a foreign country. Registration helps the Embassy to provide important services for American citizens residing or travelling abroad. Some of these services include:

Locating individuals in cases of family or personal emergencies,

Relaying important travel and safety information about the region,

Arranging evacuation transportation in cases of natural disaster or civil unrest,

Issuing replacement passports when originals are lost, and

A number of other administrative services relating to personal documentation.

Without the information provided through registration, the Embassy is severely hindered in its ability to provide these services. Many of these services involve emergency situations and time constraints, therefore failure to register will almost certainly lead to delays at moments when you can least afford them.

Think about what you are leaving behind and the first day in New Zealand

Do you have pets to consider -

If so make sure you have provided what you require in advance of the dates you leave.

Stop services you have-

Once your travel is booked, you should look into placing "stop" orders on any regularly occurring deliveries or services. These may include postal mail, newspapers, housecleaners and the like. If you want particular services to continue (such as landscaping), consider paying in advance if this is not your usual arrangement. Many service providers allow you to place stop orders online;

this is particularly the case for mail delivery and most newspapers. As most stop orders require one or two business days' advance notice, make sure you take care of this at least three days before you travel.

Have your first day planned –
Most people have come a long way and need to catch up so they can enjoy the trip.
The first day of your trip is often lost to logistics and unfamiliar surroundings. First you have to haul yourself and your stuff to your first place you stay or get oriented with a camper van. Then you have to figure out exactly where you are, what attractions are nearby and how best to use your limited time. Planning ahead will help you make the most of that first confusing day. Don't rush the first day. Try to sit back and enjoy it and get a good night's sleep the first night.

Map Out Your Drive – (or get a personal itinerary from me is the best answer to having a relaxed and easy trip while in New Zealand)
 Or if not and wish to do it on your own it may be worth mapping out the route ahead of time. Figuring out how to get where you are going in an unfamiliar location from a one-page map choked with advertising is risking more than just your time. How many times in your life have you been just one street over from where you should have been. This book will be a big help…

Important item for driving in New Zealand -
There is one item that has become an essential packing item: the cell phone earpiece. Pack your cell phone earpiece in your carry-on bag and you will not find yourself on the side of the road with a red siren whirling in your rear view mirror. In New Zealand it is the law that you must not use a cell phone while driving.

Passport Protection:

Your passport is the most important document on your packing list; protect it. Having your passport lost or stolen could turn your otherwise flawless trip into a disaster. Read on for ideas about how to protect your passport -- and tips for what to do if it's lost or stolen while you're travelling abroad. I had all kinds of trouble with the US Embassy in Costa Rica when after my sailboat caught fire and I spent six days in a life raft I arrived at the embassy thanks to an Exxon ship rescue without anything. They could care less about my predicament and if it hadn't been for Exxon who provided a hotel room and cash I would have been placed in a Panama jail. When they sent a request to Washington for my passport details they made me wait several days and they charged me a fee. You can guess how I feel about US embassies. I have heard about other horror stories also.

Before you Leave Home

Make two copies of your passport identification page. Leave one copy at home with friends or relatives and carry the other with you in a separate place from your passport. It's also a good idea to bring along two or three passport photos; these should be identical 2" x 2" photographs taken within the last six months, featuring a front view of your face on a white background. Be sure you also have another form of photo ID and a copy of your birth certificate (or another document to prove your citizenship). If your passport is lost or stolen, having these will speed up the replacement process.

Also, if you plan to be abroad for more than two weeks, you may want to register with the embassy in the country you are visiting. You can send the information via the internet.

Insurance –

Rather important in today's travelling environment. With the combination of political unrest, financial troubles of major tour operators and airlines, and the prevalence of non-refundable airline tickets it is wise to try to be covered for the worst. Makes a more relaxed vacation…

There are several different types of travel insurance policies available, ranging from trip cancellation insurance to emergency medical evacuation, all of which vary widely by company in what their coverage includes and how much it costs.

Look at the insurance policies you already have to see what they will cover. Some medical insurance policies will cover medical emergencies overseas while others will not. Many home owner's policies cover baggage loss. Also, many credit card companies (particularly gold cards) offer their members baggage loss, international medical assistance, and accidental death and dismemberment insurance if they simply charge their airline tickets on their credit card or for a small additional fee.

The first thing to check is with your credit card company and insurance company to see how their travel insurance works.

Vehicle Rental in New Zealand:

One of the most asked question I receive is about the rental car insurance required. All New Zealand vehicle rental companies have a required insurance on every rental that will require an excess to be paid. No matter if you can get coverage through your own insurance you still must pay the required minimum.

Each company has its own terminology but what it conveys is the amount you pay extra dictates what your excess is.

Here is an example:

Such as <u>Standard Cover</u> that will show heavy excess such as $1000 and $2500 per single vehicle accident.

Next it may be named the <u>Silver Cover</u> whereby the excess is dropped to $100 single accident still $2500.

Next it may be named the <u>Gold Cover</u> whereby the excess is just $100 overall with windscreen, tyre cover, extra driver

Next it may be named the <u>Platinum Cover</u> whereby the excess is $100 but other coverage is offered same as gold plus baggage and personal injury.

Remember the Accident Compensation Corporation (ACC) provides comprehensive, no-fault personal injury cover for all visitors to New Zealand free.

Contact me direct for help in getting a vehicle rental you can trust and get a free personal itinerary in the deal.

<u>Traveler's Check List -</u>

Okay you have made all the plans and have all the itinerary and all paperwork to leave on the big vacation holiday. One area be sure to pay attention to is a "before you go" check list. There's nothing worse than realising you have forgotten to do something important when you are already at the airport.

So let's go through the list………………..first a month or two before:

1. Check to make sure your passport will be valid during your trip and make a photocopy to carry with you.
2. Check your itinerary – Ensuring dates, times, baggage allowance and seat allocation are correct, any changes should be attended to immediately.

3. Always let the airline know of any special requirements you may require.
4. Have valid photo identification – At the airport you may need photo identification in addition to your passport.
5. Be sure you have travel insurance– I have covered this more specifically in another section
6. Check with your doctor and get a letter about any prescriptions you must carry with you.

Then a week before your trip:
- Get copies of your passport, insurance policy, itinerary, traveller's cheques, visa and credit card numbers.
- Make sure you carry one copy in a separate place to the originals and leave a copy at home with a friend or family member.
- Check that all your credit cards are okay to use and let the bank know of your trip. Sometimes they refuse payment if they think the card has been stolen. Make sure you take a small amount of cash.
- There is an area in the book I have discussed the custom laws of New Zealand but it wouldn't hurt to have a look at the website.
- The same is true of the immigration laws just to make sure.
- Mark down the telephone numbers and where your embassies are located in New Zealand. I have a list of the US in the book.
- Check the regulations in regards to size and weight of your carry-on bags. It is important to keep all valuables in your carry-on baggage just in case your checked luggage is misplaced. I generally carry everything of importance in a small strap bag that lies in the small of my back when travelling.

- Be familiar with the latest baggage allowance relating to the airline you're travelling with. Be sure to attach a lock and an identification tag to your bags for security reasons. Any medication must be correctly labelled and attached to a subscription. Mark your bag for quick identification on the baggage carousel. Use something you will readily spot.
- Be aware of which items that are prohibited in carry-on luggage – Flammable or sharp objects are not allowed in hand luggage as well as a list of other items.

Day of Departure:

- Now we are getting down to it. Don't panic.
- Check again you have all the correct paper work – your tickets, passports, photo identification, insurance policy, itinerary, money, Visa and credit cards.
- Wear comfortable clothing and shoes – The flights to New Zealand are quite long so comfortable clothing will help make your flight as relaxing as possible.
- Be sure to arrive at the airport early – at least 2 hours before your flight. In today's world be prepared for waiting time at the terminal prior to boarding.
  Be aware of what you must do to get through all the check points. Smile and be friendly and helpful. Customs have a tough job so don't make it any harder for them or you.

Medication

Medication is a very important part your bag. Be sure to bring any prescriptions that you take regularly to begin with. In addition a good selection of the proper medication can keep one from being disrupted by jet lag, upset stomach or other common travel maladies.

So what can happen. What can you hope to avoid. Here is a list of the most common problems encountered while travelling and some suggestions as how to help keep healthy on your trip.

Deep Vein Thrombosis

This is a real worry, a problem where blood clots develop in the leg. It's particularly common on long-haul flights where movement is restricted. The best strategies to prevent it are to drink a lot of water and to stand up, stretch and walk around the plane as often as possible. If you have any cardiovascular problems be sure to use your blood thinning medications.

Motion Sickness

Motion sickness is caused by a disturbance in the balance in the inner ear. Some people get it very easily when under movement that is not familiar or normal to their every day lifestyle.

Several over the counter aids are available such as Dramamine and Bonine. There is also a small patch (scopolamine) to stick behind your ear and one that you put on your wrist that stimulates acupressure points. and I understand ginger is effective.

Remember also you will more than likely take the ferry between the North and South Island known for possible wave action and also perhaps enjoy some boating in our vast boating area. Be prepared.

Sleeping on the plane
This is not the easiest thing to do for many people. Coupled with the excitement of the trip there are all the noises and disturbances aboard. Ambien a prescription drug is considered the best by many travellers and I understand it doesn't leave one groggy.

Ear Infections

This has always been one of my biggest discomforts as I injured my ear scuba diving and it always gives me trouble on flights as I find it hard to clear the ear by holding my nose and blowing to adjust to the cabin pressure. Sometimes the pain is unbelievable. Try to use a decongestant, nasal spray or sinus medicine before you board.

Travelers Diarrhea
Known as Montezuma's revenge and other colourful names it is quite common when one changes location, food and water.
Keep Imodium or Pepto Bismol handy. It's probably the most unpleasant minor traveller's malady. Unfortunately, it's also probably the most common. 20% to 50% of travellers suffer with it.
New Zealand is a very low risk area. Our water straight from the tap is drinkable. Make sure, again, to drink lots of water. You may have 48 hours of diarrhea before you get relief.
On the flight or before do not eat fast foods or drink to much alcohol or carbonated drinks.

Don't catch a cold on the flight !

A long distance flight such as to New Zealand exposes you
to the common cold. A recent study says you may be
100 times more likely to catch a cold on a plane than you
are in your normal daily life primarily on a single cause:
extremely low cabin humidity caused by low humidity
at high elevations. At very low levels of humidity, your
"natural defence system" of mucus in our noses and
throats dries up and is crippled, allowing cold germs to
infect us. If you make sure there is sufficient moisture in
both nose and throat you will be unaffected by the low
humidity.

How not to get affected:

1. Sipping water or some other fluid regularly
2. throughout the flight may be more effective than
3. drinking a lot of water at one time before or during
4. the flight. This will keep your protective system
5. from long dry spells. Remember alcohol and
6. caffeinated drinks can actually dehydrate you.
7. Nasal mists have been found to be very effective.

2. Washing your hands with hot water and soap is a
3. way to
4. stop picking up any germs on the area around you.
5. Wash your hands prior to eating any meals and
6. after your flight. I take along alcohol based
7. handi-wipes.

3. Use a mouth wash that will kill any germs and also
4. help keep your mouth moist. Remember to keep it
5. in a three ounce or smaller bottle to follow today's
6. carry-on rules.
7. I believe in taking vitamins as a help to add extra
8. protection to your system especially vitamin C.

9. Start days or weeks ahead of your trip.

10. Face masks also are an option but I find that a little over the top but if you happen to have a cold it would help fellow passengers. Probably not a bad idea to keep one though in your travel bag just in case. It may be a great help if all of a sudden you get caught in a situation of closeness to an affected passenger.

How to Enjoy your flight

I am sure you remember the times you been crunched into a seat from the guy in front who has his seat reclined way back! Or the person next to you overlaps the seat on to yours. We can all go on about the may scenarios that unfold on flights and the long flight to New Zealand is not easy under the best of circumstances.

What Makes a Great Seat?
Seats close to the front of the plane, exit rows or window seats are considered the best.
Exit row seats usually offer a bit more leg room, but they're not appropriate if you're travelling as a family. By federal law, no one under 15 may sit in an exit row, and infants are not permitted in the rows immediately behind or in front of an exit row either.

Bulkhead seats directly behind the physical barriers that separate different parts of the plane. With no seats in front of you often will get some extra legroom. But remember on some planes, the first bulkhead row may be cramped and uncomfortable. Go to SeatGuru.com where you can check out seat maps for nearly every type of plane on every major airline.
Also check on the seat pitch, especially if you're tall.

This is a measure of how much space there is between a seat and the one immediately behind or in front of it -- so the higher the number, the more leg room you will have . SeatGuru.com lists both seat pitch and width (when available) for most airlines. I wish they had this service years ago.

You may be concerned about safety, but there's no clear answer about where you should sit in order to fare best in a plane crash. Several studies indicate seated in the rear of the plane but then another says that the safest place to sit is near the front of the plane within five rows of an emergency exit. To me it is rather a waste to worry about a crash. Spend more time trying to find comfort during the flight.

The middle seats are usually not the best in any row. Rows near flight attendant areas and restrooms may be noisier and experience more traffic, and seats very close to cabin movie screens can be uncomfortable and aggravating if you are trying to sleep.

10 Ways to Get a Better Seat –Sourced Information from the Independent Traveller website (great website):
1. **Join a frequent flier program.** If you are lucky
2. enough
3. to fly a lot (or unlucky) you should have the
4. program. Providing your number at the time of
5. reservation goes a long way toward making sure
6. you get a good seat.

    2. Buy your tickets early. Availability for
7. pre-assignment dwindles as the travel date closes in
8. . If you can't buy your tickets at least several weeks
9. in advance, be sure to check in online as soon as

possible before your flight to select a seat, or arrive at the airport early if online check-in isn't available.

3. Consider purchasing a better seat. Several airlines now offer economy-class seats with extra legroom for an additional fee. Check to see what is offered by the airline you have chosen.

4. Select your seat when you book. Most airlines allow you to choose a seat when you purchase your ticket, or to return to your reservation after your initial purchase and make your seat selection later. In most cases this process is free. Check to see when booking.

5. **Confirm your seat at check-in.** Most airlines allow
6. passengers to check in online 24 hours before their
7. flight departs. At that point you can confirm the
8. seat you've already chosen or even choose a better
9. one.

      6. Get to the airport early. If you arrive too late
10. at your gate, you may lose your seat.

      7. When in doubt, ask. When you get to the
11. airport ask whether any new seats have opened up.
12. Other passengers may have upgraded to business
13. class or don't show up for the flight, you may get lucky and grab a better assignment.

8. Be specific. If you know exactly what seat you're
14. interested in, it can be easier for agents to get it for
15. you. Instead of asking for just an exit row or
16. "a good seat," try asking for "12A" -- you'll be more likely to get what you want (or an acceptable substitute).

9. Medical Condition. If you have a medical condition, let the agent know. Most will do their best to accommodate you.

10. Kindness counts. Approach agents in a spirit of understanding. They hear complaints and demands all day. Treat them with respect they certainly deserve it.

Lots of reasons that make it tough to get some sleep on flights. Not enough legroom. People climbing over you. Noise from movies and video games and screaming children. Sunlight pouring in your neighbor's window at 35,000 feet.
Just remember you are not alone -- but choosing the right seat, bringing the right gear and making a few small changes in your flying habits could help you sleep better on your next flight.
Here are some travel-tested tips.

Choose your seat wisely.
Try to get a window seat if possible. It provides a way to get you out of the way of other folks in your row. People won't have to scramble over you each time they need to use the bathroom. You'll also have some control over the window shade.

Think twice about bulkhead or exit row seats. The extra leg room is great, but remember some exit row seats do not recline and some bulkhead seats have arm rests that can't be raised.

Andrea Rotondo of LuxuryCruiseBible.com also cautions against bulkhead seats because they "are often reserved for families travelling with babies or young kids, and can be noisy."

Another area to avoid is the last row of the plane. Again, the seats may not recline, and they're often located right near the lavatories -- where both noise and odour could be an issue.

Seats near the rear of the plane may be noisier due to the planes' engines and noise from the galley, but it's also more likely that you'll have a couple of seats (or even a whole row) to yourself back there -- and the extra space could make up for the extra noise in my opinion.

Cut down on your carry-ons.
If you have two full carry-ons, one will probably end up under your feet, limiting your leg room and making it harder to sleep.

Forget the caffeine.
This is a hard one for me. You'll find it much harder to sleep if you have caffeine coursing through your veins. Skip the temptation to have a cup of coffee or a soda before boarding, and stick to water or juice when the drink cart comes around.

Blankets and pillows -- stake your claim.
There are never enough blankets and pillows to go around. Be sure to stake your claim early. If there isn't a set in your seat, immediately ask the flight attendant for one.

What about a neck pillow.
Many travellers swear by their supportive neck pillows. Try one out at home to see if it helps you first.

Free your feet.
This is a controversial subject. Some people slip their shoes off as soon as they get on a plane; others wouldn't think of doing it. There's the issue of keeping your circulation

flowing; going barefoot permits your feet to swell. Be sure
to have clean socks. No one likes stinky feet. Wear shoes
you can slip on and off easily.

Try a sleep aid.
Check with your doctor or pharmacist to see what they
recommend. Here are a few products used with some success:
Melatonin: This is a naturally occurring substance -- it's
the compound that triggers our sleep patterns. The level of
melatonin in our bodies declines as we age; this is why
older folks often sleep less as they advance in years. As it
is a gentle approach, melatonin doesn't seem to work for
everyone. Good idea to start using a few days prior to flight.
Dramamine: This motion sickness remedy is a pretty
common over-the-counter drug. Good for the long flights
but will still leave you feeling drowsy I find.

Use headphones with discretion.
Get more sleep by not watching the TV and movies but
listening to music can help tune out distractions and lull
you into a peaceful sleep.
Ear plugs can help.

Recline your seat -- but be courteous.
Ideally, everyone on a night flight will be trying to sleep
and seatbacks will tip backward soon into your flight.
You should always look behind you to make sure the
your neighbor is aware. Simple common courtesy applies
here.

Make sure you won't be disturbed.
Notify your flight attendant that you want to sleep --
that way he or she will know not to disturb you. If you're
under a blanket, be sure your seat belt is buckled over top
of it so the belt is visible at all times.

Stay away from the light.
The animated flash of movie screens, reading lights, cabin
lights, sunlight bursting in -- all can disturb your slumber.
An eye mask is a very good idea.

When it's time to wake up..
Set a watch or your cell phone alarm for 45 minutes before
you have to land. That will give you time to go to the
restroom, gather your gear, tie your shoes, watch the
approach to your destination -- you might even convince
an attendant to pour you a cup of coffee -- and walk off the
plane fully awake. You will be a happier traveler.

This Information sourced from website –
Independent Traveler -
http://www.independenttraveler.com

**Be sure to check this website out for great expert
information for travellers.**

<u>Missed Flights/Lost Luggage</u> –
Events beyond your control, from problems at the security
checkpoint to stormy weather, may mar even the best-
planned itinerary.
What to Do
Has your plane taken off without you? Immediately go to
your airline's desk. It is possible that your airline can get
you on the next flight.
If your airline refuses to offer a voucher for another flight,
get ready to pay up. Passengers who miss their flights
sometimes must pay full price for a new ticket -- and
prices are steep when it's the day of or the day before your
departure. Take this as a warning to always arrive at the
airport with plenty of time to spare, especially around the
holidays.

If you have missed a connecting flight and your luggage has been checked, it will most likely go on without you -- so your suitcase may be en route to the Bahamas while you're stuck in a chilly airport in Chicago. Go to your airline's ticket counter and ask if they can locate your bags. The airline may be able to hold your bags until you arrive in your destination. Always pack a change of clothes in your carry-on when you fly. Anything may happen.

How to Be Prepared
Get to the airport early! Check out your airport's Web site for recommended arrival times.

Lost Luggage
Here come the bags but, alas, yours are not there.
What to Do
Make sure you have your baggage claim ticket.
What Happens
Your airline will most likely have a counter or office in the baggage claim area; go to this counter immediately and fill out a "missing luggage" form. If you're lucky, your bag was simply delayed or put on the wrong plane and the airline will deliver it to your hotel within a few days. If your bag is lost and the airline is unable to recover it, you can file a claim for damages. In this case, you will probably have to make a list of everything that was in your bag. You will get the depreciated (not replacement) value for the items in your bag. This means that your two-year-old $400 shoes will no longer be worth $400.

How to Be Prepared
To prevent (as much as you can) your luggage from getting lost, remove any extraneous tags on your bag that may confuse the airport's scanning machines. In addition,

don't pack anything valuable or essential in your checked bag, and, as mentioned above, bring a change of clothes in your carry-on. Make sure that your name and address are clearly labeled on the outside of each piece of luggage, and put a label with your contact information on the inside of your bag in case the outside tag gets ripped off. And hang on to your baggage claim ticket!

For more on what to do if your bags go missing, check out the guide to Lost Luggage on the website
- **Independent Traveler -**
- http://www.independenttraveler.com

NOTES:

Information For Travellers from the USA

New Zealand
EMBASSY AND CONSULATE ADDRESSES
Diplomatic Representation in US:
   Ambassador: Roy FERGUSON
   Embassy: 37 Observatory Circle NW, Washington, DC 20008
   Telephone: [1] (202) 328-4800
   Fax: [1] (202) 667-5227
US Diplomatic Representation:
   Ambassador: David Huebner
   Embassy: 29 Fitzherbert Terrace, Thorndon, Wellington
   Mailing Address: P. O. Box 1190, Wellington; PSC 467,
   Box 1, FPO AP 96531-1001
   Telephone: [64] (4) 472-2068
   Fax: [64] (4) 471-2380
   Consulate(s) General in: Auckland
      Consulate(s) General:
      Los Angeles
      12400 Wilshire Bl., 11th Floor
      Los Angeles, CA 90025
      (310) 207-1605
      New York
      222 East 41st Street, Suite 2510
      New York, NY 10017
      PH: (212) 832-4038
      FAX: (212) 832-7602

Some Quick Travel Tips:

Just a top up of information to make your trip more enjoyable without the hassles.

Book Early:
Lots of availability today on the internet to check and evaluate all airlines along with their comparative pricing structure.

Remember it is important to get the cheapest seats by booking early. All airlines will sell the cheapest flights first and the price increases closer to the departure date. Those who use their rewards programs will find they must book early for the best results.

Compare the flights and the airlines:
There are many airlines now servicing New Zealand so it pays to have a check. When checking be sure to look to see if all taxes and surcharges are quoted.

Travel Warnings:
It would be rare there would be any travel warnings in New Zealand but at any given time natural disasters could occur and New Zealand does have a strong volcanic and earthquake possible presence as we have just witnessed at Christchurch. Also if you plan to travel through other countries on the trip be sure to have a look. Better safe than sorry.

Immunization:
Not required as New Zealand is free from any problems that require immunization but again if you plan to travel certain other countries be sure to check.

Insurance:
I cannot really stress the importance enough.
Anything can happen and insurance protection for
accidents or lost luggage is very important.

Passports:
Save embarrassment at the airport by ensuring your
passport is valid for the duration of your time overseas.
This has caught many a traveller out on an extended
holiday. Make sure you have copies kept separately and
copies left with friends or relatives. Don't always believe
your embassy will be of help you.

New Zealand Customs:
Good friendly bunch and extremely efficient. Please
be kind and considerate and don't break the rules. You are
the one who suffers so pay attention to what you can and
cannot do. New Zealand Customs Service has a guide for
international travellers to familiarise themselves with New
Zealand's prohibited and restricted goods laws and
personal duty-free concessions.
For a free copy visit their website.

Tourist Refund Scheme and Durty Free:
It has long been a tradition for departing international
tourists to buy items in New Zealand and claim the tax
back on these items upon their departure. The TRS
enables you to claim refunds in some circumstances for
GST and Wine Equalisation Tax on goods purchased in
New Zealand. Be sure you know what can and cannot be
claimed to avoid any surprises at the airport. Again check
on the Customs website.

Carry-on luggage restrictions:
Travel security measures were increased for carry-on
luggage at international airports. Passengers are permitted

to only carry on a maximum 100ml of liquids.
 All liquids and their containers must be sealed in a
transparent bag as shown below. This is so officials can
inspect your luggage quickly. Failure to adhere to the
100ml limit will mean confiscation of goods over this limit.
 To avoid this, store as many liquids as you can in your
checked-in luggage. Don't put that bottle of wine in your
carry-on! I had sent an expensive bottle back with a visiting
 friend from the US, back when the rules had just been
changed, to share with old classmates and it was taken as
he boarded. Never did get an answer back from Customs
as to what happened to all those bottles of wine they were
 taking back then.

Airport Security

If you haven't flown in a while, you may not be up on
the latest airport security changes. Most travelers are
aware that there are strict regulations about the amount
 of toothpaste, bottled water, and other liquid and gel
 items that travelers are permitted to bring in carry-on
 luggage. But what exactly are the rules? Just how
 much of your must-have favourite shampoo can you
bring? And are the rules different if you're flying
overseas?

Here are some answers to these and other common
questions to help you figure out your packing strategy.
 It is important to follow the guidelines -- that way you
 won't be the fool holding up your entire security line.

On international flights, you may no longer be able to
use the onboard restroom during the last hour of your
flight. There may also be restrictions on the use of
electronic devices and possession of any items
(including pillows and blankets) in your lap during
the last hour of your flight. (The captain may relax

these restrictions at his or her discretion.) Your airline may also choose to limit the number of carry-on items you may bring onboard. Currently there are size restrictions on carry-on bags on some flights.

Q. Are liquids and gels permitted in my checked baggage?
A. Yes. The new rules only apply to carry-on baggage.

Q. May I bring liquids and gels in my carry-on?
A. Yes, but only in limited amounts. Liquids and gels must be in individual containers of three ounces or less and placed inside one clear, quart-size, plastic, zip-top bag. The TSA emphasizes that containers should fit comfortably into your bag, and that only one bag is permitted per passenger. If you need to bring more than three ounces of any liquid or gel substance, it should go into your checked luggage.

Q. What about prescription medications, baby formula or milk?
A. These substances are exempt from the rules above. As long as you declare them at the security checkpoint, you may carry more than three ounces, and they do not need to be placed in a plastic bag. The TSA recommends but does not require that prescription medications be in their original labeled containers to expedite the screening process. The TSA may also make exceptions for other medical necessities such as insulin, eye drops or syringes. Make sure you have a letter from the doctor.

Q. May I pour shampoo and other liquids or gels into unmarked, travel-size containers, or do these substances need to remain in their original bottles?
A. The rules do not require that liquids and gels be kept

in their original labeled containers, though doing so may help expedite the screening process.

Q. Do solid vitamins and medications need to be packed in their original containers?
A. While the rules encourages travelers to keep their medications and vitamins in their original labeled containers to expedite the screening process, you may transfer them into more convenient smaller containers such as daily pill minders.

Q. What about makeup?
A. Makeup is subject to the same liquid and gel rules as all other substances -- so if you're bringing liquid mascara, lip gels (such as Blistex) or other liquid- or gel-like items, they will need to be placed in your quart-size plastic bag in three-ounce or smaller containers. Lipstick, powders, solid lip balms (such as chapstick) and other solid beauty products are not subject to the rules, and may be carried in your hand luggage without restriction.

Q. What about food?
Even though the rules say to "try not to over-think" the new guidelines, that can be tricky when it comes to food items. Does a cheesecake count as a gel or a solid? What about pecan pie? And can you bring your holiday leftovers like turkey, stuffing and mashed potatoes?

Turkey and stuffing should be solid enough to pass muster, but mashed potatoes are a bit too gel-like. As for baked goods, the latest word is that travelers can take pies, cakes and other bakery products through security -- but be prepared for additional screening.

You may bring solid snack foods such as pretzels, potato chips or carrot sticks for the plane -- but you may want to hold the peanut butter and jelly sandwich. Single-serving packages of condiments are permitted as long as they fit within your single zip-top bag, so you can add mustard to your ham sandwich after you get through security. All food must be securely wrapped or in a spill-proof container. You may not bring gel packs to refrigerate food (though they are permitted for medication).

The advice? If you have any doubts about an item, either check it or leave it at home. After all, you can always buy food or drinks after you pass through the security checkpoint if you need some munchies for the plane.

Q. If I purchase beverages or other liquids/gels beyond the security checkpoint at the airport, may I bring them on the plane?
A. Yes.

Q. Are there any special rules for batteries?
Loose lithium batteries are no longer permitted in checked bags. If your batteries are installed in a device (such as a camera), you may pack the device in either a checked bag or a carry-on, but loose lithium batteries may only be transported in your carry-on luggage. Certain quantity limits apply to both loose and installed batteries.
Q. What are the rules for cigarette lighters?
Common lighters are permitted in carry-on baggage, while torch lighters (which are typically used to light pipes and cigars) are not. Neither type of lighter is permitted in checked bags. For more information.

Q. May I bring needlepoint or knitting needles on the plane?
In most cases, yes, but TSA officers may confiscate your needles at their discretion if they think the needles could be used as weapons. Your best bet is to pack knitting needles that are no longer than 31 inches and that are made of bamboo or plastic (rather than metal).

Q. Are the rules different for other international travel?
A. The European Union (E.U.) as well as other countries such as Australia, Japan, Singapore, Iceland and Norway have adopted similar security restrictions to those in the U.S. You are permitted 100-milliliter containers of liquid and gel substances, packed within a clear, resealable, one-liter plastic bag. New Zealand will follow the same rules.

Q. Am I permitted to bring duty-free liquids in my carry-on bags?
Duty-free liquids, such as perfume or alcohol, are subject to the same rules as all other liquids and gels when it comes to security checkpoints -- containers must be no larger than three ounces, and they must fit into your clear, quart-size, plastic zip-top bag.

The same rules apply to the security checkpoints in the European Union and other nations mentioned above, with one exception: duty-free items purchased in airports in those countries will be given to you in special tamper-evident bags, which may be safely taken through airport security checkpoints in those countries.
However, the tamper-evident bags will not pass muster in the United States, so you must transfer the items into your checked baggage while you're in customs.

Q. May I bring dry ice in my carry-on? What about my
checked bags?
The FAA has strict regulations about the transportation
of dry ice on airplanes. Passengers may bring 2
kilograms in carry-on luggage or 2.3 kilograms in
checked luggage as long as it's stored in a package
that allows the venting of carbon dioxide gas. A DOT
spokesperson suggests that travelers avoid packing dry
ice in carry-on luggage.

Q. I have a hearing aid, C-PAP machine, pacemaker or
other medical device. How will this be handled during
my security screening?
The customs agents are used to dealing with these kinds
of medical issues and will work with you to maintain
your privacy and get you through security with your
medical equipment intact. As soon as you approach the
agent you should notify him or her of your medical
issue so that they can determine the best way to screen
you and any equipment you may be carrying. The TSA
does not require travelers to carry a doctor's note
describing their condition, but having this written
description may help expedite the screening process.
Q. How early should I arrive at the airport?
A. We recommend arriving at the airport two hours
before your flight, especially if you're travelling during
the summer, the holidays or another particularly busy
time of year. Flying internationally, you should allow
yourself even more time.

Q. What should I expect at the security checkpoint?
A. You will have to put your clear plastic bag, jackets,
jewellery, cell phones, keys and metal items into a bin
for screening before you step through the metal
detector. (Your shoes go directly onto the X-ray belt

rather than into a bin.) Laptops and video cameras must be removed from their cases and screened individually.

Save time at the checkpoint by putting metal items into your carry-on ahead of time, taking your electronic items out of their cases and wearing easily removable footwear.

Q. I'm bringing birthday or holiday gifts. What's the best way to pack them?
A. Do not pack wrapped gifts in either your carry-on or checked baggage, as the agents may have to unwrap them for inspection. Your best bet is to wrap your gifts once you arrive at your destination, or ship them ahead of time.

Q. May I bring electronic items on the plane or in my checked luggage? If so, how should I pack them?
Laptops, video cameras, iPods, and most other standard electronic devices are permitted in both checked and carry-on luggage. As noted above, you should be prepared to remove laptops or video cameras from their cases at the security checkpoint for additional s creening. Because electronic items tend to be frequent targets for security screening, you may want to pack these near the top of your bag so that inspectors don't need to unpack your whole suitcase to get to them. Keep in mind that certain electronic devices -- such as radios, cordless computer mouse or portable GPS systems -- may not be used in flight even if you do pack them in your carry-on, as they may interfere with the plane's navigational or communications systems.

Q. Can I lock any suitcases that I'm checking?

A. Yes, but you'll need to use an approved lock so that screeners can open it if your bag is selected for inspection. Screeners will simply cut off non-approved locks if they need to get into your bag.

Acknowledgement:
The above is Information sourced from website –
Independent Traveler -
http://www.independenttraveler.com
For more complete information go to their website.

New Zealand Customs Requirements:
I have listed what you can bring and not bring as you enter New Zealand. For a more complete rundown go to their website.

Duty free allowances:
Cigarettes, cigars, tobacco - 200 cigarettes, 250 grams of tobacco, fifty cigars or a mixture of all three not to exceed 250 grams
Alcoholic beverages - 4.5 litres of wine or beer and one 1125ml bottle of spirits or liquor.

Customs Restrictions:
New Zealand is an isolated country, free from many pests and diseases. To protect our unique environment and agriculture, border controls are strictly enforced and New Zealand Customs imposes heavy penalties on individuals who break these rules.
Even inadvertently carrying an apple into the country in your carry-on luggage could result in a hefty fine – so take care! There is plenty of very fine fruit and vegetables here so I request you wait to try them.

On arrival visitors must declare the following goods:

food of any kind
plants or parts of plants (alive or dead)
animals (alive or dead) or their products
equipment used with animals
straw items
wooden items and curios
sea shells
equipment such as camping gear, golf clubs,
hiking boots and used bicycles
biological specimens

We now have the dreaded didymo in our once
pristine rivers due to the fact some US trout
 fisherman had not cleaned his boots before coming
here to fish....a great loss to our natural world.

CITES: New Zealand adheres to the Convention
on International Trade in Endangered Species of
Wild Fauna and Flora (CITES). For a full list of
Endangered Species prohibited go to the website.
Weapons: The importation of weapons and firearms
into New Zealand is strictly controlled.

Cash: Anyone carrying in excess of $10,000NZ must
complete a Border Cash Report on entry to
New Zealand.

Medications: Visitors entering New Zealand with
personal medication are advised to carry a doctor's
certificate to avoid potential problems with Customs.
Drug trafficking: Drug trafficking is a serious offence
 in New Zealand. Never agree to carry packages or
bags for others, unless you are entirely sure of their
contents.

Liquids, Aerosols & Gels - Like many countries, New Zealand now has strict regulations on the amount of liquids, aerosols and gels (LAGs) that can be taken onto international flights. While you can still take duty free liquids on board the aircraft, you must purchase these items after you have cleared airport security, otherwise they will be confiscated. If you purchase your duty free at a downtown duty free store before your flight, ensure the airport pick-up point for your purchases is after the airport security check. Remember that if you stop off at another airport on your way to your final destination, you will most likely need to go through airport security again. So if you are carrying bottles of duty free liquid, it will be confiscated! The best idea is to try and buy duty free when you land, or to ensure you will have a chance to pack any duty free purchases into your check-in luggage during a stopover.

Before we move on to the actual travel and itinerary for New Zealand I would like to provide a bit more helpful information. General information I would have loved to have had before my visit here.

Food – New Zealand is superior in fresh veggies and fruits. As we travel we stop at stands along the road to get most of ours. New World super markets we feel do a great job. You should go out of your way to have venison, fresh fish (blue cod & gro(u)per are the best) but New Zealand is all coastline so the fishing is tops with lobster (crayfish), oysters, mussels and scallops (my favourite) and farmed salmon.

Plenty of opportunity for the best in food and wine here. They are way ahead of most places in the world in both categories.

Good food, wine and coffee are what we pursue in our

travels.

No tipping in NZ. Unless at a real restaurant all orders will be going to the counter and pay when ordered. Food might be delivered but no waitresses. Most food is in displays on the counter. Fresh made every day! Tea rooms are the food stops along the way in this country. If you like coffee get in touch and I will provide our list developed over the years on the road pursuing the best café coffee. I had placed the New Zealand Coffee Guide online many years but when I asked support from the cafes and roasters none would so I closed it.

The New Zealand dollar is all over the place right now so I haven't a clue what it will be when you get here. As I am writing this it is at a record high so you get more for your dollar anyhow here.

For Americans - The language is English but not American as is the spelling of many words such as some you see I have adopted. They have tyres not tires for instance.

The people are extremely warm and friendly but quiet. They will stand off a bit until they see where you are coming from. The social life of the Kiwi is at the pubs. When you see a building called a hotel that is their pub place. Tea rooms are like our cafes out in the country areas. Great to stop and grab a bite and a drink. Lots of great homemade stuff. They have a lot of hot pies here. Don't hesitate stopping at the country pubs (named hotels) you see along the way if you really want to get to know about Kiwi life. They are very down-to-earth and wonderful to have a beer with. Trouble here is almost unheard of except in the cities. Don't have any fear of going in a pub here. Queenstown is expensive and overdone but that's what it is.

Small enough though to not be over

powerful when visiting. It's New Zealand's party town and adrenalin city with people from all over the world having a ball............Join them if you want!
The scenic drive to Glenorchy is a must. You will see the true beauty of NZ and be sure to stop at the Glenorchy pub.
The driving journey itself is a destination. The drive is the most spectacular in the world. The country is so compact you enjoy the vista that is coming around the bend. Have a look at the driving times I schedule when creating a holiday....a couple hours a day and you are in a new environment. Check here for driving the country – www.ronlaughlin.net. I will gladly provide a free driving itinerary for you.
Oh yes....clothes. Don't overdress. Prepare for rain as you will be going into the Rain Forest on a portion of your trip (West Coast). There is six months difference from the northern hemisphere.
I must say every "tourist" is decked out in Columbia gear looking like they are on an African safari. May I suggest you just be at home casual. Levis and t-shirts are what the locals wear. Good footwear for hiking, rain gear, jackets for warmth when the cold wind blows up from the Antarctic now and again.
Be sure to prepare for our sandflies with giant jaws – Take massive amounts of vitamin B at least two weeks before arriving and it will help. When you get here one of the first things to buy will be repellent.
(This has to do mostly with the South Island and in particular with the West Coast..............
If you are planning for a camper van holiday (highly recommended) make sure you pick a reliable company. Why spoil your entire holiday by making the mistake of getting cheap transportation that fails you............really important to research ahead of time. I only recommend a very few that

I have trusted over the years. Contact me for
ones that have proven themselves over the years!
(and get a free itinerary in the bargain).
If you are in a camper van they are warm and toasty
hooked up to electric at the camps so no problem
and air-conditioned for the summer time needs.
Speaking of camper vans/motor homes that are
fully contained. Don't be afraid to use the toilets.
Every park has dump station. All rentals have
self-contained toilet containers that are easy to empty.
Easy to use units.
Easy to hook up to the electric in the parks.
They all have electric and water at each parking site.
They expect everyone out by 10am. You can fudge a
little as long as you are not using their facilities such
as showers that they need to clean. The kitchens
have just about anything you need (BBQ's too) so
even though you may cook in your vehicle you may
wish to clean up in the kitchens. Make sure you
have your own towels and cloths for showers.
We also carry a mat to stand on since most don't
have anything. Nice if it happens to be cold.
Top up with water at the holiday parks. Leave your
trash at the parks. If you park overnight somewhere
outside the parks just be sure you don't leave a mess.
Most rental units have the ability to play CD's so be
sure to bring what you like to listen to.
Another point is to bring your belongings in soft bags
that can pack easy when you unpack for the camper
van. It is a real pain to have big bulky hard bags in
a small living space. Some of the top companies will
store your empty bags until you return the van.
An important travel hint. All the small towns have
public toilets usually at one end of the town or the
other or both.
New Zealand should get the top points

for the cleanest toilets in the world. It is so rare to find one otherwise it is notable and there is also paper every time! Just a point I think is important when traveling.

Many of you will be driving for the first time on the left side of the road. Just remember it. We don't need to lose you on our roads. The roads are usually very, very good and well maintained. You must take care though since almost everywhere the roads are either going up or down an incline and at the same time around curves. Great for sightseeing just be sure to not take your eyes off the road too much.

Lots of one-way bridges but well sign-posted. Thankfully the roads are not crowded except around major cities. In the South Island you can go for hours without seeing another vehicle except perhaps a tractor and maybe a flock of herded sheep.

It's a shame so many people haven't the opportunity to spend more than a couple of weeks here and try to see it all. It isn't as easy to drive everywhere in a short time due to the type of driving required.....slow due to the curves and mountains.

Also be aware when you rent a vehicle based upon the lowest price. There are a lot of new vehicle rental companies out there now who have purchased old worn out vehicles from the bigger companies and are passing them off as top quality. Not the case.

I have seen several holidays ruined because of going for a cheapo. Remember what I said about the roads here.....not for weak units and the breakdown may be a long way from civilization. If you spent all that money getting here don't mess up by setting yourself up for a bad time for a few extra dollars saved (but lost).

This isn't a problem to those of you from countries

with the same measuring systems but to this old
American it was a bit confusing until I slowly
worked it out over the years especially the driving in
kilometres.

Conversions ....for those who use different measurements
1 meter = 3.280 839 895 feet
1 meter = 1.093 613 298 yards
1 kilometer = 0.621 371 192 24 miles (for quick
conversion as you drive along the road if it says
100kms think 100X6 = 60 miles.....)
1 hectare = 2.471 043 920 2 acres
1 square kilometer = 0.386 102 158 55 square mile
Centigrade to Fahrenheit – times 2 + 29

New Zealand Weather and when should you visit:
To everyone in the Northern hemisphere be aware
the seasons are opposite in the Southern Hemisphere.
If you want to identify with the time of year take
the month you are in there and add six months to get
the weather here.

General rule of thumb –

Spring - October is like the beginning of spring.
Lots of winter weather is still hanging on in the
South Island sometimes up to and including parts
for December. We usually start our South Island
tour in October but for those of you who come
during this period be ready for rain and even snow
and sleet and hail and the cold Antarctic winds
blowing up the island. Envision the spring time in the
northern temperate places and you will get an idea.

Summer – December through March and even April.
If traveling here be sure to have a look at the enclosed
information on school holidays. Over the Christmas

period all of New Zealand is on holiday and not a time I would recommend to be here in respect to having the place to yourself. I consider February the ultimate weather month to travel here.

Autumn – April, May – Great time also to cruise the islands.

Winter – June, July, August, September I do not recommend traveling the South Island unless you are seeking the winter. Great skiing and snowboarding for those into it though but many roads are temporarily closed due to weather. Absolutely stunning in the mountains if you like cold weather. We tend to go to the North Island to the Far North for the winter but find Nelson and the Marlborough Sounds actually the best weather in the country consistently.

Be aware we are more temperate than tropical and the winds from the Antarctic are brutal.

Variances, as one would expect in weather, will change all of this somewhat but it will give you a general sketch of time to go by.

Here is the New Zealand weather channel to have a look at: http://www.metservice.co.nz/default/index.php.

Enjoy the country at its best when you will be comfortable and be able to see everything.

Traveling around Wild New Zealand –

How about some information to help de-mystify getting around the country and on what to expect in general weather patterns in each area.

I will add more in the itinerary section but this will help in understanding what kind of general transport is available, the road access and the climate.

Most of New Zealand is accessible by road to at least the edges of
many of the wildest regions with sealed roads running through
much of the scenic world of this country. I don't recommend
getting off the roads and exploring here without local input. There
are two classes of roads in New Zealand – national state highways
-   numbered from 1 to 5. The provincial highways
-   are numbered10 to 99. Most of the regions can be
-   reached by train, plane or bus.
New Zealand's climate is temperate but varies accordingly due
to the many geographical styles and topography and
the remoteness of the country in its isolated position in the
south Pacific.
 The prevailing winds are from the West. The
massive mountain ranges create different climates
based upon the wind directions. It is a rain forest area
especially in the South Island where it may rain at any
 time of year.

Driving in New Zealand - My concepts
After years out here in our gypsy lifestyle 24/7 I am happy to say
 I have only seen a couple crashes and neither were fatal. After
several 100,000 kms I would say that is fairly good.
 Not saying there
aren't problems out here on the road but I see more
 infractions by Kiwis than visitors.
First... visitors driving a camper van in New Zealand.
Getting used to driving a large vehicle takes a little

practice. I suggest you might rent one at home to see
how it feels before making a rash decision to get a
large camper van if it is all new to you.

For everyone the biggest mistake I have noticed
from visitors is driving too slow in camper vans.
Always allow plenty of chances for everyone to pass.
Be observant out your back mirror is the answer.
Don't pull over if there isn't room. If you can see far
ahead and see it is safe flip your indicator and slow
down to allow someone to pass as long as it isn't on a
solid yellow line.

The New Zealand roads are well built and properly
maintained. Some of the best in the world from my
knowledge of past travels. Saying that.... the majority
are either going up an incline or down one at the
same time curving left or right and not rarely a sharp
hair-pin turn so speed is not required but diligence.
If you have a problem with heights don't look down
as you drive along but if you appreciate the vista you
won't be disappointed but do keep your attention
on the road as the driver. You never know when a cow
or a sheep or another traveler is around that bend.

The "wrong-side-of-the-road" problem happens
when a person drives out on a road from where they
were parked having just stopped to have lunch or
photograph a magic scene. Their minds are on the stop
and old habits take over. With a lack of traffic on so
much of our roads they don't adjust by virtue of what
they see. All I can say is "Think Left"!

One-way bridges may seem daunting at first but pay
attention to road signage and it will show who has
right-away (large white or black arrow yes - large
red arrow no) Don't rush to get there first. If there
is a doubt give up to the other. The majority of Kiwis
are excellent at the one-way bridges and are very polite.
Saying that I'll now express my thoughts on the Kiwi

driver. As nice and friendly as they are face to face when the majority get in vehicles they think they own the road and also simulate rally drivers. They tend to ride the back bumper of a slow vehicle and there isn't one in a hundred who knows what the white line in the centre of the road indicates on a curve. Be totally aware of the fact most will take their half out of the middle as they come around a curve whether they can see or not. If you are on the inside of a mountainous curve hug in as close as you can to keep from being hit by someone coming at you.

The worst offenders are the ones pulling boats and trailers. It seems they forget that what they are dragging along needs more room. I have had to slam on my brakes hundreds of times to keep from being side swiped by a boat or a utility trailer.

The worst are people hurrying to their weekend holiday speeding to get there. The ones coming home after work are also usually driving too fast and cutting curves. Also a lot of the people who live in the country forget they aren't still on the farm and claim the entire road as theirs.

Not being hard on my fellow Kiwi's but just advising of what I have personally encountered while being out here constantly driving as a part of my lifestyle.

By the way the truck drivers are usually very good just get out of their way when you can.

So be careful, be aware, be nice and enjoy the world of New Zealand and take home lots of pleasant memories.

Driving Tips

For your safety and comfort I have put together some driving tips which we hope you will find useful.

The most important thing to remember is that in New Zealand, driving is on the LEFT HAND SIDE of the road. This is the same as in the United Kingdom and Japan.

Travelling Times

The maximum speed limit for the open road in New Zealand is 100 kilometres/hour (US60 miles/hour). Drivers generally travel slightly under the speed limit. Please note that average speeds are lower and it takes longer to travel distances in New Zealand than might be expected. This is due to the hilly and mountainous nature of our countryside.

Rural Driving

Many roads have gravel verges. Be mindful to keep clear of the verge, especially on corners. Some isolated roads are unsealed and use gravel as the surface. In these cases, drive slowly. Note that there are some roads which are not suitable for camper vans and on which are placed restrictions. Please refer to the terms and conditions for more information.
During winter and early spring, some roads in the South Island and central North Island may be closed due to snow and ice. There will usually be an alternative route for you to take.

Seat Belts

It is compulsory in New Zealand that the driver and all passengers wear their seatbelts. This is an important safety requirement.

Camper Vans and Motor Homes in New Zealand -
An Overview
Some of the most sought after information is the rental
and use of camper vans and/or motor homes. Perhaps
with a brief outline I can provide some clarification
on what is available, what it means and how does one
go about knowing what to do.
First I must say I am very biased about seeing New
Zealand with your own self-contained vehicle as
opposed to a bus tour or even a car. I do realize many
cannot or do not wish to go that way but for those who
do perhaps the following will help:
Why is it a good way to see the country? New
Zealand is a truly scenic wonderland almost
everywhere you drive. The opportunity to stop and
relax in comfort in a unit large enough to prepare
lunch or a meal or just sit by the beach and have a
drink far removed from anyone but you is readily
available. The window space is greater and the ability
to move around is helpful. Who wants to be
crammed in the back seat of a car with small
windows? Plus staying at holiday parks is less
expensive than motels and who wants to keep
packing and unpacking every day?
New Zealand Holiday Parks are some of the
finest in the world being spacious, clean and
tidy for the better part, providing parking
spots with a pleasant outlook and have water
and electric hookups for each unit. All have more
than adequate waste disposal facilities to alleviate
any worries in that department.
I note almost daily new companies sprouting up
renting vans. All I can say is most of them have
not proven themselves as reliable. If I were spending
thousands of dollars to take that once in a lifetime
trip to New Zealand I surely wouldn't gamble on

poor equipment to get me around. I would like to know I am working with a company that will back up any problems that may go wrong. Provide equipment I shouldn't have to worry about. This is based upon my five solid years on the road every day and being with people at the holiday parks asking them questions on their rental equipment. Don't take a chance just because one is cheap. You don't need the aggravation of vehicle problems.

Yes a lot of companies are buying the vehicles taken out of service from the top companies and renting them cheap. Be careful! Work with reliable people and you won't spoil your holiday.

So what should you rent? What will work for you? First there are generally four sizes of rental units

1. Small 2 berth camper van with sleeping only
2. 2/3 berth camper van with kitchen & facilities
3. 4 berth motor home w/total facilities
   4. 6 berth motor home w/total facilities...........................
   5. .and then variations from these but these are
   6. the basics.

If you do not need much room, feel you could drive a normal camper van easier as opposed to a larger motor home then the camper van may be the option. The first one is no more than a station wagon without head room. The rest you can stand up inside and move around. (6' head room)

Most require making beds at night except the motor homes that have permanent double beds over the cab. The camper vans come with hot and cold water, shower, toilet, full kitchen with crockery, cutlery, etc. Check out the companies for the full specs.

This is just to give you an idea.

The motor homes are deluxe in their specs and really provide a home away from home. I find they are a luxury way to travel with room and storage never

having to worry about the clothes, luggage, etc.
Perfect for traveling families or two or three couples
and for a couple who enjoy more room.
Saying all that the ability to be more flexible on your
trip is a real bonus but if you park up each night at a
holiday park the van shower is generally redundant
unless during the day you took a swim in the sea or
get really dirty on a tramp or the weather got you wet
and cold (heaven forbid) and a good hot shower was
handy. Having a toilet handy sometimes is a real help!
This is just a quick summary to give you an idea of
what to look for. Check with the rental companies
that are well known and have a good reputation. Even
though with some the vehicles they rent are older
models they have been checked and re-checked to make
sure they do the job intended.
I have used many companies for hundreds of visitors
now for years and feel very confident in saying you
can get top quality camper vans without hidden costs
and value for money.
My major comment to everyone is you are about to
spend a lot of hard earned dollars to come a very
long way to be able to experience and appreciate one
of the finest natural places on earth. The one place
where you should not try to save is on the camper
van you plan to use. The heartache, hardships and
time lost is always attributed to the failure of the
vehicle one uses to go around the country.
New Zealand had extremely well maintained roads
but it is a country where 80-90% of the travel is on
mountainous terrain with twists and turns everywhere.
Hardly a flat straight road anywhere especially where
the traveler wishes to go.
Most of it is quite remote also and a breakdown can be
a long time consuming problem.
For instance I had brakes go out in Milford Sound.

It was two days of harassment getting back out of there
..........not to mention the 2 weeks it took to get back
on the road (but this was my own bus so the time of
delay wouldn't be the same).
The roads in the mountainous regions that twist
and turn are also have very steep valleys along side.
One does not need to be told how it feels to have a safe
vehicle when moving along these areas.

Check with me via email and I will advise you of the
companies that have proven themselves reliable over
the years. I have booked hundreds of visitors and have
eliminated the companies that have not been up to par.
No one needs a holiday ruined by poor transportation.
By the way it does not cost you anymore by
booking through me (sometimes less) and I provide a
free personal itinerary when you do. The same is true
when you plan to use a car rental.

What will you need when you use a camper van?
Small left over throw-away containers. We have $2 s
hops and the Warehouse that is good for cheap items
like this. Check here first when you come into the
country.
A knife sharpener might be handy to put an
edge on dull knives that come with the campervan.
Most campervan companies in New Zealand have a
detailed list of stuff they provide on their website.
Check it out to see if it will be enough for you.
Buy a measuring cup is handy and not always provided.

Place mats and napkins for the table. Just provides a better situation.

Cheap towels you can throw away at the end of the trip. Maybe two cheap shower mats. Some parks charge for showers so be sure to have $1, $2 coins handy. Also need them for the laundry.

Get some rope for a clothesline and some clothes pins. A couple of large plastic bags plus the smaller ones are real handy.

Get some of that non-skid fabric for the table. You will find it ever so handy. Perhaps even Velcro and be sure to get a roll of Duct tape. (you always need Duct tape in life!)

Tools such as a vice grip and a Swiss Army knife are invaluable.

Don't forget your eyeglass fix it kit (if you wear glasses) Make sure you get bug repellent!!! Take a heavy dose of vitamin B for two weeks before coming to New Zealand. The South Island requires it.

Bring your belongings in soft bags instead of big heavy bags. No place to store them in the camper van. Some of the companies will store them for you until your return.

Take it easy on the amount of clothes. You do not need many and the holiday parks all have good laundry facilities.

Camping in New Zealand –

Camping in New Zealand is an activity many Kiwis families enjoy for the Christmas holiday stay over at the local holiday park to the hiking through out into the wild regions staying at the huts provided or in their own tents. The love of the outdoors is an inherent concept for the Kiwi.

Many of the visitors to the country are here for the opportunity to camp in the beautiful unspoiled wilderness areas and even more are renting camper vans to enjoy a stay in our modern and well run holiday parks.

So we have many and varied types of camping to cover all facets of the outdoor world of New Zealand and provide easy access to all walks of life.

New Zealand Holiday Parks

Numerous campgrounds of a very high standard are found throughout the country. Almost all campgrounds offer full kitchen facilities, BBQ areas, TV lounges as well as washing machines and dryers.

Visitors are impressed by the cleanliness of shower and toilet blocks and the comprehensive facilities on offer. Campgrounds are often in scenic locations and the management is always happy to assist with information on local attractions and sightseeing.

It is recommended to book ahead especially during the New Zealand school holidays in December and January to ensure a powered site.

These operations are commercial operations that offer tent sites, powered and unpowered motorhome sites. Along with these the modern camps now also provide cabins and motel units so there is a place for everyone. For those who want a motel room or cabin it allows them to have a place that is more than just another room. It provides a more outdoor environment. There is quite a lot more on offer today than just an old camp ground with rustic facility. We have travelled throughout the entire country using the holiday parks and have found it is extremely rare to find one that is not top quality for cleanliness and service.

Tenting site cost is about $10 per night while the power site is around $40. Cabins vary but are usually from $50/75 per night while the motel units are around $100/150. Check as this may change from the time this book was published.

They most commonly provide:

A communal kitchen with most of the cooking gear provided

Toilet and shower complex

Laundry facility

Dump stations for the motor homes

Internet facilities

Recreation and lounge areas

Playgrounds for the children

Many have:

Swimming pools

Spa and gym

Department of Conservation Camps:
There are over 250 camping areas on the conservation land through the country and in some of our most scenic spots. The majority are operated on a trust basis with an envelope to leave the money in on site. The cost is at $6 per person per night and some are even free. The facilities may be basic with only toilets available. They also provide the standard campsite that provides toilets, tap water, barbecues, cold showers, picnic tables, rubbish bins. They also have the serviced campsites with flush toilets, kitchens, hot showers, laundry facilities.
Check with the DoC website for the lists - www.doc.govt.nz.

Freedom Camping –
We used to have great camping along the various streams, river and lakes if there was a place to pull over with the camper van. After too much abuse by visitors who left their personal trash in the woods and along the sites local councils have stopped almost all of it. I still do not understand the way a person who has come here to see the natural beauty and then leaves toilet paper and accompanying debris in the woods....
no respect....so now we all have to suffer from the freedom we once had. If you rent a camper van without full facility don't even think about parking in the wild.

New Zealand - Telephone and Postal Services
Telephone services
There are 6,500 payphones throughout New Zealand. The blue and yellow Telecom payphones will take phone cards, credit cards, Telecom TalkAway cards, Telecom Calling cards, and some will accept coins too. Telecom payphone cards come in $5, $10, $20 and $50 denominations. Five hundred indoor payphones also offer modem access.

Local calls made from payphones cost 50 cents, regardless of how long you talk. Toll calls are charged at current rates. To direct dial a national (toll) call in New Zealand, dial the national access code, 0, then the area code, then the number. For instance, to call Auckland 123 4567, dial 0, then 9 (the area code), then 123 4567. Area codes are in telephone directories, or dial directory assistance on 018.

To place a national call through an operator, dial 010. To direct dial an international call, dial the international code, 00, then the country code, then the area code, then the number. Eg, to call Sydney, Australia, 123 4567,

dial 00, then 61 (the country code), then 2 (the area code) then 123 4567. Country and area codes are in the telephone directory, or dial 0172. To place an international call through an operator, dial 0170.

Mobile & cellular phone options
New Zealand has a sophisticated cell phone network with both GSM (popular in Europe) and CDMA (popular in the US) based networks available. There is good cell phone coverage in towns and along the most major highways (eg State Highway 1 which runs the length of New Zealand) and popular holiday towns - but poorer coverage in New Zealand's mountain or remote country areas.

If you have a cell phone, you can check with your cell phone service provider (eg: Cingular or Sprint in the US, BT or Vodafone in the UK, Telstra or Optus in Australia) as to what roaming coverage they have in New Zealand. They can tell you whether your particular phone is compatible with the New Zealand networks (and any changes required to the settings on your phone) and what the calling costs are (both inbound and outbound from New Zealand and within New Zealand). Usually, the incoming calls diverted to your phone in New Zealand will be charged to you at international calling rates. Most cell phone companies also offer the option of just sending calls straight to your voice mail, which you can check at your leisure. Based on where you live, you are likely to need an adaptor plug for charging the phone in New Zealand.

You can also rent a cell phone on arrival either from Vodafone at www.vodafone.co.nz or Freephone 0800 300 021 on arrival in NZ (Vodafone have offices in Auckland, Wellington and Christchurch), or from Telecom New Zealand at www.telecom.co.nz or phone 123 on your arrival (Telecom have more than 40 stores around New Zealand). Rates and plans vary but, for frequent use, it may be cheaper than bringing your own phone.

A NZ prepaid SIM card costs $35 and comes with $15 worth of airtime. You will be able to pick up a SIM card on arrival at your NZ arrival airport from the Vodafone shop.

Top ups are available in multiples of $20 and they can be obtained from any supermarket, many dairies and Vodafone shops. Checkout counters at supermarkets issue top up vouchers direct from their till so you wont have to spend time looking for them.

The SIM card will give you access to both local and International calls. For rates on your NZ prepaid SIM card go to www.vodafone.co.nz

Telecom accepts American Express, Mastercard, Visa and Diners credit card payments for national and international calls. To place a credit card or transfer charge call through an operator, dial 010 for national and 0170 for international. In emergencies, contact the police, fire department and/or ambulance on 111 from any phone. There is no charge.

Postal services
New Zealand Post operates 316 Post Shops throughout the country, providing a full range of services from 8.30am to 5pm, Monday to Friday, with some also opening on Saturday mornings. There are also 703 post centres, which are scaled-down versions of a Post Shop and are part of an existing business, such as a dairy, chemist or bookshop.

Visitors can pick up mail at Poste Restante counters in Auckland, Wellington and Christchurch Central Post Offices and Post Shops will also hold mail if it's clearly marked. Local mail can be sent fast-post for a slightly higher postal fee. International mail should be posted in the red and white mail boxes.

Well that should be enough information to make sure you get here with minimum inconvenience. For most it will be the longest plane ride ever. Getting squared off with everything you need to know to enjoy your time here allows you a more free and easy drive around the country however you may choose to travel.

So now it is time to learn about what
New Zealand has to offer you……
from the mountains to the beaches….

Come with me as we explore the world of New Zealand

<u>**NOTES:**</u>

New Zealand from Cape Reinga to Bluff

One of the greatest holiday adventures on earth from the top of the North Island to the bottom of the South Island.

I will take you through the cities and towns and introduce you to the people who live here, what there is of interest to see and do and let you walk bare foot along isolated beaches far removed from people.

Climb or fly to the top of a glacier, boat across a turquoise coloured glacial lake. Tramp through forests of black beech and giant palm fronds. Stand in awe at the base of the Southern Alps and camp by the clear waters of a pristine trout filled lake.

See penguins, seals, albatross and other unique wildlife up close and personal.

Ocean kayak, enjoy the thrill of a jet boat ride or a bungy jump.

Visit some of the finest wineries in the world and enjoy some of the best culinary experiences such as fresh caught mussels, scallops, oysters and enjoy the taste of venison and lamb.

The restaurants and cafes rightly boast of their New Zealand foods and you too have the opportunity as you drive along to find many roadside stands full of fresh fruits and vegetables.

Take a relaxing dip in one of the many hot pools and be sure to visit the fascinating world of the Maori.

Be in the heart of Lord of the Rings country and follow the path of the hobbits to Mount Doom and beyond.

Around every corner and over every hill there is a startling vista and another adventure…..

Ready to discover the world of New Zealand?

So what are we waiting for......
let's get started.......

I am going to take you from the time your plane lands at the Auckland airport all the way to the **Far North** and **Cape Reinga** then back south through the **North Island** describing both coasts and down the middle by three different routes. Then we will cross over to the **South Island** along the top and down both coasts with a crossing over to each coast all the way to **Stewart Island**.

I will outline the routes, mention the driving time daily, point out what experiences and sights to enjoy. I will provide information for both those driving in camper vans and those in cars.

At each major region I will point out some historical facts and some personal observations I have made to help you find exactly what will make your visit to New Zealand the best travel experience you have ever had. What I will do is point out the places that are uniquely New Zealand and I have seen and experienced in my own personal travels here over the years.

Marlborough Sounds

Here is a portion of what I will cover:

From the Far North south to Wellington:
Cape Reinga Lighthouse at the very top
Ninety Mile Beach
The Dunes in the Far North
Waitangi Treaty Grounds
Bay of Islands
Tane Mahuta(God of the Forest)
Auckland – Sky Tower, Kelly Tarlton Underwater World
Coromandel Peninsula
Waitomo Caves, Billy Black's Woodland Park
Rotorua
Mt Taranaki
Wellington – Cuba Street and more

South Island:
Marlborough Sounds
West Coast (from top to bottom)
Punakaiki Pancake Rocks
Glaciers
Kaikoura Whale Watch
Lewis Pass
Hanmer Springs
Akaroa
Arthurs Pass
Mount Cook
Mackenzie Country
Oamaru Blue Penguins
Moeraki Boulders
Dunedin
Milford Sound
Queenstown

First I will introduce the major regions separately:

From the highest mountain ranges to the long expanses of beaches from the far north at Cape Reinga to Bluff I have divided the country into distinct regions and areas of interest in the North Island and in the South Island along with isolated Stewart Island. The world of New Zealand adventure beckons.

Northland -

The main approach is from route 1 to most of Northland and route 12 along the western coast. The weather is warm and humid in the summer with mild winters and rainfall. It is considered a sub-tropical area in the far north. This is generally a rugged land that has been settled since the Polynesian arrived followed by the European pioneers both groups leaving telltale signs of settlement. Prior to human invasion the entire landscape had been covered in forest.

The early Maori enjoyed the benefits of the abundance of bird life in the wilderness along with the fish and shellfish of the rivers and coastal areas. To the Europeans the forest itself was to be plundered and ransacked for timber to be used in their sailing vessels and the digging for the kauri gum in the swamps to be used for varnish. The re-build began in the mid-1990's so today the forests of Northland once again are green. Remnants of the mighty forests still can be found.

The Bay of Islands was formed after the ice age with the rising of the sea levels. There are over 150 islands that provide many deserted beaches for the boating visitor. Two historic buildings made of kauri timber from the early 1800's are the Kemp House in Kerikeri and Christ Church in Russell. In 1840 New Zealand became a British colony.

Big game fishing from the Bay of Islands was the first draw card for tourists to the area. Many a big game fish world record was recorded by Zane Grey in the 1920's. I was anxious to go there as Zane Grey also fished a lot in the Florida Keys where I spent 20 years plus I grew up reading his books and I too enjoy the fishing.

On the west coast of Northland the prevailing northerly inshore currents created many sand dunes. 29,000 hectares of sand have drifted inland to form the now famous Ninety Mile Beach. From this far north area the bar-tailed godwit leaves in March for the annual migration all the way to the Arctic tundra of Siberia.

A very unique wildlife situation takes place here with a bi-valve mollusk named the toheroa that burrows deep into the sands of Ninety-Mile Beach. It is known as the king of clams and totally disappears for long periods of time then as abruptly shows back up in the millions. No one knows where they disappear to. If you get there during the time they have disappeared the smaller and sweeter tuatua is readily available.

Most of the far north region is under protection with government reserves to protect the fragile environment for all of us to enjoy.

Saved from the ravenous kauri millers the government stopped their desecration of the kauri timber and was able to save a portion of what was once 13 million hectares of forest and is known as the Waipoua Forest now. The kauri tree may live to be 2000 years old with a girth of 16metres and a height of 55metre. Tane Mahua, (God of the Forest) at 51metres is available to be seen by everyone who enters the forest. Kauri timber in the mid-19th century was the major New Zealand export with ¾ of the forest destroyed by 1900. Driving into the forest is rather awesome and walking through to this tree is an experience. Just always remember to lock away your "stuff" when leaving your vehicle.

At the Poor Knights one will discover underwater exploration to be the best in the country. It seems a warmer sub-tropical current flows around the islands providing a quality spot for tropical fish to enjoy. The Poor Knights islands are home to the tuatara along with rare and extinct plants and many types of enchanting birds and reptiles and the Little Blue Penguin. If you want to experience diving New Zealand this is the place.

Hauraki Gulf –

Again the sea rose after the ice age (global warming) and what was left was the tops of the many volcanoes and outcroppings that became islands along with the sunken earth's crust creating the Firth of Thames and the Hauraki Plains. There are over 100 islands in the area. The sea rose over 100 metres and now provides 800 kms of coastline with another 450 kms of island shoreline. Little Barrier Island is protected. It has been the home to the stitchbird for over 100 years along with native bats and giant weta long no longer found anywhere else. The islands are sanctuary to thousands of birds far from the reach of predators and man. There are twelve breeding colonies of the petrel. It is considered a living museum.

Waiheke Island is well established as a settled area with many fine vineyards easily accessed from Auckland by ferry. Take the time to go to Waiheke Island and if you really want to enjoy the day go on the tour with Ananda Tours - **http://www.ananda.co.nz/** Now they know how to provide a real tour you will enjoy.

On the east side of the Gulf is the Coromandel Peninsula long regarded as the Auckland playground splattered with summer retreats and one of the most interesting parts of New Zealand not to be missed. I will take you up both sides of the Peninsula pointing out what to see and do. This will be a highlight of your North Island visit.

A half hour trip from Auckland also is Rangitoto Island that was an active volcano as recently as 300 years ago.

Governor Sir George Grey bought Kawau Island in 1862 to place animals from the many places he had served during his colonial service. Several have flourished and today wallabies and the kookaburra from Australia are prevalent around the historic Mansion House.

About 100kms from Auckland is the Great Barrier Island. On the west coast are rugged cliffs and ridges with bays and inlets on the east side. A small permanent population of around 500 people live there. Only a very small portion of the island has roads so if you visit be ready to walk.

The New Zealand Forest Service has created a 2000 hectare forest of native kauri, rimu, totara and tanekaha that will be the backbone of beauty for centuries to come.

Free from all predators the bird life is spectacular from the black petrel high in the cliffs of Mt Hirakimata, the highest mountain to the penguins and gannets sea side. The kaka parrot and the kakariki parakeet make a home there.

It was also the place where the last whaling station in New Zealand was located having started in 1950s and lasted a decade. It was close to the migration routes of the humpback, blue whales and orcas. They killed more than 100 humpback whales in one year. Thank goodness that is a thing of the past.

Notes:

Auckland's West Coast –

Easily accessible by sealed road from the Waitakere Ranges to Raglan and all points in between. Usually moderate temperatures throughout. The city of Auckland is located at the narrowest part of New Zealand between the Hauraki Gulf in the east and the Manakau Harbour to the west. I can recommend a company who provides several great tours in the Auckland/Coromandel region – check out these tours: **http://www.bushandbeach.co.nz**

The west coast is steep shore and rough water from the Tasman Sea. Over the past 100,000 years over sixty volcanos have erupted through out the Auckland region created by the pressures 50kms under the area. The hot springs scattered about show there still be freshly made volcanoes at any time. The area west of Auckland is known as the Waitakere Ranges and is so wild in places kauri trees still are there left by foresters unable to get them out. On both north and south of the Ranges is sand dune country some rising to 100metres or more. The sand is mostly iron rich black sand to the point in late summer it is sometimes too hot to walk on comfortably. There are very few access roads to the majority of the West Coast in this area.

With the wildest area most remote is Whatipu. There are quite a few walking tracks but not for anyone not in shape and experienced. The most used area is the beach at Piha famous for its surf, swimming and fishing. It is a treacherous coast not to be taken lightly as many can attest to.

Other beaches one can visit are at Bethels Beach and Muriwai Beach. The variety of volcanic action and erosion have provided very interesting rock formations along the cliff faces. At the northerly end of Auckland's west coast is South Kaikara Head where one of the most dangerous sand bar entrances is into the harbour.

For the bird enthusiast this area is the home to thousands of migratory birds as far away as Alaska and Siberia. This is also the end of New Zealand's longest river the Waikato river that began 425kms south of here at Lake Taupo.

Other entry points to the northern West Coast are Raglan, Aotea and Kawhia Harbours. Raglan is internationally famous in the surfing world. I really enjoy the laid back community that provides very good cafes and shops. Well worth a visit.

The Pirongia State Forest Park dominates the western edge of the Waikato Basin with 11,748 hectares with the two mountains of Mt Pirongia at 963m high and The Cone at 945m. Mt Pirongia is a favourite to climb. The rare bird the kokako is said to be prevalent on the mountain. A road along the coastal edge of Mt Pirongia takes you to within a short walk to Bridal Veil Falls that drops 50m to the forest below.

Further south is the well known Waitomo Caves area where three caves of the 85 km of the known cave system are open to visitors. This is one of my favourite areas to visit. First is the caves and all they offer and then we have the Billy Black Show plus a whole lot of other entertaining places. This area is a must for everyone coming to New Zealand.

Notes:

Coromandel Peninsula –

This is a very special area to visit. Highway 26 goes around the Peninsula from Thames to Waihi with rough winding roads crossing at a couple of places. They have moderate weather with heavy rains in the winter. The Coromandel Forest Park runs along the entire peninsula with portions of it opened for visitors with camp grounds and walks. The Peninsula has the look of an island. It was assaulted in the early days with mining and farming, burning and milling but has maintained its wild characteristics. The western road meandering along the coast from Thames to Coromandel Town is an exciting scenic drive especially if the red flowered pohutukawas are in bloom (Christmas time).

Along these stony beaches one can find semi-precious stones such as carnelian, jasper, agate and chalcedony. Love this drive along the West Coast from Thames to Coromandel Town. When we first bought our bus we lived at a friend's place in the Coromandel where we prepared it for our home and office and tested it and us on the mountain roads of the Coromandel.

Down the east coast are the towns of Whitianga and Hahei with scenic Cathedral Cove and further on Hot Water Beach where you can scoop out your own spot in the sand to enjoy the waters. On south the road takes us along the east coast to the pleasant town of Tairua and on to Whangamata then on over the hills to the town of Waihi.

Giant tree ferns and the occasional huge kauris are a feature in the Coromandel forests. The search for gold in the Coromandel have left many of the scars that accompany it. Volcanic remnants dominate the skyline with giant vertical rock formations dotted through out the peninsula.

Rotorua –

This is the number one place anyone visiting New Zealand must visit. Highway 5 from Hamilton and access from Tauranga in the north is route 33. Rotorua enjoys a stable climate. The area is natures' cauldron of hot springs, boiling mud, geysers and the smell of hydrogen sulphide have made this thermal region world famous.

This area is a basin-like structure 16km in diameter and 300metres deep that was formed 150,000 years ago.

At Whakarewarewa south of the city of Rotorua there are more than 500 hot springs. There are two types of hot springs - chloride and sulphate. A chloride spring runs clear that over time releases enough silica to form sinter terraces where as all geysers are chloride springs. Ones to see in this area are Pohutu that has an eruption of over 18metres, the Prince of Wales Feathers and Waikorohihi. Be careful when exploring this area as much of the ground between the hot springs is warm and with steam coming from many small fissures. It is quite important one stays to the well marked paths provided. Some areas there is only a thin crust of ground over boiling mud. If you have never been around this type of terrain it will be one of your most exciting experiences.

The most violent and destructive volcanic eruption during European settlement time was by Mt Tarawera in 1886 destroying three settlements. It was this eruption that destroyed the then famous Pink and White Terraces and formed Lake Rotomahana. An interesting walk is to go to the isthmus between the Blue Lake and the Green Lake, created also by this eruption to see the actual colour difference.

One of the most interesting and most active thermal areas is at Hell's Gate. They offer a mud bath here you may enkjoy. Also Kakahi Falls a major attraction where one can be splashed in a cascade of warm water.

The Waimangu Thermal Valley did not exist prior to the eruption when ten craters were formed with some filled from the overflow of Lake Rotomahana. The three most visited in the valley are the Inferno Crater, Echo Crater and Southern Crater. Echo Crater is filled by Frying Pan Lake, one of the world's largest "boiling" lakes. Several explosions have occurred over the years with the most recent in 1973 but no one was injured.

It is only 26kms from Rotorua to Waimangu and from there a track begins that can be followed through this crater area. A quick short walk of only an hour will get you to a good portion of it but if you continue along through the area and along the lake to circle back to where you begun it will take you to some very scenic sights and views of these thermal wonders.

The large Waiotapu Wonderland thermal area 25km southeast of Rotorua is open to visitors and has crater-like pits up to 20metres across with boiling pools of muddy water at the base of some. Southeast of the pits lies the spectacular Champagne Pool and at the south end of the pool is Bridal Veil Falls. Just outside the reserve are also some excellent mud pools and also the Lady Knox Geyser which was actually artificially created in 1906. It was discovered to erupt when soap powder was introduced by the local inmates of the prison in those days when they came to wash their clothes so the Chief Warden installed a cast-iron pipe and increased the height of the geyser....

After the hot pools or maybe before you check them out is where you can get full immersion into the Maori culture. You have to visit the villages and you can't go to Rotorua without enjoying an evening meal or a hangi as it is known in Maori with its fantastic food and cultural show.

Rotorua itself as a town provides great accommodations cafes & restaurants and a good place to pick up some New Zealand souvenirs. Plan a couple of days here to really get full enjoyment of the area and what it has to offer.

Sixty-eight kms from Rotorua is the Orakei Korako themal region. One way to reach the thermal valley is by jet boat across Lake Ohakuri and a walk of an hour or so around takes you by the Diamond Geyser , the Hochstetter Hot Pool, the Rainboe Terrace and the most spectacular Golden FDleece Terrace a gigantic deposit of white silica over 5 metre high cascading down the hill side. The best known is what is called Aladdin's Cave where in pre-European times it was used by the local Maori women to adorn themselves in the mirror pools. At night glow worms bring a strange glow to the cave.

The Rotorua area has vast forests of introduced pine for logging that covers over 111,000hectares. It is one of the largest in the world employing over 1500 people producing nearly 30 cubic metres of wood annually. The Park has been opened to recreation with many tracks and huts along with camping and picnic areas.

Lake Taupo -

Highways One and Five are the access roads from Hamilton, Rotorua and Napier. The area has a stable climate. Lake Taupo is a volcano and the largest lake in New Zealand. The last eruption occurred in 130AD that it has been estimated spewed a cloud to 40 km above the volcano. Ash which had risen to the top of the cloud fell over much of the North Island.

If you like to fish Lake Taupo has the top trout fishing reputation in the country and draws sportsmen from all over the world. In 1886 Brown trout were introduced to the lake with rainbow trout hatcheries having been established in 1883. Good conservation practices have kept the rainbow trout pure as the first shipment from California.

One of the most famous trout streams is the Tongariro that enters Lake Taupo from the north. When I first got back to New Zealand to live permanently I went with friends who had a boat on the lake for a weekend. I had never seen or caught such large trout in my life.

East of Taupo is Mt Tauhara and extinct volcano and a good climb to the top and return in a couple of hours for those hardy trampers.

You can drive completely around the lake on a 150km round trip with Route One running close on the eastern side but with limited access to the western and northern areas.

The Waikato River flows from Lake Taupo meandering north to west of Auckland dumping into the Tasman Sea. From Lake Taupo the river flows for 354kms. Here the river narrows to 15metre wide to cascade over the **Huka Falls** and drop 11metres to a large pool. The Falls area can be accessed by a road that brings you directly to the falls. This is one of the natural highlights of the North Island and I highly recommend a visit.

Another small thermal park of interest is the Craters of the Moon. It has the Karapita geyser along with mud pools and steamy grounds.

In this area the Waikato River power is being harnessed for electricity. Quite significant amounts have been established. By 1979 the power station in this area provided enough to provide 5% of the nation's requirements. Quite significant.

<u>Tongariro National Park</u> –
The main road to Whakapapa Village is highway 48. Rain and high winds have spoiled many a tramp in the park and the winter snow falls are welcomed by the skiers. Here you will find the highest mountain, Mt Tongariro (2797mrtres) in the North Island one of the three volcanos and the high desert country.

The volcanos are still active with eruptions from all three - Mt Tongariro, Mt Ruepehu and Mt Ngauruhoe the most active. In 1894 it became the first national park in New Zealand and now covers over 75,000hectares. Summer time there are many walks throughout the park to enjoy and in the winter Mt Ruepehu has three ski fields that are easy access. To the east of Mt Ruapehu is the Rangipo Desert. Lake Rotopounamu only 10 metres deep fills a crater and has several sandy beaches reached by a short track less than 2 km from the Te Ponanga side road.

At the top of Mt Tongariro the crater is filled with hot sulpherous water covering around 17hectares. Several times the lake has spilled over causing problems below with one event in 1953 taking out a bridge and a train load of people below killing 151 people. The water is highly acid so don't be inclined to take a dip. The volcano is still in a very active state but still thousands enjoy the winter activities on its slopes.

The area abounds with bird life with the Little Brown Kiwi, a forest recluse, coming out at night to forage. The alpine region is fabulous in summer with many small flowering plants such as the mountain buttercup.

Mt Ngarauhoe is continually active usually with eruptions of gas and steam. The Ketetahi Springs on Mt Tongariro remained in Maori title as it was considered a sacred spring that produced curing waters. It can be reached by a good track from the National Park-Turangi Road and is around a half day walk. If you do go there be sure to stay on the marked track. There are many streams that begin in Tongariro including the Wanganui River, North Island's second longest. This is a great river to kayak or canoe with over 90 rapids below the town of Taumarunui.

For the keen hikers - a track across a volcano - one of the most spectacular walks in New Zealand – The Mangatepopo Track, the first segment is between Whakapapa village skirting Mt Ngauruhoe and onto the Mangatepopo Hut a 10km rather easy three hour walk. Most of the track goes through tussock country with some beech forest and low bush.

The longest section of 15kms is the traverse of Mt Tongariro and includes several steep climbs (five-six hour walk). After the hut for around two kilometres the track follows the Mangatepopo Stream. At the head of the valley you get a great view of Mt Ngauruhoe to the left with Soda Springs on the right. From here the climb is steep. The track continues across South Crater climbing to Red Crater at 1820metres the highest point of the walk.

The track down on the other side is steep and requires care. At the base are the Emerald Lakes. The next kilometre is crossing flat Central Crater then climbing to the Blue Lake crater where a fabulous view of the volcanic area is fantastic. The end of the track at the Ketetahu Hut is only another 1 ½ kms from here and another two hours to the road through the Ketetahi thermal area.

The entire track can be done in nine to ten hours by a very fit tramper but staying at both huts it is an enjoyable walk of around 2 ½ days. You can drive to within an hour of the Mangatepopo Hut whereby a fit walker can do the Tongariro and Keteahi Tracks in around eight hours.

White Island – Bay of Plenty –
Named by Captain Cook White Island is an active volcano 50kms off shore from Whakatane. It is a small island of 1.5km in width to 2.7km length.

There are commercial boats to take visitors to the island. It is a dangerous place with the mud and water strongly acid and many holes emitting gas. You do need a gas mask. Early exploration and mining of sulphur ended in the death of all hands and mining was abandoned. It is a very hostile environment but quite fascinating for the adventure minded. The best access to the area is the town of Whakatane a pleasurable place to visit and stay.

East Cape -

The most remote area of the North Island with the sea on one side and the boundary of the Opotiki to Gisborne Highway on the interior and separated by the physical barriers of the Raukumara Ranges and the Urewera National Park.

The Maori have been predominant here from the time of their early arrival in the area by canoe at Whangaparaoa Bay. There are three major rivers on the East Cape that all provide excellent canoeing through real isolated rugged country.

Most of the back country is not accessible with few major roads. Not a place to venture out into without local knowledge. Two routes - the coastal route between Gisborne and Opotiki and the inland route that is 480kms roundtrip but worth it if you want to see what the East Cape is all about.

The Waioeka Scenic Highway is a sealed road that goes through the very scenic Waioeka Gorge along the Waioeka River.

The mountain of Hikurangi is the first place that the sun rises at the beginning of the international date line in New Zealand. So if you happen to be here for a New Year's morning maybe you would enjoy being one of the first person on earth to see the sunrise on a new year.

Two roads provide access from the north highway 2 from Opotiki and highway 35 around the coast and is not recommend in wet weather. From Napier it is route 2 with an alternative route of 36 from Wairoa.

The climate is generally mild and sunny. It is an isolated area and nor many tourists take the time to go around the East Cape. I really enjoy the route 2 drive through the gorge to the city of Gisborne that is a fabulous place to visit and is Young Nicks Head.

Hawkes Bay and the Wairarapa Coast –

Route 2 from Napier to Wellington is the access in this area. The south coast is exposed to high winds and weather changes. From Napier to south to Cape Pallisar has a coastline of golden sand and wild surf.

Below Napier is Cape Kidnappers where the only know mainland colony of Australasian gannets exists. There are many fine beaches all along the coastline. The name Cape Kidnappers came from an attempted taking of a young cabin boy from Capt Cook's boat the Endeavour. Firing upon the canoe the boy got away and swam back to the boat.

November and December are the best months to visit the gannet colony. If you want to walk to the Cape it is about 8kms starting at Clifton Domain south of Napier. Plan for two hours each way.

Don't start your walk from Clifton earlier than three hours after high tide and leaving the Cape be sure to not begin later than 1 ½ hours after low tide…

In the area Ocean Beach and Waimarama Beach are beautiful golden sand beaches to enjoy but as one travels further south the coastlines become more hostile all the way to Cape Palliser. One of nature's wonders inland from Cape Palliser and 17kms from Lake Ferry, plus a walk of about an hour, is the Putangirau Pinnacles a natural area of massive vertical pillars and fluted cliffs created by erosion.

Taranaki Region - Egmont National Park –
South on Route 3 takes you to the Taranaki region, New Plymouth and the Egmont National Park.

Three approaches to Mt Egmont off route 3 with access to Dawson Falls Lodge, Stratford Mountain House and North Egmont Chalet.

As with most mountains the weather can rapidly change. Clouds generally hang around the upper level except perhaps in the early morning.

New Zealand's most climbed mountain at 2518metres. In the late 1800's a route was created to the lower slopes of the mountain and in 1881 the mountain and the land around it to 9.6 km of the summit was to be protected. Roads circle the mountain and from them roads to three mountain houses can be reached at the 900m level.

Three prominent waterfalls in the Park: Dawson, Bells and Curtis Falls all in easy reach by the vast number of tracks cut into the mountain amounting to over 300kms total.

The climb to the top is easy enough in good weather.

Mt Egmont

I have briefly provided a background and a general insight to the major areas of the North Island so you can get an idea of what and where you will get the most out of your holiday time while here.

Next I will do the same for the South island and then I will begin the in-depth coverage of the country so you will not miss anything you might want to experience.

I want to make sure when you leave here the memories you take with you will be positive and for a lifetime.

Notes:

Now on to the
South Island regions.......

Marlborough Sounds -

Highway Six from Nelson and Highway One form Blenheim to Picton. There is great back road (sealed but winding) between Havelock and Picton through the Sounds. Also there are several roads into the Sounds but not really recommended for visitors.

Fine weather throughout the Sounds in summer but can get very windy in the winter but still a very pleasant place to be.

The sea has made deep bays and filled valleys of what was once the northern portion of the Richmond Range of mountains from the rise of water after the ice ages plus the entire area seems to be continually tilting into Cook Strait.

Captain Cook used it as his base. He discovered a good harbour that he named Queen Charlotte the location now known as Ship Cove. The Queen Charlotte Sound is one of two entries into the Sounds and the one that all ferries arrive or depart between the North and South Islands through the Tory Channel. The other is on northwest and is the Pelorus Sound where the Pelorus River flows into.

The entire Sounds is a boating dream with bays and inlets everywhere along with a generous dollop of small islands. In the area of Port Underwood was a whaling town in the late 1800's known for its hell raising population all over the Pacific.

Heavy forest covers a great deal of the Sounds and wild pigs abound many descendants of those turned loose by Capt Cook. Much of the Sounds is reached by road but there are many homes scattered all over that can only be reached by boat. Picton and Havelock are the major towns of entry. Cook Strait dividing North and South Islands takes on the ferocity at times of the area it lies in called the Roaring Forties. Crossing at times can be upsetting with massive winds and strong currents.

Golden Bay and the Able Tasman National Park -
Highway 60 from Nelson and highway 6 from Westport are the roads to get to the Bay and to the Abel Tasman Park.
Golden Bay has a sunny, mild climate with light winds generally and a really pleasant spot. There is one road to this isolated area reached after a climb over the Takaka Hill or as it is mostly called "the Marble Mountain".
The drive is very scenic and picturesque both going up and then down on the other side. The first glimpse of Golden Bay from the outlook at the top of the mountain shows a Shangri-la with rich farmland encompassed by mountains all the way around with the bay disappearing off into the mist of the sea toward Farewell Spit.
Great marble caves have been discovered along with rich and diverse plant and animal life which is one of the defining aspects of this special area.
The Able Tasman Park provides one of the best coastal playgrounds in New Zealand with golden sand beaches and wooded tracks perfect for boating, swimming, camping and walking.

The Park came into public controlled existence in 1942. Native forest has slowly begun to regenerate throughout the Park. For the adventuresome (not recommended for motor homes though we took our seven metre bus there) a dirt road on the top of Takaka Hill curves and jogs through marble and schist outcroppings and tussock to what is known as Cannaan Downs. At the end of the 11km road there is a short walk through the forest to Harwood's Hole which drops 360 metres into the centre of the mountain.

Over 100 million years the Marble Mountain has had its depths carved by acid water into a honeycomb of caves and tunnels. April 2010 three cavers found the first 1 kilometre cave in New Zealand under Mt Arthur south of Nelson in the Ellis basin system that is 33.4km in length.

The Abel Tasman area is for adventuresome souls where white water boating, caving and wilderness travel are highlighted but it also provides plenty of places for the less adventuresome who want to visit scenic areas by car or short walks. In the Golden Bay area one of the top tracks for trampers is the Heaphy Track and the Mt Arthur Tableland.

The Heaphy Track is a 3 to 4 day walk of 70kms with comfortable huts not over 5 hours apart plus good bridges crossing all the major streams. The Tableland is a two day easy walk from Flora Saddle on the Motueka side to Cobb Road on the Golden Bay side.

IN 1862 James Mackay cut the track used today by modern trampers starting at the Aorere River in Golden Bay to the Heaphy River 11.5 kms north of Karamea on the West Coast. The track begins in beech forest then enters Gouland Downs an area of red tussock and multitudes of herbs and flowers with over 26 species of orchids along with lilies and daisies. 448 species of native plants have been found here many of them rare. From here the track is into valleys and forest becoming more tropical along the way leading into coastline.

There are several places worth visiting in the Golden Bay area such as Pupu Springs, one of the clearest springs in the world, the Te Anaroa Caves near Rockville, the Whanganui Inlet, Westhaven (up the Wairoa estuary at high tide by boat) and the Kaihoka Lakes Scenic Reserve but the one truly awesome spot to experience is Farewell Spit, a curve of sand 26kms long extending past the Centre where the road ends. There are excursions available out the Spit from Collingwood a really great place to stay when in the area.

This area is a migratory bird heaven with over 100 species been recorded. In March and April thousands of godwits start for their breeding grounds in the Siberian tundra, the longest migratory excursion in the world and returning in September. This sand spit was formed and continues to increase at the rate of 3 cubic metres a year from rock ground into sand by the glaciers and swept out to sea from the Southern Alps.

The Humpback whales in their migratory path north to their breeding grounds sometimes get stranded here.

Nelson Lakes National Park and the Buller River –

Access from the north is by route 6 from the Nelson area and route 63 from Blenheim. Pleasant summers with more rain in the western ranges. Through the Park runs the Alpine Fault, the western boundary of the Southern Alps, and to the east is the mountain range of St Anaud enclosing over 57000 hectares of land mostly mountainous country and forested valleys.

Lake Rotoroa and Lake Rotoiti formed by glacier and are enjoyed by everyone visiting the area. From Lake Rotoiti flows the Buller River for 170kms to the Tasman Sea on the West Coast and I consider it one of the most beautiful rivers I have seen.

Several easy walking tracks around Lake Rotoiti or perhaps the climb up Black Hill that takes about an hour or to the top of Mt Robert for the view. There is a road skirting the lake and goes to Robert's Lookout. There is also a track along the Hukere River to Lake Angelus where there is a tramper's hut.

There is a road (rough and narrow) coming off Route 6 at Gowan Bridge that goes along the Gowan River to Lake Rotoroa. From the Spenser Mountains the Sabine and Durville rivers feed Lake Rotoroa.

Lake Rotoroa is the place for visitors who want peace and quiet or perhaps a chance for a trout as it is considered one of the best lakes for fishing in the country. There are several tracks around Lake Rotoroa with the easiest being the Porika Track about a half day walk and the full day walk on the rougher Rotoroa Track but Lake Constance with mountain reflections is considered one of the most beautiful in the country and close by also of exquisite beauty is Blue Lake, surrounded by beech forest on the west branch of the Sabine River.

The Buller River named by the early European explorers, Brunner , Heaphy and Fox doesn't quite fit as well as the Maori name I prefer of Kaatiri, meaning "swift and deep" which sums up this beautiful length of water.

At the junction of the Buller and Gowan rivers the waters flow aggressively through steep gorge for 75kms that can been seen from the road that parallels it a majority of the way to Murchison where it gentles down a bit.

Along this section of the river one can see the scars from the 1929 earthquake and at Inangahua it is worth a stop at the old building they have by the road that contains photos and information of the quake destruction then and in 1968.

Past here the river enters the Lower Buller Gorge also quite spectacular. The drive around Hawkes Crag is quite daunting as it is narrow and carved out of the vertical cliff face. The Buller River enters the Tasman Sea at Westport.

Ten kms to the west is Cape Foulwind where a walk to the lighthouse is well worth it. When you stop in the parking lot the local Weka are sure to check you out for a possible food source. This is one of New Zealand's native birds that is visitor friendly and a delight to watch.

The Kaikouras
Route One from Picton to Christchurch is the main South Island road. Winds are light and the summers are warm but there are winter squalls. From Blenheim one passes through vineyards and the desolate hills until finally coming to the East Coast via route one.

As you get to the coast far to the left untouched by roads is Cape Campbell and from here the land rises and forms into two mountain ranges – the Seaward Kaikoura and the Inland Kaikouras. The Clarence River runs for over 70kms along a fault that separates the two ranges.

Also following a fault is the Awatere River and just north in parallel another fault rift has the Wairau River flowing. From the Clarence River south to just north of the Kaikoura Peninsula heavy rocky coast line and grey sand and rock beaches where giant kelp and seals call home and lobster fishing is at its finest. The towering mountains inland are impressive and have snow on their peaks most of the year.

The coast south of Kaikoura is quite rough and rocky with jagged reefs and large expanses of the giant kelp. Limestone caves named the Maori Leap Caves are just south of town filled with stalactites and stalagmites and the fossilized bones of seals and penguins.

This is the primary place to see and enjoy the seal colonies and the home to the whales either by boat or plane.

Arthur's Pass National Park
Arthurs Pass is Highway 73 from Christchurch to route 6 to Kumara Junction south of Greymouth. Long periods of unsettled weather with strong westerly winds at times. Be aware of driving during winter with snow being a factor.

You can also catch a train ride also across from Christchurch and Greymouth is considered one of the world's great train rides.

In 1865 it was decided to cut a road across to the West Coast as gold fever was upon the land. A thousand plus men through the bitterly cold alpine winter with only hand tools and explosives created a road in less than a year. Arthur's Pass is the highest and most spectacular road crossing the Southern Alps. It is 160 kms from Springfield in the east to the old gold mining town of Kumara now but a crossroads.

A startling difference of vegetation with the east side of the Main Divide being forests of beech and on the west it is rainforest. Many a waterfall can be seen along this route.

The Craigieburn Range is ski country in the winter and beyond is Lake Pearson famous for its trout fishing and close by also is Lake Grassmere. The road follows the Waimakariri River that travels for 150kms to the Pacific Ocean.

This area has had four major periods of glaciers over 500,000 years and with erosion, raid, avalanche and earthquake this stark rugged country was formed.

In the upper Waimakairi can be found a tramper's paradise. In a matter of just a few hours four huts can be reached. Glaciers are still to be found high in the river's watershed. This is also a great area for mountaineer and climbers to tackle. There are over 16 mountains over 2000metres. Throughout the park also can be found the pesky bird, the kea, a parrot-like bird known for his curiosity and destruction of rubber auto trimmings such as around the window and the wiper blades.

Major earthquakes are still active in this area. The Taruahuna Pass is but a large pile of earthquake debris and in the Otehake Wilderness just beyond hot springs still merrily bubble.

This area of Edwards Valley has many good walking tracks. The Bealy Valley where the town of Arthurs Pass is located is the heart of the park. Less than a kilometre from the town is the location of a giant waterfall falling 150m named the Devils' Punchbowl and nearby is the Bridal Veil waterfall.
 If you cross the Pass in summer you will be rewarded on the west side with the beautiful flowering trees, the rata, with its scarlet flowers covering the slopes.
One of the major magic drives in New Zealand with the Otiri Gorge bridge being a spectacular man-made inclusion along the route.

Banks Peninsula (Akaroa) –

A good sealed road is available from Christchurch Highway 75. Variable weather with cool summers and cold southerly gales bring snow to high levels.
It was named by Captain Cook in honour of his botanist, Sir Joseph Banks, who had been with him on his 1769-70 voyage. Banks Peninsula was formed by two volcanoes.
On the road to Akaroa on the right lies Lake Ellesmere a shallow coastal lake famous for its flounder and eel fishing and a population of thousands of black swans.
From the town of Little River one soon begins the circuitous drive up the mountain to reach the top for a scenic view of the town of Akaroa and the harbour.
The historic French town is the result of early French settlers who founded a colony there in 1840 but discovered the British had got there before them with a formal claim. They didn't mind and stayed anyhow so today the town has the French charm of streets named Rue Lavaud, Rue Croix and more.
There is more to the Peninsula than Akaroa for those more adventuresome.

Take the Summit Road above Akaroa Harbour that goes on to the bush reserve of Otepatotu, 37 hectares of forest with a walking track 755m to the top of Lavericks Peak.

In the eastern bays there is Le Bons Bay and Okaines Bay where a small museum houses artifacts from the early Maori and pioneers to the region along with many walking tracks.

We enjoy Akaroa for its semi-isolation and great restaurants.

Mackenzie Country –

Highway 8 through the Mackenzie Country to route 80 into the National Park. This is the Southern Alps and the weather in the summer is fine but in the winter is heavy snow at times

The bare brown tussock world of the Mackenzie Basin is accessed from the east via the town of Fairlie. This is the beginning of the Mackenzie Country and access on route 8 from the south and from Central Otago through the awesome Lindis Pass to Omarama.

The three lakes of the region are Lake Tekapo, Lake Pukaki and Lake Ohau that provide the power for the hydro-electric stations and through canals to be stored at Lake Benmore for more power stations.

If you enter the area from route 83 you will pass through the length of hydro-electric lakes. The lakes were naturally created over 17.000 years ago being dammed by glacial moraine.

Several small lakes can be seen from the top of Mt John where the University of Pennsylvania has established an international observatory due to the clarity of the sky in this location. A great vista to drive up to and photograph.

Mount Cook National Park –

One of the major spots one must visit in New Zealand the area known as the Mackenzie Country inland southwest of Christchurch.

New Zealand's highest mountain, Mount Cook (3764metres) and Tasman Glacier, longest glacier area in the park plus fourteen more peaks over 3000metres and four other glaciers with over 150 mountains over 2000metres. The park covers 70,000 hectares. The Maori name for Mt Cook is "Aorangi" meaning cloud in the sky.

Lake Pukaki and Lake Tekapo waters are of glacial beginnings and are of the cloudy light blue colour caused by the grinding force of the glaciers on the mountains creating what is known as rock flour.

Mountain climbers have been attacking Mount Cook since 1882. One being New Zealand's world famous Edmund Hillary, who made history as the conqueror of Mt Everest in 1948. The first ascent was actually by another New Zealander, Tom Fyfe, in 1894.

The Tasman Glacier is one of the longest in the world 29 kms long and 3kms wide. From the Mt Cook Village there is a road to Blue Lakes and from there a short walk to the glacier terminal. From 13,000 years ago the glacier has been melting. Surveys show the ice is around 600metres thick at Ball Hut. The glacier provides top quality skiing also reached by ski-plane.

This mountainous area has a wild population of the chamois climbing through its heights from an original release back in 1907. The thar is also living in the region.

The Copland Pass at 2133metres separating the barren rocky eastern part of the Southern Alps to the western region of lush rainforests provides an accessible walking route over the Main Divide. It is a three to four day tramp with three huts available. Alpine tramping experience is required and Feb/March the best months to attempt it.

For those who wish a short trek of around three hours (11kms) start at the Mt Cook Village taking the Kea Point track into the Hooker Valley track taking you over two swing bridges above the Hooker River and close to the face of the Hooker Glacier.

The majority of New Zealand's native plants grow exclusively in the mountainous areas and in the Mount Cook National park where there are over 400 species alone.

Westland National Park –

The West Coast is a narrow strip of land 238kms long from Greymouth to Haast with the Tasman Sea on the coastal side and the entire wall of the Southern Alps to the east where at certain intervals the mountain ranges border the sea.

The Westland National Park is 160kms of this area. Entry to this area is Route six all the way through the West Coast. The twelve rivers all begin in the mountains rushing wildly to the sea. Swamps and lakes are interspersed through the area with rain forest and glaciers being an integral part of the scenery. The warm current of the Tasman Sea keep the temperature on the coast from becoming too cold but it does have a tendency to be wet.

There is 24kms of steep winding road between Franz and Fox Glaciers. This is rainforest country.................so do expect it! If you want to go up the glaciers try to get there early is best.

Lake Mapourika is the largest lake in this region of 1813hectares having filled a hole left by a glacier. Lake Ianthe is surrounded by a matai forest that has a giant matai tree over 1000years old that is 5.3metres in girth. White herons and the royal spoonbill nest only in the Okarito Swamp here.

The Franz Josef Glacier is a mere 7000 years old and is 11kms long having advanced and receded many times in its life. It comes within 19kms of the coast. You can drive close to the terminal base to see it at that area where it feeds the Waiho River.

Several walks in this area such as just off the approach road is a five minute walk to the dramatic, clear Peters' Pool. The Sentinel Rock walk is an easy walk to a scenic outlook of the glacier.

More fitness and time are required for the Robert's Point Track and the hours trek to Lake Wombat. On this walk one can discover a plant hanging from the ferns, little hanging straps with tiny needles pointing down. This plant's ancestors were common before modern plants 160 million years before dinosaurs.

The full days walk to Christmas Lookout requires good fitness and gear but worth it to be in the mountain meadow of alpine flowers in the summer.

Fox Glacier is 13kms long its base reached by a narrow road through forest for 5kms. The surface of the glacier has a pristine whiteness on its surface with the hollows create by water are a beautiful turquoise showing the criss-cross patterns created by the grinding action of constant movement. A track can be taken (with the right footwear) to the top of Mt Fox where panoramic views are fabulous as are the overlook of the glacier on the track up.

 From Fox Glacier Village take the road to Gillespies Beach to Lake Matheson, the most scenic lake with the reflections of the Southern Alps providing a photographic quality especially early in the morning before the wind ruffles the water. It is an easy walk around the lake through the forest lined with ferns and moss and the joy of having the fluttering of fantails that come to chat at you and the sound of bellbirds rings through the canopy.

You can also take a branching track for 1 ½ hours to discover Lake Gault deep in the forest. This lake has most bird life around it and the view of the mountains is even more dramatic than Matheson.

To continue the road to Gillespies Beach will take you to an area that once was populated to the size of a small town during the gold rush (the gold found in the beach sand) from 1860 to 1890. A short walk around the area one can discover an old miner's road and a tunnel and also a resident seal colony.

Travel on south on route 6 crossing over the Karangarua River and the western end of the Copland Track on south through forest lakes, river and swamps. One comes back to the ocean and the west coast beach at Bruce's Bay, passing by the trout filled Lake Paringa and then Lake Moeraki and then coming back to the coastal lookout of Knight's Point.

From here it is a roller coaster drive with swamp and trees closing in on the roadside until finally reaching the Callender-Hamilton bridge, the longest one-way bridge in New Zealand, over the Haast River.

Mount Aspiring National Park –

Continuing along Highway 6 it goes through the Park. It is a good chance it will be raining as you drive through. Not bad though as there are plenty of fabulous waterfalls to see then. I consider this one of the top drives of New Zealand.

Mount Aspiring, the Matterhorn of New Zealand, dominates the park at 3027metres second only to Mt Cook. The park was established in 1964 and stretched from the Haast River to the Humbolt Mountains by Lake Wakitiopu near Glenorchy. There is permanent snow above 2000metres.

One of the greatest ranges of alpine vegetation in the world between snow line and tree line is here with 94% of the vegetation found only in New Zealand. The Haast Pass is the lowest pass on the Main Divide.

It wasn't until 1965 that the road was completed through to form this portion of route 6. It is 146kms from Haast Pass to Wanaka. To me this is one of the most dramatic drives in New Zealand.

On the western side it is wet with the mean annual rainfall recorded at Roaring Billy is 5840mm and rain falls on 182 days a year. One of the most dramatic scenic areas is at the Gates of Haast bridge where the Haast River plunges through giant schist boulders as it crashed down the mountain side.

Two kms south of the bridge is Thunder Falls where with just a 100meter walk through the beech forest brings you to the edge of the river and across from the 30 metre waterfall spectacular.

The whole area from the Olivine River to the Naihi River, 68 km to the north has been proclaimed as a wilderness area. The area of the Arawata and the Waiatoto rivers is some of the most remote inaccessible place in the country.

The Arawata river meets the sea northeast of Jackson's Bay, settled since 1875, remotely reached by a road from the Haast area. It is a world of whitebaiting in the rivers of the area and also known for its lobster and paua.

Lake Wanaka/Lake Hawea -

Lake Wanaka is 45kms long and 4.8kms wide with its deepest point being 311metres. It is the source of the mighty southern river known as the Clutha.

Lake Hawea is 31kms long and 8km wide and a depth of 410m with its waters well stocked with trout and land-locked salmon.

Tracks -

The <u>Rees-Dart</u> track is marked, easily accessible and safer than many alpine tracks.

The <u>Routburn</u> track – This popular track can be accessed easily from either end from the Fiordland National Park by the Hollyford River or from the Routburn in the Mt Aspiring Park. There are several well placed huts along the walk first come first served November to May and only two nights.

Central Otago –

Highways 6 and 8 traverse Central Otago. Wanaka is linked with Queenstown also via the Crown Range - highway 89. This is the highest road in New Zealand closed in winter and not recommended any time. Rental vehicles are not allowed.

One of the most spectacular drives is from Queenstown to Cromwell on route 8 through the Kawarau Gorge. The climate is extreme with hot summers and cold winters and the lowest rainfall in the country.

A giant schist plateau rising over 600metres above the coastal area with the Dunstan Mountains, St Bathans and Hawkdun Ranges are the northern boundary to the Garvie and Umbrella Mountains to the south.

The area has the most popular tourist areas of Queenstown, Lake Wanaka, Lake Hawea and Lake Wakitipu within and Dunedin is at the southeast limit of the region.

Extreme weather from the hottest in the summer to the coldest in the winter is what to expect plus the dryness and the hills barren and arid.

Once upon as time less than 1500 years ago there was vegetation and forest but the early Moa hunters set fire to everything to drive the birds out to kill. Along with sheep grazing and unlimited amounts of rabbits the area has been totally denuded. Remoteness and desolation is what one finds with open blue skies that I actually find very beautiful in its starkness coupled with the solitude and open space. Pillars of rock 6-9metres high create a strange landscape in the Ida Valley and the Maniototo Plains.

In 1861 Gabriel Read discovered gold 5km out of the present town of Lawrence and the New Zealand gold rush began with over 11,000 prospecting for gold in just a couple of months in this area. Naseby was one of the early gold strike areas and today is where the sport of curling takes place.

The Roxburgh area is known for its fruit orchards. The original town of Cromwell was destroyed for the hydro lake all but a very small area now at the edge of Lake Dunstan and the present newly built Cromwell.

Beyond on the road to Queenstown area one drives along the Kawarau Gorge one of the most exciting drives in New Zealand. The Roaring Meg stream was named after a loud-mouthed redhead woman who tended a bar during the early gold mining days.

The towns of Clyde and Alexandra are both small towns of Central. The Clutha River, starting from Lake Wanaka, winds its way all the way to the Pacific through Central Otago and has an influence in its path. Central Otago wine is now being sought internationally for its quality especially the Pinot Noir.

The 800meter long and 50metres s deep Blue Lake at St Bathans was created in the search for gold…

Lake Wakitipu is 77kms long, 4.8kms at its widest and 378meters deep. At the junction of the south arm and the central arm of the lake lies Queenstown. The 50km drive to Glenorchy along the lake is one of the most scenic drives in the country. Just outside of Queenstown on the right a side road of 7kms takes you to the awesome Moke Lake DoC Camp one of our favourites to stay at.

Arrowtown came into being by gold discovery by William Fox in 1862 and is a fabulous small town to walk around plus a visit to the Chinese Village down by the river is recommended. You can also still find gold in the Arrow River.

The road to Wanaka over the Crown Range and via the Cadrona Valley is 70kms. The views are panoramic.

Lindis Gorge – (one of my favourite drives) is a linking road between Central Otago and the Mackenzie Basin through the Lindis Gorge via the Lindis Pass nestled between the Old Man Peak to the south and Longslip Mountain with Omarama 32kms to the northeast and Tarras 40 kms southwest. There is quite sparse vegetation with mostly tussock but the scenic value is extremely high.

Fiordland National Park –

The Milford Road is the only main road into the Park from Te Anau. It runs for 125kms through one of the most beautiful drives in the country. Even though you may be driving around New Zealand I recommend taking other transportation so you do not have to worry about the road and get the chance to really enjoy the scenic ride.

Fiordland is one of the wettest places in the country with unpredictable weather at all times. The extreme southeast of the South Island is the wettest, wildest and most isolated part of New Zealand. The valleys have broad, flat floors and almost vertical mountains. This area is greatly affected by the gales of the Roaring Forties.

The rainfall on an average at Milford Sound is 7274mm a year making Fordland one of the wettest places on earth. The land rises from south to north to the summit of the Darran Mountains.

The ice age ground out troughs and on the west coast these became the fiords and in the east lakes formed. Lake Te Anau is the largest lake in the South Island with a shoreline of over 500kms.

A half-hour trip from Te Anau to the base of the Murchison Mountains are the glow worm caves.

Deer farming sprang from the wild deer released in this region that once became so plentiful they had to be culled to protect the vegetation and over population. There is also Lake Manapouri said to be the most beautiful in New Zealand. A power project at the lake is probably one of the most interesting trips one van make in the region. Water is taken down vertically to turbines 213metres below lake level where it is discharged along a 10km tunnel and out to sea at Deep Cove.

The fiords exploitation began in the late 1700's with the sealers and then the whalers followed by gold prospectors as late as in the early 1900's.

When seals were almost exterminated and the whales became less and less and the gold veins petered out the fiords were left alone to be appreciated by explorers and lovers of nature. The Fordland crescent penguin breed only here.

The Milford Track is well known through the world by trampers. It is a three day hike for those who are fit and well prepared especially for the rain. One of the finest treats of the walk are the waterfalls such as the Sutherland Falls dropping over 580metres to the valley below, the fifth highest falls on earth and Giant Gate Falls considered the most beautiful.

Milford Sound –

Considered one of the great drives in the world is the one into Milford Sound. Passing the Mirror Lakes and on to the beautiful bush Hollyford Valley and on to the Homer Tunnel that was completed in 1953. The steep descent through the mountain with the tunnel dripping wet is an excursion on its own not so daunting now that there are lights in it. Then it emerges into the Cleddau Valley on many sharp curves of road to the valley below. One of the most photographed mountains in New Zealand is Mite Peak that forms the south wall of Milford Sound and reaching skyward to 1412 metres.

Looking down the Sounds from the parking lot and the Hotel beyond Mite Peak there is Bowen Falls and Mt Pembroke, the Lion and beyond id Sterling Falls.

In 1878 Donald Sutherland made this area his home and the present hotel stands where he began. A boat trip out through the Sounds takes you to the base of Sterling Falls which cascades directly into the sea and on to Anita Bay ad the Tasman Sea.

The Hollyford Track begins 8kms from Gunn's Camp on the Hollyford River. The first day's walk takes you to Hidden Falls on the river. Next day the track takes you along Bridal Falls after crossing the Little Homer Saddle. Guided walkers are picked up by jet boat and taken to a hut while those on their own have another 90 minutes to the public hut on the shores of Lake Alabaster and on to Lake McKerrow and along Demons Trail to the area once inhabited and known as Martins Bay.

The Catlins –

Sealed road now through the Catlins with highway 92 from Invercargill to Balclutha and highway One from Edendale. The climate is variable with shelter from the Southern Alps, low rainfall and constant summer sunshine with the winter storms bringing snow and sleet to low levels. One of New Zealand's least known regions bordered by the sea between Invercargill and Balclutha with Owaka being the major small settlement of a few hundred. The forests were immense and in the early 1870s it was the busiest timber port in the country. Today the timber is long gone, the small farms were not prosperous leaving the area quiet. The Catlins State Forest Park protects what is left of the forest. One of the main landmarks is the lighthouse at Nugget Point and can be reached by leaving route 92 at Romahapa past Kaka Point. Seals and shore birds prevail on the rugged kelp fringed coastline. The Catlins is a natural place with virgin roan forests covering the hills along golden sand beaches scattered along broad estuaries and towering cliffs.

Cannibal Bay, named by early settlers after finding human bones there, can be reached by a road from route 92. It is a bay of broad sands for a kilometre and across the dunes is another beach at Surat Bay and the entrance of the Catlins River and upstream is the tidal Lake Catlins known for its sea-run trout. Close by is Jacks Bay with high cliffs and where the Tuhawaiki Island cliffs are honey-combed with little blue penguin burrows, sooty shearwaters and muttonbirds. Jack's Blowhole a 55metre deep chasm at the end of a long tunnel is an interesting sight when the sea surges through at a roar.

From Ratanui the Takakopa Beach road leads to the Purakaunui Falls Reserve 500 hectares of native bush which has been preserved since 1905.

Studies have shown the Catlins were perhaps the last known area where giant flightless Moa existed.

South of Papatowai from Florence Hill one gets a panorama of the golden sand beach of Tautuku Bay. In this area is true dense green moss-hanging rain forest where except for the bird song all is quiet and peaceful. One of the roads that penetrate the forest goes to Waipati Beach Scenic Reserve and a 20 minute walk to the Cathedral Caves that are 30 metres high and reach into the cliffs more than 100 metres.

I recommend turning south along Waikawa Harbour and Porpoise bay to see the petrified forest at Curio Bay created 160 million years ago when a sub-tropical forest was overwhelmed by sand. At low tide you can see the now silica tree trunks up to 30 metres long.

Stewart Island – Air service daily from Invercargill and ferry service from Bluff. Very changeable weather and the effect of the southerlies from the Antarctic are apparent. The least known and the least populated of the three main islands Stewart Island has remained largely a wilderness with exploration mostly on foot. The only settlement is Oban in Half-Moon Bay. The island itself is a part of the top of a large granite mass lying in the sea south of the island.

The island can be reached by a 20 minute air flight or the two hour boat ride from Bluff. The plant life shows its difference after 10,000 years of isolation. Many tracks available but the majority require experience and fitness. Early inhabitants were the sealer and whalers. This ia where the young of the sooty shearwater, known as mutton bird, are harvested each year this right being reserved for the descendents of the southern Maori who lived here when Steward Island was sold to the British.

The large Brown Kiwi can be observed here in the daytime. My wife tells the story about when her and her first husband lived a winter there in their sailboat in Glory Bay/Little Glory Bay. They were possum trappers for the fur in those days. Red deer were over abundant and upon occasion they would shoot one on the beach from the sailboat for food. There was also a salmon farm there and the local seals would terrorize it causing the salmon to scatter. So they had wonderful meals of venison and salmon whenever they wanted. Their excursions into the bush allowed them to observe the Brown Kiwi on many occasion during the day. The rare native ground parrot the kakapo lives o the island and is protected. Some interesting history – In 1810 sealers came ashore near South Cape and were massacred with the exception of 16 year old James Caddell who for the next 12 years became a Maori in all aspects marrying the chief's daughter and became a chief in his own right.

Now off we go..................

First stop is Auckland...

<u>**Auckland - http://www.aucklandnz.com/**</u>

Welcome to Auckland New Zealand International Airport. Our custom officials are very sharp but very nice and polite. Our laws are very highly regarded as far as what you can or cannot bring in. Don't spoil a good trip by bringing in something you shouldn't. A big worry is the introduction of something that will harm our ecosystem. If you have tramping or sports gear make sure it isn't contaminated with contact in another country especially your boots. Didymo is now in our once clean pristine rivers thanks to a fly fisherman's dirty boots from the US.

Dependent upon how you feel after a major flight or a late arrival it may be that you would prefer getting a room and chill out before beginning your sojourn. Best to get acclimated to the new time zone so as the rest of the trip will be pleasant.

Auckland, the major city of New Zealand, as far as population size and a port of entry for international air flights. It is known as the "City of Sails" based upon the magnificent harbour and marina at the base of the main downtown area that is dedicated to a vast array of sailboats and yachts. America's Cup was sailed and won from here by New Zealand. You may want to visit Sky City and ride the glass-fronted lifts up to the Sky Tower — this is the tallest building in the southern hemisphere — for the 360-degree panoramic views of Auckland and its harbours. There is also a casino at Sky City, if you feel so inclined with restaurants and shops. Auckland offers top quality entertainment, diversified restaurants many showcasing the large Asian population that abounds here.

Top Things to do in the Auckland Region:

Get an inside look of the area on a Bush & Beach Tour -
http://www.bushandbeach.co.nz .
Take the free city circuit Red Bus -
http://www.aucklandnz.com
Go to the Kelly Tarlton's Underwater World -
http://www.kellytarltons.co.nz/
Visit the Sky Tower and maybe a sky jump -
http://www.skyjump.co.nz/
Sail aboard the 70ft classic schooner SV Haparanda -
www.deckedoutyachting.co.nz
Go out to Waiheke Island for a taste of top wines -
http://www.waihekenz.com/
Take a walk on Rangitoto Island and climb a volcano -
http://trampingtracks.co.nz
Tour the War Memorial Museum -
http://www.aucklandmuseum.com/

Auckland Bridge Climb and bungy jump -
http://www.bungy.co.nz/auckland-bridge

Central Auckland

It is 21 kilometres (13 miles) from the International airport to downtown Auckland. One of the best ways to get there is by the Airbus - **http://www.airbus.co.nz/home/** departing every 15 minutes every day of the year and takes about 45 minutes.

The main street is Queen Street that runs from top of the central area to the base at the waterfront. There is a visitor information centre, 299 Queen St on Aotea Square , close to the waterfront and another in Sky City. Whatever you do, be sure to have a good Auckland city map and be aware walking is the best option in the downtown area but if you wish to go further afield check out the free **Red Bus** to get an idea where everything is located and then get either a bus or a taxi.   Enjoy world class dining and shopping

Downtown retail hours open:
Monday-Thursday, 8.30am -5.30pm;
Friday, 8.30am - 9pm;
Saturday & Sunday, 10am-4pm

Auckland's North Shore -
http://www.tourismnorthshore.org.nz/
Across the harbour Bridge is the area known as the North Shore with the suburb of Takapuna and down on the harbour is Devonport one of my favourite spots that offer great cafes, restaurants and shops. Devonport can easily be reached by ferry from the harbour side in Auckland.

What to do in Auckland's North Shore
Walk through Devonport streets and enjoy the shops
Dine out and have a perfect coffee at a Devonport café'
Spend a summer's day on beautiful Takapuna Beach
Explore one of the area's 400 parks and walkways

Hauraki Gulf - http://haurakigulf.aucklandnz.com/
There are several islands in the Hauraki Gulf worth a visit.
First is Waiheke with its vineyards, the beaches of remote
Great Barrier, walk the volcano of Rangitoto Island and the
island of Tiritiri Matangi. The Hauraki Gulf is a great place
to explore and enjoy a harbour cruise and
visit the native birds on Tiritiri Matangi Island.

Waiheke Island is special. It is a 35 min ferry ride from
downtown Auckland. There are 30+ boutique vineyards
producing a range of varietals, predominantly Bordeaux
Blends, Syrah, Montepulciano, Viognier, Chardonnays and
Pinot Gris and some delightful summer Rose`. Mature
olive trees now adorn many of the island's hillsides
producing Gold medal olive oil. There is a wide selection
of restaurants and many art galleries, gardens, native bush
and coastal walks and white sandy beaches. **Ron
recommends the Ananda Tours** for a real day of fun and
exploration on not to be missed Waiheke Island:
Ananda Tours invites you to enjoy a wonderful day tasting
award winning wine, olive oil and other local produce for
which Waiheke Island is world-renowned. Visit local artists
and galleries, explore one of the many eco-trails or wander
along a pristine beach. On the way, stunning scenery is
absolutely unavoidable!
To contact them:
Phone: 09 372 7530
Mobile: 027 233 4565
Website: www.ananda.co.nz
West Auckland
This area is the location of the rugged Waitakere Ranges
and some of New Zealand's most stunning surf
beaches. Piha, Muriwai, Bethells and Karekare are popular
black-sand beaches, known for excellent surf conditions.

To really see it right take one of the Bush & Beach tours –
http://www.bushandbeach.co.nz

What to do in West Auckland, New Zealand

Visit the Arataki Visitor Centre -
http://www.arc.govt.nz/parks/our-parks/arataki-visitor-centre/
Surf or soak up the sun at Piha or Bethells Beach -
http://www.pihabeach.co.nz/ Wander one of the many
Waitakere forest tracks -
http://www.arc.govt.nz/parks/whats-on-in-parks/activities/waitakere-ranges-walking-tracks.cfm

South Auckland
South Auckland is the home to our Pacific Islanders :
Samoan, Tongan, Fijian and Cook Island cultures
intermingle here, making Auckland the largest Polynesian
city in the world!

What to do in South Auckland, New Zealand
Visit the Otara Markets for a real taste of Pacific food,
art & culture. -
http://www.viewauckland.co.nz/insidersguide/otara-market-feature-2726.html
Have a family day out at theme park - Rainbow's End -
http://www.rainbowsend.co.nz/
Visit the beautiful Auckland Botanic Gardens -
http://www.aucklandbotanicgardens.co.nz/

Some helpful hints:

After landing I will suppose you will be picking up a rental
vehicle as your next priority. After that if you wish you can
go into the Auckland city area. Remember it is a city with

all the problems one has with parking and driving so be sure you have come to terms with driving on the left side of the road. (What I usually recommend is to go to your accommodation already booked the first day or two and then when you get ready to start your road trip make arrangements with the rental company to pick you up and take you to their terminal and leave from there).

If you drive the Auckland region offers everything one would wish from such an environment. Usually you can get a park at the waterfront downtown. Turn off Motorway on Fanshawe Street and follow all the way through to the end at Quay Street, turn left and park in the **America's Cup Village Marina** Parking lot. Good idea to pick up an Auckland map at the airport. You can park right by the Museum and enjoy the city. (make sure you get some change for parking metres while at the airport) Have a stroll around the waterfront area where the America's Cup Race was staged. The best way to tour the inner city is to take the free bright red "City Circuit" bus that runs every 10 minutes.

You may want to bungy jump off the **Sky Tower**, the tallest tower in the Southern Hemisphere.(or just watch) You can base jump 630 feet (192m) falling for around 16 seconds at 75kph. Please book first. There are also three viewing platforms and the glass bottom lift that will give most of you enough thrills. Live entertainment, casino, bars and restaurants Sky City has it all.

Princess Wharf will provide you with plenty of bars, restaurants and shops but if that is not enough shops be sure to go to **Victoria Park Market** with over 85 shops handling just about everything you may want to take home. If you are looking for Auckland's restaurant strip go to Ponsonby Road where it is the happenin' place.

Catch a **Fuller's ferry** from the docks at the base of Queen Street and take a ride across the bay to the beautiful seaside village of **Devonport**. Lots of studios and galleries tucked in among the cafes, restaurants and shops.

Take a short drive on Quay Street, the one along the waterfront and the one you enter after the parking lot, to one of the finest attractions in New Zealand the: **Kelly Tarlton's** Antarctic Encounter & Underwater World, 23 Tamiki Drive or you can grab a free bus ride from there on Quay Street at the base of Queen Street.

Your itinerary time and your personal interests will decide the amount of time you will devote to the Auckland area.

Auckland waterfront – Take a sailing dinner cruise

Time to move on if you want to see the magic of the rest of New Zealand........................

North of Auckland to Cape Reinga and back.......

First let's go north from Auckland and see rural New Zealand and get introduced to its early history where **Northland - http://www.northlandnz.com/** was the first to be settled both by Maori and Europeans in the **Bay of Islands - http://www.bay-of-islands.co.nz/** area. Direct driving time from the airport to Paihia is 2 ½ hours (246kms) but there are many interesting places in between. Hopefully you are in no hurry....

By the way for those of you used to miles a quick way to convert kms to miles is to multiply by six - ex: 100kms x 6 = 60 miles. (that's the top speed allowed on the roads here).

If you are in a camper van and need to stock up on supplies for your trip or even if you are in a car and require items you felt best to buy here than carry aboard the plane there is a large shopping complex by the exit from the airport that is easy to access and will have everything you may need. For the movanners don't overstock as there are more than enough places along the way to find plenty of fresh fruit, veggies and meat. We have a lot of roadside markets that are a cornucopia of delights.

From Auckland north on route one the city and suburbia begin to dissipate and smaller villages and the countryside take over the scenery.

Take route one to the turnoff on route 17 to the town of **Orewa - http://www.orewa-beach.co.nz/** and enjoy one of the finest beaches in the country. Before Orewa just north of the village of Silverdale there is the turnoff right to the

Whangaparoa Peninsula - http://en.wikipedia.org/wiki/Whangaparaoa_Peninsula you can visit one of the areas major marina development at Gulf Harbour. Also a chance to stop at the Shakespear Regional Park and the **Gulf Harbour Country Club - http://www.gulfharbourcountryclub.co.nz/layouts/terraces/Template.aspx?page=home** .
We lived in this area when we first came back to New Zealand and enjoyed it very much.

When leaving this area stay on route 17 out of **Orewa** as opposed to the toll road so you can see the best of the scenery here. Just north, after crossing the Waiwera River on the right, is a good rest stop at the Wenderholm Park. Route 17 then finishes when it links back up to route one north. On to the **Waiwera Thermal Resort and Spa - http://www.waiwera.co.nz/** if you wish to take a break. Then on the left not too far along is the Bohemian Village of **Puhoi** and a place to try out some of their fabulous cheeses. Well worth a quick cruise through the village. Now on north the next place of interest is the town of **Warkworth - http://www.warkworthnz.com/** . On the north end of the town off route one take the Matakana Road through the local **wine region - http://www.matakanawine.com/** . In the area there are over thirty wineries. I enjoy Heron's Flight for their tasty Sangiovese wine.I am a little bit prejudiced as I was there talking with the owner David Hoskins in 1993 and he excitedly revealed his plans for the planting of the Italian grape as we looked down over a barren hillside now completely covered with the Sangiovese vines. So glad it has become a success. We also stop by the Ascension Winery. Plenty of galleries in the area also.

On to the village of **Matakana -** http://matakanavillage.co.nz/ . If you are here on a Saturday there is a brilliant market going one.

For the adventuresome on through to the town of Leigh and on north on the Pakariki Road then Whangaripo Valley Road that circles through the countryside to end up back on route one at Wellsford then on north. Out of Leigh is Goat Island NZ's first fully protected marine reserve and a brilliant spot to dive and snorkel. Good café at Leigh the Sawmill Café.

For a scenic side trip take at Kaiwaka take the route to the right out to **Mangawai** and **Mangawai Heads - http://www.mangawhai.co.nz/** on the Mangawai Harbour then continue on Cove Road to **Lang's Beach** and the coast to **Waipu – (love the museum) - http://www.waipumuseum.com/html/index.htm** and back to route one north the next major town being **Whangarei – http://www.whangareinz.com/**

The northern most city and the major hub of activity for Northland. Whangarei is a water world playground of 100 beaches, pristine harbours and off-shore islands. Enjoy some of the world's best sub tropical diving, walkways, or go to town to have a walk through the many fine galleries and cafes and visit the Town Basin Marina complex.

Close by is **Tutukaka** the jumping off spot to dive the world famous Poor Knights Island Marine Reserve.

Our favourite camp ground to stay at here is the Whangarei Falls Holiday Park - **http://www.whangareifalls.co.nz/** .

The best restaurant in our opinion is

A Deco – www.a-deco.co.nz

Five Top Things to Do in the Whangarei area

- Dive at Poor Knights Island - **http://www.doc.govt.nz/conservation/marine-and-coastal/marine-protected-areas/marine-reserves-a-z/poor-knights-islands/**
- Stop and see the Clapham's Clock Museum - **http://www.claphamsclocks.com/**
- Visit Whangarei Falls (the most photogenic in New Zealand) - **http://www.whangareinz.com/things_to_do/activity/whangarei_falls**

- Take a walk in the Kauri Park - **http://www.whangareinz.com/things_to_do/activity/a h_reed_kauri_park**
- Take a walk through the Town Basin

On north a beautiful isolated spot for camper vanners is **Whananaki - http://en.wikipedia.org/wiki/Whananaki** reached by the Marua Road out of Hikurangi. Good stay at the holiday park - **http://www.whananakiholiday.co.nz/** .

Continuing north on route one before you get to Whakapara take Whananaki Road North on the right to Pigs Head Road (junction at Opuawhanga) and then Kaiikanui Road and Webb Road to one the top spots I really enjoy stopping at is the **Helena Bay Gallery & Café.**

Best to then return to route one at Whakapara on Russell Road. Next stop is **Kawakawa**. Be sure to stop here and see the public toilets (strange but true) a startling piece of work by **Hundertwasser** an internationally acclaimed artist) **http://www.teara.govt.nz/en/northland-places/9/5/1** .From Kawakawa to route 11 and to the playground of Northland –

<u>Paihia and the Bay of Islands</u> - http://www.bay-of-islands.co.nz/

The Bay of Islands is considered one of the premier New Zealand holiday destinations and definitely the place to go if you go north of Auckland to explore. The Bay of Islands is made up of several small towns very close together. 150 islands comprise the archipelago of small islands in the Bay of Islands. Most of them are uninhabited and many still unexplored. About the only island which has some facilities is Urupukapuka Island lying northeast of Russell.

Maritime and historic park

There are some forty sites on the islands which are part of the Bay of Islands Maritime and Historic Park. The Park's Visitor Information Centre is at Russell. These islands have many walks and historical sites, as well as recreation reserves. Full information is available at Department of Conservation information centres.

Attractions and activities

The Bay of Islands is a world of water sports and recreation. This includes many scenic and unique attractions that may be enjoyed with the local boat tours.

Activities include scuba diving, swimming with dolphins, sea kayaking, fishing. The Bay of Islands became a major destination for American western writer Zane Grey in his pursuit of the mighty marlin.

The first time I came here in 1989 I was invited out onto a big game charter boat that was in a tournament. My partner, Howard, and I spent the day with the group aboard swapping tall tales of our big game fishing experiences in the Florida Keys where once upon a time I had been the dockmaster at the Islamorada Resort.

History

The Bay of Islands is the cradle of New Zealand nationhood with historic Waitangi here. In 1769 Captain James Cook dropped anchor in the Bay of Islands and began the settlement by the English. It was Cook who named the place Bay of Islands and it was here that English settlers first set up home in New Zealand.

The birth of New Zealand nationhood goes back to 1840 Waitangi when Maori tribal leaders and the English colonisers forged a treaty which still serves as the official document for uniting New Zealand's various peoples into one common nation. There is still much contention and argument over rights by the present day Maori.

Top Five Things to do in the Bay of Islands -
- Visit the Waitangi Treaty Grounds - **http://www.waitangi.net.nz/**
- See New Zealand's oldest buildings at Kerikeri - **http://www.kerikeri.co.nz/OurTown.cfm**
- Experience historic Russell - **http://www.russellnz.co.nz/**
- Take a boat cruise around the bays from Paihia
- Go big game fishing

Festivals in the Bay of Islands:
Country Rock Festival - **http://www.country-rock.co.nz/**
Jazz and Blues Festival - **http://www.jazz-blues.co.nz/home**

Tours:
Mack Attack – see Cape Brett, Hole in the Wall and Cathedral Cove - **http://www.mackattack.co.nz/**
Dolphin Cruises - **http://www.dolphincruises.co.nz/**
Scenic Cape Reinga tours - **http://www.dolphincruises.co.nz/cape-reinga/**
Overnight Cruise - http://www.dolphincruises.co.nz/overnight-cruise/

Kerikeri - http://www.kerikeri.co.nz/
This town is at the northern end of the Bay of Islands inland on the Kerikeri River. It is home to New Zealand's oldest buildings, Kerikeri is a historic destination filled with art, crafts, water based activities, walks and one of the world's top golf courses!

Top five things to do in Kerikeri, New Zealand
- Visit the historic Stone Store built 1832-36 - **http://kerikeri.co.nz/feature.cfm?wpid=2323**
- Visit also Kemp House oldest building in New Zealand - **http://kerikeri.co.nz/feature.cfm?wpid=2323**

- Drop by Pete's Vintage & Classic cars - **http://www.petesmuseum.co.nz/**
- Indulge yourself with Makana hand made chocolates - **https://secure.makana.co.nz/Default.aspx**
- Take a steam boat cruise - **http://www.steamship.co.nz/**

plus:

- ✓ Golf Course - **http://www.kerikerigolf.co.nz/Kerikeri_Golf_Club/Home.html**
- ✓ Great walking tracks in the Puketi and Omahuta Forest also Rainbow Falls Walk(10 minutes) - **http://www.doc.govt.nz/**
- ✓ Rewa's Maori Village - A reproduction of an unfortified Maori village called a kainga. It is across from the Stone Store.
- ✓ Kororipo Pa - or Maori fortress on the marked 10 minute historical walk.

Bay of Islands Café/Restaurants recommended:
Waikokopu Cafe
Posh Nosh
Marsden Estate Winery
Only Seafood
Campgrounds:
Beachside Holiday Park – Paihia
Kerikeri Top Ten
When in the Bay of Islands area stay at a fabulous B&B:

You are invited to come and share a haven of peace and luxury. Landing Cottage is boutique accommodation for up to 6 people, in Kerikeri, the jewel of the Bay of Islands.

A delicious full breakfast each morning from our menu is included in the price.

Situated in an acre of beautiful, private garden, they offer a fully-serviced guest-wing of 3 luxuriously appointed spacious bedrooms, (King, Queen & Twin), suitable for families or groups of friends of up to 6 people.

Guests have their own private lounge, modern bathroom with bath, shower and twin-basins and a separate toilet. Guests also have their own entrance and private patio which gives a wonderful view of the garden.

Our exclusive *SINGLE-PARTY BOOKING POLICY* ensures your privacy and comfort.

Contact:

Website: **www.landingcottage.co.nz**

AND:

Luxury Bed & Breakfast Accommodation
Kerikeri - New Zealand

Looking for the perfect place to stay in Kerikeri? We invite you to indulge yourself at **Bed of Roses, a Romantic French Country Accommodation**. We would love to treat you to a stay that you will never forget. Bed of Roses sits on top of a hill with panoramic views over the historic river basin; the meeting of Kerikeri river and the sea inlet. The property is large with no near neighbours to disturb the peace and quiet.

Perfectly located close to the Stone Store (the first shop in New Zealand), Bed of Roses is one of the few buildings in Kerikeri that is part of the historic precinct and the town is only a few minutes walk away.

We offer three completely refurbished luxury guest suites, each with its own ensuite, and a spacious guest lounge where you can relax and unwind.

When you stay at Bed of Roses you will receive one of our famous breakfasts. We love creating delicious, beautifully presented breakfasts that utilise the finest local produce.

Your hosts, Cliff and Louisa, have the ability to offer exceptional service without being intrusive.

Website: **www.bedofroses.co.nz**
165 Kerikeri Road, Kerikeri, Bay of Islands

Paihia - http://www.paihia.co.nz/

The major Northland tourist destination it is known as the place to take a boat trip to enjoy a dolphin encounter, fishing, scuba diving, snorkeling and sailing. Boats, bikes and kayaks are for hire. Great place to wander around visiting the shops and cafes plus there are great restaurants to enjoy. All styles of accommodation available.

Top Five Things to do in the Paihia area:
- Catch the ferry across the harbour to Russell
- Take a cruise around the Bay of Islands
- Kelly Tarlton's Shipwreck Museum – an old sailing ship by the Waitangi River
- Visit the Waitangi National Reserve and visit the Haruru Falls
- Take one of the walks in the Opua Forest
- ✓ **For the children:** Lily Pond Farm Park with farm animals, black swans and horse and pony rides.

Russell - http://www.tapeka.com/russell.htm

Once the capital of New Zealand now a laid back spot with charm. One can reach Russell by land but not really recommended as it is quite a circuitous route. The best is to catch the ferry over from the Paihia dock.

Top Five Things to do in Russell:
- Russell Museum – it has a working scale model of Capt Cook's ship the Endeavour

Christ Church – New Zealand's oldest church built in 1835.
- Pompallier House – One of the country's oldest houses
- Flagstaff Hill – A scenic lookout area where Maori chief threatened to tear down the flag of the Pakeha
- Oneroa Bay beach – a pleasant 15 minute walk from the wharf.

Plus:
- ✓ Cape Brett Walk - **http://www.capebrettwalks.co.nz/**

I recommend several days stay in the Bay of Islands if your itinerary provides the time.....try to allow for it...

North to the top at Cape Reinga

From the Bay of Islands now take route 10 north. On the East Coast there are several beautiful bays you can visit and stay if you are a camper vanner such as one of our favourites – **Tauranga Bay** off Wainui Road - **http://www.taurangabay.co.nz/**

Route 10 also takes you to one of the best fish & chip shops in the country at **Mangonui** - **http://www.doubtlessbay.co.nz/** .

Route 10 joins with route one at **Awanui** - **http://en.wikipedia.org/wiki/Awanui** where I recommend stopping to see the woodwork of the giant Kauri trees and actually walk up inside one they have as their stairway to their second floor exhibitions - **http://www.ancientkauri.co.nz/** .

Inside the Ancient Kauri Kingdom

Now the road goes all the way north up the peninsula to the end and **Cape Reinga and Spirits Bay.** It is at the top of the North Island 100 kms one-way north of Kaitaia at the northwestern tip of the Aupouri Peninsula and the end of route one on this one-way drive through the peninsula. Here from the vantage point of the lighthouse you can witness the dramatic clash of the Pacific Ocean and the Tasman Sea as they meet in an oceanic maelstrom.

On the way through you may see some of the wild horses that live in the Aupori Forest area and be sure to go out to the sand dunes....

<u>Five top things do on the Aupouri Peninsula</u>
- ✓ Visit the Cape Reinga lighthouse
- ✓ See the Pacific Ocean & Tasman Sea meet
- ✓ Cruise along isolated 90 Mile Beach
- ✓ Visit Spirit Bay
- ✓ Go boarding on the sand dunes at Te Paki stream

<u>**Walks:**</u> From the lighthouse car park you can join part of the New Zealand Walkway System. A track leads down to Werahi Beach and continues on to Te Paki Stream. A track above the car park winds around the coast to the Department of Conservation campsites at Tapotupotu Bay and Spirits Bay. Other walks listed on the Dept Conservation website.

Now you have been there and done that for the Far North and the East Coast so it is time to start <u>back south</u> on the West Coast.

From the Peninsula it is south to **Kaitaia - http://kaitaia.co.nz/** on route one to Kaitaia-Awaroa Road south through Herekino and on to Kohukohu on the **Hokianga Harbour - http://www.hokiangatourism.org.nz/** and take the ferry across to Rawene -

**http://www.hokiangatourism.org.nz/listings/hokiangaferry.ht
ml** . Love this area.

Hokianga Harbour Ferry

Tane Mahuta

Then south to Oponui and Omapere on route 12 and into the **Waipoua Forest** - with massive kauri trees some over a thousand years old. One Kauri tree, **Tane Mahuta** (God of the Forest) is 51.5metres high, 13.5 metres girth estimated at 1200 years old. The road leads through the forest and a walking track is provided. **http://www.doc.govt.nz/parks-and-recreation/places-to-visit/northland/kauri-coast/waipoua-forest/**
It is 64kms from here to **Dargaville - http://dargaville.co.nz/ and Baylys Beach - http://thisistheplace.org.nz/index.php? option=com_kttw&view=storydetails&story_id=194&Itemid =28**

For the camper vanner I recommend to stay at the Baylys Beach Holiday Park -
website: **www.baylysbeach.co.nz**.

This Holiday Park offers accommodation for every type of traveller – whether you are on a family holiday or you are travelling the world with your backpack. This holiday complex is situated only a short walk from the spectacular long remote sandy beaches of the west coast of Northland, has freedom quad bike hire on site and the famous **Funky Fish Café** next door. Activities at Baylys Beach include coastal walks, quad bike riding on the beach, golf, surfing, horse trekking and beach tours by 4-wheel drive bus and something I found really interesting is a small night private (open to the public) sky observatory called the **Skydome Observatory**.

From Dargaville head south on route 12 cuts back across the country to route one. Be sure to stop and visit the **Kauri Museum - http://www.kauri-museum.com/** and I recommend the superior accommodation only a few steps away from the famous Matakohe Kauri Museum:

Matakohe House B&B is a purpose-built, modern B&B in a colonial style befitting the historical significance of the area. Lyn and Alex invite you to their 'comforting, colonial getaway' on the wonderful Kauri Coast. Their accommodation features period furnishings, peaceful decor and friendly, down-to-earth service.

Matakohe House Café

The cafe is open daily for morning and afternoon teas and delicious lunches; all our food is cooked on the premises, the service is friendly and caring. Evening meals are available; however, bookings are essential.

Contact Details:
24 Church Rd · RD1 · Matakohe
Phone: +64 9 431 7091 · Fax: +64 9 431 6002
Email: **mathouse@xtra.co.nz** ·

Website: **www.matakohehouse.co.nz**

Some Interesting Historic Information on Matakohe –

Matakohe is an area of historic significance to New Zealand in relation to both pioneering and the kauri industry, Matakohe is now home to the largest undercover attraction in Northland, **The Kauri Museum**. The magnificent kauri tree and New Zealand pioneers are the themes of the museum. Displays include a huge 22-metre slab of kauri, kauri gum exhibits and working equipment, a completely furnished 1900s kauri house, panels of New Zealand native trees and magnificent early New Zealand furniture. A pioneer church, school and post office are part of the complex along with vast collections of original photographs and pioneering memorabilia. This is a stimulating insight into New Zealand's heritage and is a must see when visiting the North – remember to allow at least a couple of hours to see the Kauri Museum.

For a quality B&B stay in this area I recommend <u>Petite Provence</u> -

The eco-friendly Kaipara country retreat 2 hours north of Auckland on the Kauri Coast.
Petite Provence is a quality Matakohe Bed & Breakfast accommodation overlooking rolling farmland and the distant Kaipara Harbour.
Situated 10 minutes from the Matakohe Kauri museum, 45 minutes south of Dargaville and 1-1/2 hours south of the Waipoua Forest.
Contact: Guy & Linda Bucchi
Phone/Fax: +64 9 431 7552
Email: **petite-provence@clear.net.nz**
Website: **http://www.petiteprovence.co.nz**
Address: 703C Tinopai Road, Matakohe\
At Brynderwyn turn back south on route one. Now you can either continue on route one on through the Auckland region or you can take route 16 on the right out of Wellsford to the northwest of Auckland into the **Waitakere Ranges, Piha Beach, Bethels Beach area - http://en.wikipedia.org/wiki/Waitakere_Ranges.** This is an area really worth visiting.
The Auckland region has around 100 vineyards and wineries. The region is home to some of New Zealand's oldest established vineyards and some of the finest wine produced in the country.

The Waitakere Ranges Regional Park includes more than 16,000ha of native rainforest and coastline. Its 250km of walking and tramping tracks provide access to beaches, breathtaking vistas, spectacular rocky outcrops, streams, waterfalls and farms overlooking the wild west coast. There is plenty to do in the Waitakere Ranges - swimming, surfing, fishing, boat launching, horse riding, relaxing, or exploring the 250km of walking and tramping tracks.

Some of the ranges' main attractions are the four popular surf beaches, Muriwai, Bethels Beach, Piha and Karekare. The beaches are all black sand. There is an extensive network of bush walks and tracks and panoramic views of the east and west coasts and of Auckland. Scenic Drive runs a good portion of the length of the ranges from Titirangi to Swanson.

Let's move south of Auckland and explore the remainder of the North Island.

(1)I will take you east to the Coromandel Peninsula and south along the east coast to the Bay of Plenty and around East Cape and Hawke's Bay then south to Wellington.

(2)Another route will be down the middle of the island visiting Hobbiton, Rotorua and Lake Taupo and the Tongariro National Park and on south to Wellington.

(3)The route along the West Coast will point out the surfing town of Raglan and on the Taranaki region with New Plymouth and dominated by Mount Egmont on around south to Wanganui and on to Wellington.....(maybe even show you the Forgotten World highway).

By the time I have explained everything you can see and do you will be able to visit the North Island and know exactly where you want to go and what you want to experience. .

So I have covered the entire area north of Auckland from down the middle and along both coasts. Now it is time to move south of Auckland and explore the remainder of the North Island. I will take you east to the Coromandel Peninsula and south along the east coast to the Bay of Plenty and around East Cape and Hawke's Bay then south to Wellington.

Another route will be down the middle of the island visiting Hobbiton, Rotorua and Lake Taupo and the Tongariro National Park and on south to Wellington.

The route along the West Coast will point out the surfing town of Raglan and on the Taranaki region with New Plymouth and dominated by Mount Egmont on around south to Wanganui and on to Wellington.....(maybe even show you the Forgotten World highway).

By the time I have explained everything you can see and do through here you will be able to

Visit the North Island and know exactly where you want to go and what you want to see and do.

So off we go..........................

on south of Auckland -

There are several routes available and mostly it is dependent upon the time you will have. You can shoot straight through to Wellington and cross over to the South Island. You can go to the east and travel around the Coromandel and then south a couple of routes. You can go to Hamilton and then take the routes to the west coast and the Taranaki region or you can move back and forth across the island and get most of all of it in.

As I said I will explain several routes and cover most of everything you can discover and experience so you can then decide which is the best itinerary for you. If not get in touch and we can sort it out......

First if you have arrived at the Auckland airport and have a camper van booked and are heading south or just want to get to a park and chill out after a long and gruelling flight here is the best one to go to that is out of the city and quiet and peaceful. They also have accommodation for almost everyone. Check them out as place to stay when in and around the Auckland area.

For a close van park to the city but not in it I recommend **Clarks Beach** - taking Linwood Road out of Papakura just south of the airport.

Only 40 minutes south from the Auckland CBD and airport

I always stay here when in close to the city . Close but far enough away to enjoy the peace and quiet.

Clarks Beach Holiday Park is a beautiful spacious family camp on the shores of Manukau Harbour with panoramic views of the adjacent golf course and beach. This vacation spot is ideally suited for leisurely holidaying and is a popular base for large groups.

Clarks Beach Holiday Park has plenty of things to do with an indoor swimming pool, mini-golf, pool room, archery, croquet, harbour cruises, fishing charters and there are also kayaks and dinghies for hire as Clarks Beach also happens to be a great fishing and scallop gathering spot!

The park has a variety of affordable holiday accommodation including motel units and kitchen cabins, onsite caravans with cabanas (permanent awnings), cabins suitable for groups of up to 48 people and 100 spacious powered campervan sites and non-powered tent sites.

It is a quiet secluded paradise tucked away in peaceful surroundings yet it is only a short drive to many of Auckland's major tourist attractions such as Rainbow's End, also Pukekohe Raceway, Spooker's Haunted House and Maze and 5 golf courses all within 20 minutes of the park.

Contact:

226 Torkar Rd Ext, Clarks Beach,

Auckland, 2122,   New Zealand.
Ph +64 09 232-1685   Skype: mark.richards820
Email: cbhp@ihug.co.nz

Website: www.cbhp.co.nz

Notes:

Itinerary One -North Island –
East Coast Itinerary –
to the Coromandel and Bay of Plenty
south to Wellington

First let's go east to the Coromandel Peninsula -

Take route one south of Auckland to Bombay then turn left on route 2 to route 25. One of our favourite campgrounds is at the **Miranda Hot Pools** area:

Just down the road is a special place for people interested in bird watching - http://www.miranda-shorebird.org.nz/events.html .Over 100 species of migratory birds live around the waters edge. http://www.miranda-shorebird.org.nz/ .

Now we are off on route 25 across the one-way bridge over the Waihau River to the town of **Thames**. It is a very scenic drive north along the Firth of Thames and the west coast of the peninsula to get to the top and **Coromandel Town**. This area is one of our favourites.

The **Coromandel Peninsula** is a very special region known as the playground for the Auckland region with the summer season filling the local baches (summer houses).

The peninsula provides scenic coastal roads on both the east and west sides with the mountains providing a spectacular drive throughout the area.

Top Things to do in the Coromandel:
- ✓ Dig your own hot pool at Hot Water Beach
- ✓ Explore the Pohutakawa-lined coasts
- ✓ Take the spectacular, historical Pinnacles Walk
- ✓ Cruise to picturesque Cathedral Cove
- ✓ Dive, snorkel or kayak the stunning coastline
- ✓ Browse Coromandel Town's art studios
- ✓ Catch a wave at Opoutere Beach, **Whangamata**

Thames
A quiet but energy filled small town just north of the one-way bridge crossing over the Waihau River. For the motor home traveller they provide a good super market. There are two museums in town describing the early gold mining in the region. From here north along the western coastline of the peninsula is one of the most scenic.

If you happen to be here during the Christmas period the bright red flowers of the pohutakawa trees brightly showcase the area.

Good place to stock up with supplies especially if using a camper van before the drive around the Peninsula.

Coromandel Town

The drive up the west coast from Thames will be around an hour. Coromandel Town is a fabulous village that is very enjoyable to walk around and visit the craft shops, cafes and restaurants. Several accommodations in and around the area available.

For the adventurous go north to "almost" the top of the peninsula on the west coast road to just past Port Jackson and from the east side to Stony Bay.

One way is to go on the Coromandel Discovery bus especially if you want to do the Coromandel Coastal Walkway.

http://www.coromandeldiscovery.co.nz/Presentation/CoromandelDiscoveryPres.aspx?ID=14195

Or perhaps go to the Fletcher Bay campsite -

http://www.naturespic.co.nz/NewZealand/image.asp?id=39073

Now the pleasant drive down the east coast of the Coromandel Peninsula.

The drive from Coromandel town to the coast takes you through some winding hills over to Mercury Bay.

Whitianga - http://www.whitianga.co.nz/

A popular Coromandel settlement on Mercury Bay with a good harbour and a ferry across to Cooks Beach. A popular starting spot for all the water activities in the region.

The **Lost Spring Thermal Pools** are a major attraction along with the vast amount of water activities such as

kayaking, wind surfing, sailing, scenic cruising or maybe a ride on the banana boat and there are lots of charter fishing opportunities. On land there are quad bikes and scooters for hire and perhaps a visit to an animal park, go horse riding or visit the Rapaura Water Gardens. Check out the bone carving and pottery and other craft shops. For the history buff don't miss the Whitianga Museum. Catch the ferry over to Cooks Beach.
Several good restaurants and cafes such as the Mill Road Bistro and perhaps a visit to the
Mercury Bay Estate the home to Coromandel wines.

Check out the many walks -
http://www.whitianga.co.nz/walks.html

Ron recommends when in the Coromandel be sure to stay at:

SANDY SHORES ACCOMMODATION

host: Thelma Bailey
14 Buffalo Beach Road, Whitianga, Phone (0064) 7 866 4561 | Mobile 0272 178 577 | Email:
welcome@sandyshores.co.nz

Website: http://www.sandyshores.co.nz/

Whitianga & Mercury Bay

Located on the east coast of the Coromandel, Mercury Bay's main town of Whitianga has attracted visitors for more than a thousand years, since Maori explorer Kupe first settled here around 950A.D. But it was Captain James Cook who gave the area its name, when he anchored in the bay in 1769 to observe the transit of Mercury. Now an established tourist resort, the Bay's spectacular coastline is dotted with islands and its relatively sheltered waters are perfect for all water sports.

There is a large range of activities to enjoy. Buffalo Beach - named after the H.M.S. Buffalo wrecked here in 1840, this beach offers safe swimming, plus good fishing and shellfish collecting. Whitianga Wharf - the centre for boating and fishing activity, where you can take the passenger Ferry to Ferry Landing and Flaxmill Bay or the shuttle to Cooks beach, Hahei, Hot Water Beach and Cathedral Cove. Mercury Bay Museum - located in the old Dairy Factory, the museum offers fascinating relics from the areas past.

Cooks Beach - http://www.whitianga.co.nz/cooks.html

This is a beautiful beach with three kilometres of golden sand and safe waters. We always access this area by road and on the way stop at the Colenso Café by Whenuakite. Cooks Beach can be accessed via State Highway 25 taking the Hot Water Beach turn off. As I had said you can also get to Cooks Beach by taking the passenger ferry from Whitianga to Ferry Landing originally built in 1837.

Haihi - http://www.hahei.co.nz/
The most visited of the Coromandel and one of the best
areas in the Coromandel to really enjoy the coast. The area
offshore is a marine park and provides a top area for all
water sports along with the Hahei Beach to enjoy with
Cathedral Cove accessible by boat or on foot.

Hot Water Beach - http://www.mercurybay.co.nz
What can I say this is the not to be missed world famous
place to dig a hole in the beach sand and enjoy your own
thermal pool. Be sure to check the time as the tide is the
critical determination. Try for one hour either side of low
tide.
There are two volcanic fissures at Hot Water Beach issue
water as hot as 64°C (147°F) at a rate as high as 15
litres/minute. This water contains large amounts of salt,
calcium, magnesium, potassium, fluorine, bromine and
silica from underground. I stay at the Hot Water Beach
Holiday Park - http://hotwaterbeachholidaypark.com/ and
don't miss going to the Moko Art Space Gallery across the
street from the beach parking lot.

Tairua - http://www.tairua.org.nz/
Tairua is a small but developed beachside town 42km south
of Whitianga. The town's attractive combination of surfing
beach and sheltered harbour makes it exceedingly popular
in summer. A major drawcard is the opportunity for
explorative historic walks in the Coromandel Forest Park.
Tairua has all the amenities you require, including around
15 cafes, restaurants and takeways.

There's a bakery, hardware store, gifts and art galleries, chemist, clothing, hairdressers, real estate agents, liquor store. Tairua has its own well stocked supermarket and large city style supermarkets are less than 40 minutes drive away in Whangamata, Whitianga or Thames. Highspeed internet and both Vodafone and Telecom mobile phone networks are available in Tairua. Good location to stop and relax.

Opoutere/Whangamata – http://www.whangamata.co.nz/
We lived here for a year staying with a friend on her farm at Opoutere. This is where we converted the bus to our travelling home. Spent a lot of time at the beach…!
I recommend taking the ride out to the Opoutere Beach. It is the last undeveloped white sand beach on the Coromandel Peninsula accessible to the public. It is protected from development by a forested reserve running almost its entire 5km length that serves as a sanctuary for the nesting shorebird the Dotterel. Exceptionally clear water for swimming, surfing and surfcasting, safest for children at low tide.

 Whangamata is known for its surfing and beach. The sea conditions here are suitable for all along the 6km length of beach or in the estuaries that lie at each end of the beach. This area is also popular for big game and recreational fishing. The Coromandel Forest Park and Tairua Forest bordering the town is perfect for walks and biking. There are trails from the forestry roads that lead to isolated beaches away from the rest of the world. You might even be lucky and get there for the annual Beach Hop - http://www.beachhop.co.nz/

Ron recommends staying here when in the Whangamata area:

Kotuku B&B

A Quality Bed & Breakfast in Whangamata,
on the Coromandel Peninsula, New Zealand

Peter and Linda invite you to stay with them in their Bed and Breakfast when you visit Whangamata or the Coromandel. Homestay comfort with ensuite bedrooms - A self- catering studio unit - Easy access to the rest of the Coromandel Peninsula and/or Tauranga - Kayaking on the estuary or out to the bay islands - Swimming and surfing at the beach - Golf (two courses) and Bush Walks - A drive to Hot Water Beach and Cathedral Cove.
Contact Us:
Your hosts: Peter and Linda Bigge
Address: 422 Otahu Road , Whangamata , New Zealand
Phone/fax: *+64 7 865 6128*
e-mail: bookings@kotukuhomestay.co.nz

web: www.kotukuhomestay.co.nz

Now it is time to leave the Coromandel Peninsula and head south. Winding roads through the mountains but soon reaching the farm land of the northeast corner of the North Island. Our next community to explore is the town of Waihi.

Waihi - http://www.waihi.org.nz/
It is a historical gold mining town and still has the Martha's Mine a working gold mine to visit along with museums and historical sites to explore. Close by is Waihi Beach to enjoy. Good spot to check out is the Waihi Art Market - http://www.artmarket.co.nz/

At Waihi you are back now to route 2 and we continue south to New Zealand's fascinating mural town of Katikati - http://www.katikati.org.nz/ .
Take a walk down the main street and enjoy the many murals and stop at the Museum.
If there in January stop to enjoy the Katikati Avocado Food & Wine Festival.
Check also for the dates of the New Zealand Mural Contest & Arts Festival.

Waihi Beach - www.waihibeachinfo.co.nz.
A side road takes you out to Waihi Beach from Waihi. This popular destination with a population of only 2000+ offers over five miles of white sand beach. Good accommodations and cafes make for an enjoyable stop. We used to enjoy the café right in the middle of the town.
For those of you who enjoy walks one of the most popular is the Orokawa Walkway that offers miles of scenic views along the coast to the secluded beaches at Orokawa Bay and Homunga Bay. Nestled into an area just south is the small community of Athenree that offers the very pleasant Athenree Hot Springs Holiday Park where we used to enjoy staying when in the area.

Katikati – www.katikati.org.nz.
Twelve miles south of Waihi Beach Katikati is known as the "mural town" with around 3500 population. For you people who enjoy walking here again is a spot to check out with the Kaimai-mamaku Forest Park walks and the 1 ½ mile walk along the Uretara River where a local artist has carved stones along the way with Haiku verse. Quite impressive. It is worth a stop in the town to have a walk around and enjoy the art work on the buildings.

Now into a more populated area ....from Waihi Beach along route 2 inland to the mural town of Katikati south to the cosmopolitan city of Tauranga and its popular seaside resort of Mt Maunganui then continuing along Whakatane and finally to Opotika. This is the region referred to as the **Bay of Plenty** named by Capt Cook upon his discovery. Here you will find the home of the kiwi fruit and rich in other horticulture such as oranges, cherries, olives, plums, avocados, macadamias, pistachios and persimmons. You will enjoy the many roadside stands packed with delicious goodies.

It is also the home to several vineyards. It includes an active volcano on White island and miles of beautiful sand, surf and native bush along the way.

On south on route 2 and you come to Tauranga - http://www.tauranga.co.nz/ one of the larger communities in the country and nestled in by the sea the very popular Mount Maunganui – http://www.mountmaunganui.co.nz/ one of New Zealand's most popular summer destinations.

For those interested in the Hobbit films going this route you may wish to side track from Tauranga on route 29 inland to route 27 to the Hobbit Town of Matamata -
http://www.matamatanz.co.nz/home
where you can visit the movie set -
http://www.hobbitontours.com/ .

Tauranga - http://www.bestoftauranga.com/ (Insiders Guide to Tauranga)
The major centre for the region the city of Tauranga has a population of around 120,000. It is a port city (Port of Tauranga) with a large natural harbour that hosts cruise ships and is a popular spot for water sports. Plenty of opportunities to charter fishing and dive trips perhaps to explore the reefs and wrecks in the area plus underwater volcanic areas. The city offers some great cafes and restaurants many offering the local produce that is so plentiful. Just 15 minutes away is the beautiful and pleasant McLaren Falls Park. Great place to just enjoy the waterfalls and outdoor area.
If you are into kayaks or canoes you can't pass up the Waimarino Adventure Park - http://www.waimarino.com/ where you may want to kayak to the glowworm canyon or do a river tour Game On - a three-in-one venue, with combat laser tag, laser claybird shooting, and blokart sailing – the locally invented land yachts for something different or stop at Comvita to pick up some of its health food products made here.
The Western Bay is also known as the place to watch and swim with dolphins.

Mount Maunganui –

A suburb of Tauranga but a life of its own with a golden sand beach front lifestyle at the dormant volcanic cone known as the Mount. Plenty of top cafes and restaurants and an exciting boutique shopping area.

The Mount Hot Pools and Cultural Heritage Centre. Located at the base of Mount Maunganui they remain a must do attraction – especially if you combine a climb to the summit for spectacular views and then a hot pool soak. They are the only hot sea water pools in the country using naturally heated salt water.

Or perhaps visit the Aquatic centre. The heated wave pool is designed for fun featuring a state-of-the-art wave machine that pumps out 8 different waves, and features a 68-metre hydroslide, a 25 metre lap pool, fitness centre, café and crèche.

Ron recommends staying at Accommodation Te Puna when in the area:

Only 8 minutes drive to central Tauranga, 15 minutes to Mount Maunganui beaches, one hour to Rotorua & Whakatane, 1.5 hours to Hamilton and two hours to Auckland Airport. Handy to 6 golf courses, hot pools, horse riding, wineries, kayak & adventure park, harbour boat ramps and many other great tourist attractions and scenic walks.

Contact:
Phone: +64 7 552 5621
Email: info@accommodationtepuna.co.nz
Website: http://www.accommodationtepuna.co.nz/
Address: Corner Minden Road & Auckland Waihi Road (SH2),
Te Puna RD6, Tauranga

Te Puke – http://www.tepuke.co.nz/

The Kiwifruit Capital of the World is Te Puke south of Tauranga with 3000 to 4000 hectares (2.47 hectares to an acre so tis a bunch).

New Zealand's booming kiwifruit industry had its beginnings here and is now a major export crop. Hundreds of local growers produce millions of trays of the traditional 'Green' and the luscious 'Gold' that are shipped out worldwide.

There are over 80 million trays of kiwifruit exported to 60/70 countries each year. Can you imagine during harvest in ½ million kiwifruit will be picked a day. Stop at Kiwifruit 360 for the grand tour and maybe you will be lucky to come by when they have the Kiwifruit Festival.

You have to stop here for a taste of the New Zealand kiwifruit and have a close look at how it grows and is harvested. By the way here is how the kiwifruit is prepared to eat:

Cut it in half and then use a spoon to get the fruit out from inside the exterior. I mention was quite frustrated when I first tried it until this method was pointed out by a local (who usually enjoy watching the tourist trying to eat a kiwifruit). Well worth the effort by the way.

Notes:

Along the Bay of Plenty to Gisborne

Stay on route 2 east as it skirts along the Bay of Plenty with its long expanse of great surf fishing beaches through Maketu and to the town of Whakatana.

This area is historically significant to New Zealand Maori. Part of the original migration landings made their first New Zealand landings in the Bay of Plenty and at Maketu it was the landing place for the *Te Arawa* canoe after the early migration. The Polynesians came here around a thousand years ago long before Capt Cook in 1769.

Whakatane - http://www.whakatane.com/
Fifty miles along route 2 from Tauranga is the town of Whakatane a very pleasant small town on the banks of the Whakatane River with a population of 15,000.
A good place to take a whale and dolphin tour of the Bay of Plenty plus the bays of the wildlife sanctuary of Whale Island.
This is also the place to set up your tour of the active marine volcano of **White Island -**
http://www.whiteisland.co.nz/ just 30 miles off the coast.
As you drive through the area the volcanic smoke is quite evident. Be sure to enjoy the miles of beach at Ohope close by. We like to stay at the Ohope Beach Holiday Top Ten Park when here in the bus.

Ron recommends while in Whakatane enjoy the roof top pool at:

QUAYSIDE LUXURY APARTMENTS
11 George St, Whakatane
Ph: 0-7-306 0466
 Email: info@quaysideapartments.co.nz
Website: www.quaysideapartments.co.nz

Featuring large & comfortable two or three-bedroom apartments designed to maximize the stunning views. Recreational area with gym, sauna and rooftop pool. Walking distance to all attractions.

And what is there to do while here?

Visit the live volcano on White Island
 Scuba dive, fish, kayak
 Enjoy the 3000 acre adventure farm at Tui Glen
 Swim with dolphin and seals
A fabulous mountain bike park or visit the amazing maze. Perhaps the thrill of a jet boat tour to the Aniwhenua Falls. Check out the night sky at the Astronomical Society
 and don't forget to stop for a treat at Julian's Berry Farm. There are tons of hiking tracks in the area
 and for the golf enthusiast there is a large selection of 18 hole golf courses available.

If you would enjoy a fabulous stay in the country I recommend:

Whakatane Homestay:

Jim and Kathleen welcomes you to the Leaburn Farm:

We are "young oldies" with wide interests. We came to this property many years ago. 50/50 sharemilkers manage our two farm properties, milking a total of 420 cows. We also grow citrus fruit and breed a small flock of black and coloured sheep. Jim has been a member of Whakatane Lions Club for over 40 years and is also a keen bowler. Kathleen's interests are in genealogy, organic gardening and crafts. Travel is a particular interest. One of our sons lives in England and we have an AFS son who lives in Ohio, USA.

Contact information:

Whakatane Homestay - Leaburn Farm
237 Thornton Road || RD4 || Whakatane 3194
Phone: +64 7 3087487 || Fax: +64 7 3087437
Email: info@whakatanehomestay.co.nz
Website: www.whakatanehomestay.co.nz

Now after Whakatane on to the East Cape from **Opotiki** where you now have the driving option of continuing on route 2 south through the Raukumara Forest Park and a very scenic drive through the gorge along the Waioeka River to Matawai, Te Karaka and on to the city of **Gisborne** - http://www.gisbornenz.com/ or take route 35 that skirts the top of the Cape and goes through interesting places such as:

Hicks Bay – http://www.gisbornenz.com/about-eastland/heritage-and-historic-information/hicks-bay-wharekahika/ ,

Tokomaru Bay – http://archive.gisbornenz.com/default.asp?id=26 and **Tolaga Bay** - http://archive.gisbornenz.com/default.asp?id=25 .

This is a great website for historical information on this area - http://archive.gisbornenz.com/ .

Seemingly far removed from the rest of the island I have only travelled up here all the way around the cape a few times on route 35. It is roughly a six hour drive around. The area is the first in the world to see the new day. The population is mostly Maori with a long history in the area. The major city is Gisborne. Check out Whangara - north of Gisborne and take a guided tour of the place where the movie *"Whale Rider"* http://www.whaleriderthemovie.co.nz/ was filmed. Visit the home where much of the filming actually took place and listen to the story that inspired the film. Tours are approximately 2 hours and start at Whangara. Other cultural tours of the area are also available. Min 4 persons – bookings are essential.

The area is basically a quiet laid back spot where the Maori culture can be visited along with great beaches and quality wines. Freedom camping during certain months is encouraged by permit only.

Opotiki - http://www.opotikinz.com/

The beginning (or end) of this part of the trip around the East Cape is at the town of Opotiki. It is a district of diversity, ranging from beautiful coastal vistas, stunning beaches, secluded valleys and crystal clear mountain streams. One of the most interesting is the 2000+ year-old Puriri tree, Taketakerau found on in Hukutaia Domain - Woodlands Road, Opotiki. Approx eight minutes drive from town.

Macademia Orchard

Pacific Coast Macadamias is a small orchard, processing plant and café/shop set in what must be one of the most beautiful places in New Zealand. On the Pacific Coast Highway (SH 35), half-way between Opotiki and Hicks Bay you will find an orchard tucked in the bush against the hill overlooking Whanarua Bay. A plantation of Macadamia trees grows in the warm coastal climate. Nut products are offered for sale in the orchard shop and visitors are welcome to linger in our small café.

Mount Hikuranga

Hikurangi is the first place to see the sun of every new day, because of its special location in relation to the international dateline. It is 137km from Gisborne City and 205km from Opotiki. The mountain stands at 1754 metres.
The Hikurangi track is located on Pakihiroa Station 3km from the turnoff from SH35 (signposted). This track runs through private land, and may be closed from time to time.
Te Runanga O Ngati Porou is the custodian of the hut which is located 10km up the mountain from the bridge and Pakihiroa Station entrance. 4 Wheel Drive Tours are available. Hut fees $15 per person.

Hicks Bay

ON route 35 (Pacific Coast Highway) around the East Cape starting either from Opotiki or from Gisborne in the south. This is a sleepy isolated area of New Zealand known for its beaches and fishing.

Rangitukia

Te Aio o Nukutaimemeha is a 45 metre long waka (Maori canoe) which lies at the mouth of the Waiapu River. It is still considered one of the largest Waka Taua of its kind in the world. Ten years in the making, this Taonga (treasure) belongs to the descendants of Maui-Tikitiki-a-Taranga. Te Aio o Nukutaimemeha is situated in Rangitukia on private land, and may be closed from time to time. Te Runanga o Ngati Porou are the custodians of the Waka. Entry fee $5 per person. History tours are available.

Tolaga Bay

It is both a bay and small town on the 45 kilometres northeast of Gisborne.

It was named Tolaga Bay by James Cook but the original Māori name is Uawa, and some local residents now refer to the area as Hauiti. The region around the bay is rugged and remote, and for many years the only access to the town was by boat. Because the bay is shallow, a long wharf - the longest in New Zealand (600m) - was built to accommodate visiting vessels. In the 1830s there was a thriving flax trade involving early European traders. Now the locals are trying to save the wharf from deterioration.

Gisborne   -

http://en.wikipedia.org/wiki/Gisborne_Region

Visit the first city in the world to see the new sunrise. It has much to offer with its cafes and restaurants and fine wine from the region. Every time we go there we wonder why we don't come here more often.

The Top Five Things to do in Gisborne:

- ✓ Check out the wines of the region
- ✓ Stop by one of the excellent cafes and restaurants
- ✓ Visit Rere Rockslide and do a slide
- ✓ Stop by the Tairawhiti Museum
- ✓ Take a stroll along the beach and maybe do some surfing
- ✓ **and be sure to see the Eastwoodhill Arboretum -** http://www.eastwoodhill.org.nz/

The National Arboretum of New Zealand, encompasses 135 hectares of exotic and native trees, shrubs and climber plantings. It has walking trails for all levels of fitness, the nationally significant Homestead Garden, accommodation, tours for groups big and small, function venue and catering services. Eastwoodhill is situated approximately 35 kilometers northwest of Gisborne - a 30 minute drive through the picturesque Ngatapa Valley on the Wharekopae Road.

On we go south of Gisborne to Napier

Leaving Gisborne on route 2 south you pass Poverty Bay. Captain Cook first sighted New Zealand on October 6, 1769 and two days later his ship the Endeavour anchored here. On October 8, 1769 he landed in **Poverty Bay** and the landing party was attacked. Poverty Bay stretches for 10 kilometres from **Young Nick's Head** -

http://www.teara.govt.nz/en/1966/young-nicks-head/1

in the southwest to Tuaheni Point in the northeast. The area is known for its very fertile area and famous for its Chardonnay, fruit, vegetables and avocados.

From here the next place of interest is the:

Mahia Peninsula - http://www.voyagemahia.com/. Great spot for all kinds of outdoor activities with surfing, fishing, boating walks and tramp heading the list. It is a beach-fringed promontory jutting into the Pacific and a paradise for fishermen, surfers, divers and those looking for the perfect beach holiday.

Inland from Mahia on the highway between Gisborne and Wairoa are the **Morere Hot Springs** set in a nikau-predominant native bush reserve with superb walking tracks.

Morere Hot Springs -
http://www.morerehotsprings.co.nz/

Off route 2 at Morere this area is in 364 hectares of native bush. The Morere Hot Springs provide modern bathing and spa facilities in a beautiful natural environment. They are a tranquil haven where the mineralised waters are said to be amongst the most rejuvenating and unique in the world. The heated non-sulphurous water is original sea water from the nearby Pacific Ocean. A quarter of a million litres of it emerges each day from springs beneath the rainforest after travelling for thousands of years through superheated subterranean vents. The springs have a long history of recreational and therapeutic bathing dating back to the 1890s.

Next community south to visit is:

Wairoa

Wairoa, is 99km south of Gisborne on the banks of the broad Wairoa River, and is the southern gateway to Eastland and is also the gateway to the wilderness playgrounds of Te Urewera National Park and **Lake Waikaremoana**.

Lake Waikaremoana is one of New Zealand's finest lakes. Located in the Te Urewera National Park it is surrounded by dense beech forest - offering bush-walks and bird-watching - and filled with trout for fishing!

You can enjoy trout fishing, boating, day walks and a multi-day walking trip around magnificent Lake Waikaremoana, **one of New Zealand's 10 Great Walks**.

Te Reinga Falls - http://www.world-of-waterfalls.com/new-zealand-te-reinga-falls.html

Located 35Km inland from Wairoa just off SH 36 (Tiniroto Rd). Turn onto Ruakituri Road at Te Reinga, cross the bridge over the river. The car park is at the western end of the bridge. A few minutes walk from the car park and picnic area takes you to the lookout to view the spectacular 35 metre falls of the Hangaroa and Ruakituri rivers combine to form the Wairoa River. Duration of the walk is only 15mins.

Now we are into the heart of the Hawke's Bay -

Napier - http://www.napier.nz.com/

Plenty of visitor activities - There are golden beaches, theme parks and rivers to explore, swim with dolphins or view the world's largest mainland gannet colony plus jet boat rides, hot-air ballooning, surfing, paragliding, hiking 17 heritage trails, hunt in the ranges, fish for trout, or play golf.

Napier's Art Deco Walk is a popular attraction. Buildings not to be missed include the **National Tobacco Company** in Ahuriri, the Daily Telegraph Building and the residences of Marewa. Pick up a pamphlet or take an informative Art Deco tour.

For the outdoor lover and hiker:

Ball's Clearing Scenic Reserve, 65km north west of Napier, is a magical environment of enormous native trees standing side by side, the oldest being 600-700 years old.

Lake Tutira north of Napier is a wildlife refuge and park. Fringed with weeping willows, Lake Tutira is an idyllic picnicking and camping spot. There are walking tracks leading to waterfalls and splendid views of the Pacific coast.

On the way to Napier, stop to hike the Tangoio Walkway in the Tangoio Falls Scenic Reserve. The track follows the Kareaara Stream to the Te Ana Falls; Tangoio Falls are a little further on.

A walk along Napier's Marine Parade, with its beautiful Norfolk Pines, is a pleasant way to start or end the day. Take note of the iconic 'Pania of the Reef'. This statue is sometimes compared to Copenhagen's Little Mermaid and is now safely back on her stand after she was stolen for 9 days in October 2005.

Hasting's Frimley Park features a magnificent circular rose garden with more than 5500 roses.

Climb up Te Mata Peak, just south of Havelock North, for panoramic views of the Ruahine, Kaweka and Maungaharuru Ranges and Cape Kidnappers. Well-maintained walking tracks provide access to the park's bush areas and fossil-rich limestone cliffs.

The Top Five Things to do in Napier

- ✓ Go to the National Aquarium on the waterfront
- ✓ Check out the New Zealand Wine Centre
- ✓ Take an Art Deco tour of the city's amazing architecture
- ✓ Visit the Hawkes Bay Museum & Art Gallery
- ✓ Have a coffee at one of the cafes

New Zealand Wine Centre -
http://www.newzealandwinecentre.co.nz/

located in Napier's iconic AMP Building, is the ultimate wine experience in New Zealand. It is the perfect place to experience everything and anything to do with wine. From a state of the art interactive wine tasting adventure, to aroma awareness rooms, school of wine, wine museum and specialist wine shop – it's simply a wine lover's haven!

National Aquarium of New Zealand -
http://www.nationalaquarium.co.nz/

This is a truly exciting and informative underwater adventure. Watch Izzy the crocodile laze around, visit the kiwi house or the seahorse display. Travel under the Oceanarium on the moving walkway and view many marine wonders gliding by. There are sharks, stingrays and hundreds of fish species to see. Then watch a fabulous diving display at 10am or 2pm. If you've always wanted to see how an aquarium operates, then take a 'Tour Behind The Scenes' at either 9am or 1pm; bookings are essential. Another option for those wanting added excitement is to swim with the sharks. You don't need to be a qualified diver and our experienced staff will supervise you while you enjoy this wonderful experience. Make your aquarium visit the highlight of your holiday!

Hawke's Bay Museum & Art Gallery -
http://www.hbmag.co.nz/

Home to Hawke's Bay's great treasures: Hawke's Bay Museum & Art Gallery is a place of stories, heritage, art and artefacts - a place where visitors can explore New Zealand's vibrant art and cultural history. . To find out more about Hawke's Bay Museum & Art Gallery's redevelopment project visit our website: www.forus.org.nz

Explore Napier's fascinating Art Deco city centre on a guided Art Deco Walk

10am daily from the Napier i-SITE Visitor Centre and 2pm daily from the Art Deco Shop. The compact morning walk is $14 and the original afternoon walk $20. 1.5-hour evening walks are available 26 December-31 March - depart Napier i-SITE Visitor Centre at 5.30pm; $16.

Try the VINTAGE DECO CAR TOUR. See the remarkable National Tobacco Company Building, historic Ahuriri, and the Deco suburb of Marewa. Cost: $130 for up to 3 passengers. This tour departs at a time to suit you.

The DECO BUS TOUR takes you outside the city centre. Includes the National Tobacco Company Building and the grand Hawke's Bay Club. 75 minutes - cost $38pp.

Phone the Art Deco Shop or Napier i-SITE Visitor Centre. You'll find the world's best Art Deco Napier souvenirs and gifts at the Art Deco Shop.

NOTES:

I recommend staying at : Mon Logis Bed & Breakfast

It is a little piece of France nestled in the heart of beautiful wine growing Hawkes Bay

Boutique Napier Accommodation at the Beach:

Originally built as an English terrace house in the 1860's this Colonial building was extended into a private hotel accommodation in 1915. It was one of the city buildings to survive the 1931 Napier Earthquake. Only a few minutes walk to the city centre, this grand two storey Colonial Villa overlooking the Pacific ocean, has a fascinating history as a private hotel since the early 1900's. In 1991 it became Mon Logis, meaning 'My Lodge'. Mon Logis Napier accommodation recreates a French tradition of a boutique hotel in Hawke's Bay.

Contact:

415 Marine Parade, Napier,
Hawkes Bay, New Zealand
Phone: +64 (0)6 835 2125

Email: monlogis@xtra.co.nz

Website: http://www.monlogis.co.nz/

Leaving Napier Route 2 south takes you to **Hastings** - http://www.visithastings.co.nz/ a vibrant city of over 73,000 people and the area of over 65 wineries. Regarded as the twin city of Napier I really enjoy the way they have hanging flower baskets throughout the town with its Spanish Mission architecture style.

This is where you can enjoy a really great Sunday's Farmers Market.
It also boasts the location of New Zealand's only theme park – **Splash Planet** - http://www.splashplanet.co.nz/ and a lot of festivals and events to enjoy.

 Here also is **Cape Kidnappers** location of the world's largest Gannet colony - http://en.wikipedia.org/wiki/Cape_Kidnappers and a fabulous par 71 golf course - http://www.capekidnappers.com/Cape-Kidnappers/Course_IDL=28_IDT=3577_ID=20800_.html .

The Cape Kidnappers Gannet Colony is a must for wildlife enthusiasts (November to April is the best time to visit)

Great weather and beautiful beaches are a part of the scene with sun and surf. There are more than forty vineyards to explore many with top international reputations.
For the golf enthusiasts there is the Cape Kidnappers Golf Course rated 41st best golf course in the world.

Havelock North -
http://www.havelocknorth.com/visitor.html
The village of Havelock North is a pleasant spot to roam
around. Visit the Grower's Market at the Black Barn
Vineyards on Saturdays in the summer.

**For a real panoramic view of the area climb Te Mata
Peak -** www.tematapark.co.nz/

on south to Wellington -

Going south on route 2 you pass through the towns of
Waipukurau -
http://www.chb.co.nz/discover_waipukurau.shtml and
out of the Hawkes Bay area into the Tararua District and the
town of
 Norsewood - http://www.norsewood.co.nz/ a town of
Scandinavian heritage
Dannevirke - http://www.dannevirke.net.nz/
Woodville - http://www.thisiswoodville.co.nz/
Mount Bruce – http://www.doc.govt.nz/parks-and-
recreation/places-to-visit/wairarapa/wairarapa/pukaha-
mount-bruce-wildlife-centre/ home to Pukaha, the
national wildlife centre worth stopping to visit and next
into:
Masterton - http://www.wairarapanz.com/?
q=masterton-0
among other things is the home to a New Zealand famous
beer **Tui**.

From Masterton you can take the back road into the wine
country and

Martinborough or continue along route to the towns of
Carterton - http://www.wairarapanz.com/?q=node/22
Greytown - http://www.wairarapanz.com/?q=node/23
and
Featherston - http://www.wairarapanz.com/?q=node/24 .

From Featherston if you want to explore the ocean side go to
Cape Palliser -
http://en.wikipedia.org/wiki/Cape_Palliser
and to **Lake Ferry** on the coast –
http://www.newzealand.com/travel/sights-activities/scenic-highlights/lakes/scenic-highlight-details.cfm/businessid/63675/highlightcategoryid/5/startrow/3/endrow/0/seed/0.html

Along the road to Cape Palliser, you can walk up to the
Putangirua Pinnacles, formed by 120,000 years of erosion –
http://www.doc.govt.nz/parks-and-recreation/places-to-visit/wairarapa/wairarapa/aorangi-forest-park/features/putangirua-pinnacles/
For the wine lovers it is a must to visit this region of vineyards in New Zealand.
A $200 bottle of Martinborough pinot noir beat out in a blind tasting a $7000-a-pop rival from France and a host of renowned wines from around the world.

Castle Point
It is a small settlement 69 km north-east of Masterton famous for its lighthouse, annual horse races on the beach, and 160-metre-high Castle Point rock. It is popular for holidays and fishing, and has a safe swimming beach and tidal lagoon.

Cape Palliser

Southern-most tip of the North Island, Cape Palliser features some outstanding coastal scenery with the largest breeding colony of fur seals in the North Island.

Climb the 258 steps to Cape Palliser Lighthouse or take a walk up to Putangirua Pinnacles eroded landforms 10 km south-east of Lake Ferry in Aorangi Forest Park. Soaring like skyscrapers, the pillars are made of old alluvial gravels. The pillars formed as heavy rain washed away softer rock, leaving more resistant rock behind. In time individual earth pillars developed, protected by a boulder or hard surface on top. Some are thought to be over 1,000 years old.

Wairapara Lakes

The southern Wairarapa has two major lakes. About 18 km long and 6 km wide, Lake Wairarapa is shallow – mostly less than 2.5 metres deep. Covering 7,800 hectares, it is the biggest wetland in the lower North Island, and has long been an important Māori eel fishery. Lake Wairarapa drains into tidal 650-hectare Lake Ōnoke, to the south. Lake Ōnoke is separated from the open sea of Palliser Bay by a 3-km gravel spit. Lakes Wairarapa and Ōnoke are among the North Island's most important wetlands.

The lake edge supports over 40 species of native aquatic turf plant, such as swamp grass, raupō and flax. At the edge of wetlands there are large areas of mingimingi, kānuka and mānuka.

There are also stands of kahikatea and cabbage trees. Crack willow, hawthorn and alder are the main exotic species.

The eastern side of the lake is the most significant area for wildlife, providing a habitat for the bar-tailed godwit, golden plover, banded dotterel, Japanese snipe and Caspian tern. The lake supports a range of waterfowl, including grey and mallard ducks, grey teal, and paradise shelduck.

Three species of shag and the pied stilt also live in the wetlands.

Two nationally threatened fish species, the brown mudfish and giant kōkopu, live in the wetlands. Eel and black flounder migrate from the sea from midsummer to autumn. Exotic fish – brown trout, perch and (noxious) rudd – are established, but their impact on native species is not known.

Martinborough - http://www.teara.govt.nz/en/wairarapa-places/9

Martinborough is best known for the 30+ wineries sprinkled about town. Established by Irish immigrant, John Martin, Martinborough's streets are laid out in the shape of a Union Jack and are named after places Martin visited before New Zealand.

Grapes for wine production were planted near Martinborough in the late 1970s. Since then, the wine industry has had a dramatic impact on the town.. Many cellar door sales and new restaurants for visitors. Hotels and homestays were set up and historic buildings were moved from other places and placed in the main street to create a 'wine village'. An annual wine and food festival, Toast Martinborough, was first held in 1992. Along with the twice-yearly Martinborough Fair, it attracts thousands.

Masterton - http://www.teara.govt.nz/en/wairarapa-places/3

Famous for its annual "Golden Shears" sheep shearing competition, Masterton is also home to a museum, gallery, heritage trails, vineyards, farms and nature reserves. Masterton has few striking natural features, but has a number of parks and reserves. Queen Elizabeth Park, with its mature trees and well-tended gardens, is the most impressive. The art and history museum Aratoi has helped foster a cultural resurgence in the region.

Close by see native birds at Pukaha Mt Bruce National Wildlife Centre or head north for a Tui Brewery tour at Mangatainoka.

Greytown - http://www.teara.govt.nz/en/wairarapa-places/6_

Greytown was New Zealand's first planned inland town. The main street boasts lovingly restored colonial buildings –

now boutique stores and cafes. With its quiet pace, Greytown is a great place to rest before exploring the wider Wairarapa.

Greytown has recently become Wairarapa's wealthiest and most fashionable town.

Situated 15 kilometres north-west of Greytown on the edge of the Tararua Forest Park, the spectacular Waiohine Gorge was carved out by the Waiohine River. It is a popular swimming, tubing, camping and picnic spot, and a long swing bridge spans the gorge.

Carterton - http://www.teara.govt.nz/en/wairarapa-places/5_

Fourteen km south-west of Masterton Stretching along High Street (State Highway 2), Carterton promotes itself as New Zealand's daffodil capital, hosting a spring festival where crowds flock to pick flowers in outlying fields.

Nearby is Holdsworth the main eastern entrance to the Tararua Forest Park, 25 km north-west of Masterton. Holdsworth has short bush walks and longer tramps up Mt Holdsworth and beyond. The picturesque Atiwhakatu Stream flows through the area, providing swimming holes, with camping and picnicking spots on its banks.

Stonehenge Aotearoa is a full-scale replica of Stonehenge in England, on privately owned land 10 km south-east of

Carterton. When viewed from the centre, the stones mark the daily rising and setting positions of the sun. The stone circle also forms a Polynesian star compass, showing the bearings taken by Polynesian seafarers travelling to and from New Zealand.

Featherston - http://www.teara.govt.nz/en/wairarapa-places/8_
It is the southern gateway to Wairarapa, 34 km south-west of Masterton at the foot of the Rimutaka Range. Featherston is a rural servicing and distribution centre, and home to many Wellington commuters. Antique and collectible stores line the main street, along with cafés .The Fell Engine Museum houses the world's only Fell engine (once used on the steep Rimutaka Incline, over the Rimutaka Range).

Top Five Things to do in the Wairarapa
- ✓ Enjoy world famous wine in Martinborough
- ✓ Check out the scenery and seals at Cape Palliser
- ✓ Visit Stonehenge Aotearoa near Carterton
- ✓ Learn about NZ's sheep shearing history in Masterton
- ✓ Explore spectacular Castle Point

……..and now over the hill to the suburbs and the city of Wellington:

From Featherston it is through the Pakuratahi Forest and over the Rimutaka Hill and down into the outlying suburban areas of Upper Hutt and Lower Hutt and into the city of Wellington itself.

My favourite city in New Zealand. I lived and worked in the heart of the city for eight years and enjoyed every day. One of the positives of Wellington is it is a very compact and easily walked city to just about everything you want in a very short time. It is the capital and political heart of New Zealand and the country's second largest city.

It is a cultural, cosmopolitan centre everyone can enjoy. The population is around 164,000. Average summer temperature is around 20 degreeC and around 6 degreesC winter with average sunshine and rainfall. It is a windy city at times reminding me of Chicago.

Driving time from major North island cities:
Auckland to Wellington: 658km (404mi) - 9 hours 25 minutes
Rotorua to Wellington: 460km (289mi) - 6 hours 35 minutes
Taupo to Wellington: 380km (238mi) - 5 hours and 25 minutes
Napier to Wellington: 323km (140mi) - 4 hours 35 minutes

 It is a great city for cafes, restaurants, some of the best in the country along with live music venues, bars and night clubs, shows and entertainment both Kiwi and international. Be sure to check out funky Cuba Street and Courtney Place for great entertainment day and night. Lambton Quay and Willis Streets for shopping.

Walk the waterfront and be sure to visit Te Papa the Museum of New Zealand while there and also the Maritime Museum. For the motor home visitor there is a park to stay right downtown but expensive. Coming in on route 2 there are two parks outside the city to stay at.

At the Te Papa Museum, check out the interactive technology that allows you to take a virtual ride in a Maori canoe, make a bungy jump, feel a simulated earthquake or experience the eruption of Mount Ruapehu. Te Papa means "Our Place" and a fully functioning Maori meeting house involves you in Maori ceremonies. In its more traditional role, the Te Papa Museum houses invaluable collections of the arts and artefacts of the country and its history.

Check out our Parliament and the "Beehive" with a free tour where they hang out and be sure to take the cable car to the Botanic Gardens.

Top Five Things to Do:
- ✓ Visit Te Papa - the Museum of New Zealand
- ✓ Check out Cuba Street
- ✓ Take the cable car to the Botanic Gardens
- ✓ Do a Lord of the Rings Tour
- ✓ Visit Zealandia

Zealandia   -
http://www.visitzealandia.com/site/zealandia_home/
This is a beautiful 225ha (550 acre) eco-sanctuary for your best opportunity to see some of New Zealand's rarest birds, reptiles and insects in the wild ten minutes from downtown.

Museum of City & Sea -
http://www.museumofwellington.co.nz
Right on the waterfront downtown and one of the best museums you will see.

Lord of the Rings Tours -
http://www.activities.nz.com/wellington/lord-of-the-rings/
See where Peter Jackson and crew created the Lord of the Rings movies

It would take up way too much space if I listed all the cafes and restaurants we really love in this city but here are a couple off the top of my head.
First for the coffee nut you will be in Nirvana. More cafes here per capita than there are in New York City and some really awesome coffee roasters creating top quality coffee. If you see a Mojo coffee sign go in and the same with Supreme Coffee.

On Cuba Street - http://www.cuba.co.nz/
For breakfast I prefer either Plum café or the Matterhorn (great menu).
Logan Browns is one of the best restaurants in New Zealand
The Hotel Bristol has jazz night on Thursdays.
Best Turkish restaurant is Istanbul
Indian is Tulsi

And around the city is:
The White House, Oriental Parade
Monsoon Poon, Blair Street
Shed Five, Queens Wharf
Arbitrageur Wine Room, Featherston St
And as I said so many more…………………………..

So this itinerary has taken you from Auckland to the east coast of the North Island and all the way around down to Wellington.

Te Papa on the waterfront

Visit the Wellington website -
www.wellingtonnz.com

Now we go back to begin again in Auckland but down the west coast to New Plymouth and the Taranaki region, Whanganui and again to Wellington.

NOTES:

Itinerary Two -North Island -
West Coast Route – from Auckland to Wellington

Route one south it takes a drive of about 2 hours to the city of **Hamilton** - http://www.visithamilton.co.nz/ and the Waikato region. A New Zealand area with farming a major industry with many and varied activities for visitors to enjoy. The Waikato River flowing through the middle of Hamilton and much of the Waikato region is the life force of the region. Let's not overlook a place just 30+ minutes out of Hamilton (take Route 23 west) approx 50kms - less than an hour's drive) worth visiting for those with time

Raglan - http://www.raglan.net.nz/
A small wonderful community built on a surfing laid back lifestyle but now boasts quite a town of interest. Great place to park up and stroll around. The cafes all produce top quality coffee.

The Waikato River
The name 'Waikato' comes from Maori and translates as 'flowing water'. The longest river in the country (264 miles) runs from Lake Taupo to Port Waikato and eighteen hour journey and flows through 8 hydro-electric dams. The mighty Waikato generates about 13% of New Zealand's total electricity needs.
The eight artificial lakes created by the power stations are very popular recreation areas for fishing, boating and swimming.

Mount Pirongia
Mount Pirongia at 959 meters is the tallest mountain in the region. Half way between Otorohanga and Ngruawahia sits the tiny settlement just 35 minutes drive south of Hamilton is famous for its regular craft markets. This Ancient volcano is a great spot for hikers and hosts many in its Dept of Conservation Lodge.

The Agrodome - http://www.agrodome.co.nz/
Agrodome provides visitors an insight to Kiwi farming and the opportunity to meet the goats, cattle, deer, alpacas and ostriches and take part in the world famous sheep show. For

those who wish an more exciting experience how about bungy jumping, zorbing and more!

Waitomo Caves - http://www.waitomo.com/
A must stop to explore the caves, see the glowwarms and even blackwater raft through the caverns. One of my favourite spots and be sure to visit the
Billy Black Show - http://www.woodlynpark.co.nz/ .

Waitomo comes from the Maori words 'wai' meaning water and 'tomo' meaning hole. The village is a popular tourist spot to discover the magic of the glow worm caves on guided tours. Vast caves provide the thrill of black water rafting, caving and abseiling. Above ground activities include 4WD biking, horse riding, Angora rabbit show, wildlife park and drive-yourself jet boats. Extensive bush provides scenic attractions including the natural Limestone Bridge, Marokopa Falls and many areas to hike.

The Waitomo Caves region where one can explore the many caves and underground rivers. One of those don't miss places in New Zealand to visit. Go to http://www.waitomo.com/

There are fifty kilometres of caves that provide an underground world of limestone beauty. In Waitomo go to the Museum of Caves to organize the 45 minute tour of the Glow Worm Cave with its underground river is the main attraction where you follow a guide through the cave to board a boat on the underground river where in the dark the world of the glow worm is scattered above you like twinkling stars in the overhead dome of the glow worm grotto a true natural wonder.
There are more exciting underground tours such as the 45 minute walking tour of the Aranui Cave with its hollow stalactites and the most exciting Ruakuri Cave that

provides a black water rafting tour. This is a true underground adventure that requires a wetsuit and a caver's helmet with light and an inner tube to hang on to. One of the adventures takes about three hours where you will float through the pitch black world lit by your helmet light, go over a waterfall, and go though a glow-worm passage.

Take a ride into the Glowworm Caves

Black Water Rafting – http://www.waitomo.com/black-water-rafting.aspx

A true adventurous spirit is required for the black water rafting and I suggest it should only be done by those of you who are fit. It all begins with getting in the wetsuit and fitting the caver's helmet with light on your head along with an inner tube to hold onto while cruising along afloat through the underground rivers and caves that are adorned with limestone formations. One of the adventures is three hours long and has a waterfall to leap over, glow worms and a spectacular cavern environment. For the true caver and adventurer you are offered a six hour expedition that along with the black water rafting includes a 30 metre abseiling. Training is provided for the abseiling. I suggest you book ahead for this if visiting during the busy summer months. Both black water rafting experiences end with a hot shower and hot soup.

Blackwater rafting bookings may be made at the Museum of the Caves. Book well in advance during the busy summer holiday period.

Top Five things to do In the Waikato Region

- ✓ Visit the Waitomo Caves to raft or see the glow worms
- ✓ Visit Hobbiton in Matamata
- ✓ See kiwi and kiwiana in Otorohanga
- ✓ Go surfing in Raglan or just grab a coffee
- ✓ Visit the Agrodome

Hamilton

Hamilton is the heart of the Waikato. The city offers art galleries, museums, cafes and riverside walks as well as the world famous Hamilton Gardens.

On the south end of Victoria Street is a statue of the iconic Riff Raff character from the cult status movie The Rocky Horror Picture Show.

The statue commemorates the development of the idea and the writing of The Rocky Horror Picture Show by Richard O'Brien - who actually lives in Hamilton now.

Then there is Waterworld that is one of the largest indoor/outdoor aquatic facilities in NZ. Features include: Python hydroslides and Screamer speedslides, Splashpad, the ultimate water playground for under eight year olds, indoor and outdoor pools, children's playground, BBQ and picnic areas, a cafe and gym facilities.

Hamilton Lake in the heart of Hamilton has a 2 ½ mile path creating an approximate 45 minute circular walk around one of the city's hidden paradises. Relax in the picnic area, enjoy the playground, or just choose a park bench and enjoy the world around you.

Hamilton is home to many golf courses to suit all playing levels. A well know golf course in Hamilton is the Hamilton Club (St Andrews), St Andrews gold course is know to be one of the best conditioned courses in the country.

Top Five Things to do in Hamilton
- ✓ Visit the beautiful Hamilton Gardens
- ✓ Go to the annual Balloons over Waikato event
- ✓ Cruise the mighty Waikato River
- ✓ Take in a Waikato Chiefs rugby game
- ✓ Follow the heritage trail to learn of Hamilton's history

Other towns in The Waikato Region –

Cambridge
Known as the 'Town of Trees' Cambridge is home to Waikato's thoroughbred stud industry. Nearby Lake Karapiro is the national home of rowing and wake-boarding.

Huntly
Huntly is surrounded by rich farmland and lakes that are ideal for yachting, water skiing, windsurfing and canoeing. It is recognised as one of the main coal mining centres of New Zealand and produces over 10,000 tonnes of coal per day. The Huntly Waikato Coalfields Museum displays the history of local coal mining.

Matamata

It is well known for its thoroughbred industry, dairy farming heritage, and the historic Firth Tower Museum. Since the launch of the Lord of the Rings movies Matamata has become a major stopping off spot for Hobbit enthusiasts.

Otorohanga

Commonly know as the Kiwiana capital of New Zealand. Displays and murals depicting Kiwiana (national icons) are found around the town. See & Do: **Otorohanga Kiwi House** and Native Bird Park, Ed Hillary Walkway, Otorohanga Museum and Farmers/Garden Market every Saturday 8.00am to10.30am.

Putaruru

Putaruru has an affluent farming community, and predominant timber industry. The nearby Te Waihou Walkway, leading to the ultra-clear Blue Spring is a highlight. The pure water from the Blue Spring is bottled, and represents 60% of New Zealand's bottled water. On the local waterways trout fishing, swimming, tubing, kayaking and snorkelling are popular.

Te Aroha

Te Aroha is a spa town, where visitors have come for over 120 years to 'take the waters' at the Te Aroha Hot Springs Domain. The hot mineral pools and the world's only hot soda water geyser are located at the base of Mt. Te Aroha. Hiking and exploring old gold mining sites and mountain biking are some of the key features popular with visitors.

Te Awamutu

Te Awamutu - The Town of Roses - is the town with famous rose gardens. It is the hometown of Tim and Neil Finn of the music bands, Crowded House and Split Enz. The Te Awamutu Museum is home to Unenuku, a powerful symbol of the Tainui (Maori) people. Outdoors enthusiasts enjoy the nearby Pirongia Forest Park, Yarndley's Bush, Lake Ngaroto and Mount Kakepuku. Rock climbers are just minutes away from prime spots.

Te Kauwhata
Above beautiful Lake Waikare, is the small town of Te Kauwhata. Set in the research station built by Italian viticulturist Romeo Bragato in 1902, lies Rongopai Wines, the birthplace of New Zealand winemaking research and one of the leading producers in NZ of botrytised wine. Numerous medals and awards make Rongopai a great source of wines in the local market and internationally.

Te Kuiti
Te Kuiti is known as the 'Shearing Capital of the World' due to the annual New Zealand Shearing Championships, and the town's 7 metre shearing statue reminds visitors of this event. Another annual event is called, The Running of the Sheep, where 2,000+ sheep are let loose in the main street.

Tirau - http://www.tirauinfo.co.nz/
Tirau was originally known as Oxford, and today is famous for its corrugated iron icons - the largest corrugated iron sheep and sheepdog in the world! The i-SITE Visitor Information Centre is housed in a building in the shape of a dog, which was built to complement the sheep-shaped building – a wool and craft shop. Attractions include garden walks, the local honey industry, a deer farm, early New Zealand museum, jade factory, and a toy and doll museum.

Driving directions:
From Hamilton you can take route 3 on south directly or do the round trip to Matamata (Hobbit Town) via route 26 to

route 27 to Tirau and back route one to Cambridge then south to route 3 and Otorohanga, Waitomo and Te Kuiti.

Continue on route 3 to the west coast. You will reach the colourful route along the Awakino River before finally reaching the west coast at the town of **Awakino -** http://www.toa.co.nz/Taranaki%20Towns/Awakino %20and%20Mokau.htm .
The rivers along this stretch are known for whitebaiting - http://www.fishingmag.co.nz/Whitebait-New-Zealand.htm .
Good place to get your introduction into one of the country's top culinary delights. A couple of great holiday parks to stop at in this area right on the ocean.................

This route will be continued below after this side trip you may want to do................

But first......
This is an alternate route not many visitors know about to take - South of Te Kuiti take route 4 to route 43 known as the **The Forgotten Highway -** http://www.aatravel.co.nz/101/MustDo_The-Forgotten-World-Highway.html

One of my favourite trips. I always stop at the pub in the isolated settlement of **Whangamomona**, a small village declared a 'republic' by residents back in 1988. New Zealand's first heritage trail, this scenic route winds over four mountain saddles, alongside the spectacular Tangarakau Gorge and passes through the 180-metre-long, single lane, Moki tunnel. View stunning vistas of Mt

Taranaki, Mt Ruapehu, Mt Ngauruhoe and Mt Tongariro to the east. Other highlights include the Mount Damper Falls and easy walk from the road. Route 43 ends in Stratford.

Now continued from above...........................on to Taranaki......

Soon you will find the road beginning the climb up Mt. Messenger, a twisting and turning route, that will eventually bring you back down to along the ocean. After about 80 kms out of Awakino you will be in
New Plymouth –
http://www.newplymouthnz.com/VisitingNewPlymouth/
A very forward thinking community that provides a pleasant place to stop. Everything in this region is dominated by **Mt Taranaki.-**
http://www.taranaki.info/visit/content.php/page/mt-taranaki-and-egmont-national-park .

This is a great place to visit and see across the miles from on the edge of the mountain where the volcanoes north of here are dominant. Paula's grandfather took me up for the first time. His father has surveyed the area in the early stages of discovery so it was a real treat to be escorted by someone with a great history in the area.

As a visitor you should take the circle Route 45, the surf highway, around the mountain stopping at **Oakura** and **Opunake** to check out the shops and galleries. Also don't miss **Okurukuru** - www.okurukuru.co.nz, New Plymouth's first commercial vineyard, between New Plymouth and Oakura. Perched on the edge within the vineyard is an architecturally supreme restaurant with one of the most startling coastal views in the country plus the added feature of Mt Taranaki dominating the scenery to the east.

It is a good idea to take a side road up the mountain out of Stratford and perhaps a visit to Dawson Falls. A day or so in the region would be most rewarding. The region offers great scenery with fabulous beaches that has world class surfing. The entire region is centrally focused on Mount Taranaki (Egmont) providing top alpine recreation.

Taranaki is a primary place to visit. The major hub of New Plymouth offers on of the finest walkways along the coast of anywhere coupled with stunning parks and gardens along with top class festivals. The region's principal economic activities are dairy farming and oil and natural gas exploration and production. The region has 20 golf courses, ranging from nine-hole country courses where you have to move the sheep, through to Ngamotu Links – consistently rated one of the best golf courses in New Zealand. All 20 golf courses are within an hour's drive of each other.

The Top Five Things to do in the Taranaki region
- ✓ Walk or cycle along New Plymouth coastal walkway
- ✓ Explore the mysterious Forgotten World Highway
- ✓ Take a drive along Surf Highway 45
- ✓ Walk up, on or around iconic Mt Taranaki
- ✓ Take in the art galleries and the Museum

New Plymouth
The heart of the Taranaki region this city boasts numerous beaches, over 50 walking tracks, ocean and alpine views and a vibrant inner city. It is named after Plymouth in Devon, England from where the first English settlers came.

New Plymouth District has a population of 68,901 - nearly two thirds of the total population of the Taranaki region. This includes - New Plymouth City (45,228), Waitara (6,288), Inglewood (3,090), Oakura (1,359), Okato (531) and Urenui (429).

New Plymouth has won multiple awards for its advanced design thinking with notable features such as the botanic gardens – Pukekura Park - the 4.3 mile coastal walkway alongside the Tasman Sea, a 148 foot tall artwork known as the Wind Wand, and the constant views of Mount Taranaki/Egmont.

Right next to the Coastal Walkway is the Todd Energy Aquatic Centre, with indoor and outdoor pools, a diving pool, wave machine, hydroslides, spa, sauna and gym.
The New Plymouth District has a reputation as an events centre, with major festivals (the annual TSB Bank Festival of Lights, Taranaki Rhododendron and Garden Festival, WOMAD and the Guitar Festival, and the biennial Taranaki Arts Festival), sports (including international rugby, cricket and tennis matches, and the annual ITU World Cup Triathlon) and music concerts by top international names.

The world's first purpose-built, fully integrated museum, library and information centre that tells the stories of Taranaki in a variety of interactive media is in New Plymouth. Since its opening in 2003 Puke Ariki has won multiple awards for design, delivery, technology, innovation and architecture.

Top Five Things to do in New Plymouth, New Zealand
- ✓ Visit the celebrated Art Gallery and Museum Puke Ariki
- ✓ Walk or cycle the New Plymouth Coastal Walkway
- ✓ Enjoy the beauty of Pukekura Park

- ✓ Don't miss one of the many festivals and events
- ✓ Check out the world's largest surfboard at Oakura

Stratford

Named after Shakespeare's birthplace, Stratford where many of the street names stem from the great Bard's plays.

Top Five things available to do in Stratford
- ✓ Hike in nearby Egmont National Park
- ✓ Explore the Forgotten World Highway touring route
- ✓ Watch a Shakespearean scene at NZ's only glockenspiel tower
- ✓ Ski at nearby Manganui ski field
- ✓ Enjoy golf, mountain biking and short bush walks around the town

Opunake

Opunake is a favoured seaside location having one of the top beaches that are very popular with surfers, swimmers and windsurfers.

The Surf Highway 45 is a coastal 105km stretch of State Highway.

Top Five Things to do in Opunake
- ✓ Cruise the Surf Highway 45 touring route
- ✓ Surf one of NZ's top surf beaches
- ✓ Explore nearby Egmont National Park
- ✓ Visit historic Parihaka Pa
- ✓ Have a coffee in Opunake & take in the town's wall murals

Time now to drive out of Taranaki on Route 3 south..........................

We pass through vast acreages of dairy farms (corner of SR#3 and Wehareroa Road is the Dairyland Visitor Centre, the largest dairy manufacturing site in the world) on our way to the city of **Whanganui** and on to **Wellington** (about six hours drive from New Plymouth to Wellington) on Route One after the town of **Bulls**. At Bulls you can take the detour through to the town of **Palmerston North** and **Fielding** then either return to Bulls and south on route one or take route 57 south to join up with route one again below **Levin**.

It is a drive of 2 ½ hours to **Whanganui** and the **Manawatu** region from Taranaki. Situated by one of the majestic rivers of New Zealand up through the Manawatu Gorge this area has long been a place of importance to the local inhabitants and visitors alike. Located on the northwestern side of the river and close to its mouth Wanganui is 200 kilometres north of Wellington at the junction of routes 3 and 4.

This area was settled early by pre-European Maori with the first Europeans arriving in 1831. In 1854 the name of Wanganui was established but in 2010 local Maori petitioned it to be changed to Whanganui.

This was the scene of the Land Wars of the 1860's between the Maori and settling Europeans. The conflict still goes on to the present day.

The Top Five Things to do in Whanganui
- ✓ Explore the Whanganui National Park
- ✓ Go boating on the Whanganui River
- ✓ Visit the Sarjeant Gallery
- ✓ View local glass art works
- ✓ Enjoy one of the many local parks and reserves

Ron recommends to stay at: Whanganui River TOP
10 Holiday Park
The only Qualmark 4-Star-Plus rated holiday park in the
Taranaki/Wanganui/Manawatu area.

Contact:

Whanganui River TOP 10 Holiday Park

Website: http://www.wrivertop10.co.nz/
Ph. +64 6 343 8402
Fax. +64 6 343 8406
Reservations only. 0800 272 664
Address: 460 Somme Parade, Wanganui

Now on south……………..

Ron recommends staying at the:
Himatangi Beach Holiday Park
- in Manawatu (near Palmerston North) Two hours north
of Wellington's inter island ferry on the west coast of the
North Island of New Zealand - is the ideal spot for
campervans, caravans, tents and holiday-makers seeking
comfortable, tidy cabin accommodation.

Owners Margaret and Dennis invite you to come and experience their unique, award-winning brand of real Kiwi hospitality.

Contact:

30 Koputara Road

Himatangi Beach 4891

Phone: 06 329 9575

Fax: 06 329 9576

Email: info@himatangibeachholidaypark.co.nz

Website: www.himatangibeachholidaypark.co.nz

Palmerston North

Palmerston North is offers many shops, restaurants and accommodation. It is home to Massey University and the National Rugby Museum and the main service centre to rural Manawatu, Waiouru Army Camp and Ohakea Airforce Base,

The Top Five to do in Palmerston North, New Zealand

- ✓ Visit the famous National Rugby Museum
- ✓ Take some photos of the city's iconic clock tower
- ✓ Stroll Palmerston North's town square
- ✓ Enjoy the active nightlife!
- ✓ Walk the popular Manawatu Gorge Track

Feilding

Feilding is the major centre of rural Manawatu with an Edwardian-style town centre and a population of 13,000 voted "New Zealand's Most Beautufuil Town" 14 times

Top Five Things to do in Feilding

- ✓ Walk the streets of 'New Zealand's most beautiful town'
- ✓ Do a saleyard tour for an authentic rural experience
- ✓ Visit the weekly Farmers' Market
- ✓ Take a stroll along the pretty Camellia Walk

✓ View some of the many beautiful gardens

Levin

A great starting point for the outdoors adventurer with the town in between the ocean and farmland of the region with Lake Horowhenua nearby as well as the Tararua mountain range.

Five things to do in Levin

✓ Go bird watching at Papaitonga Scenic Reserve
✓ See the De Molen windmill at nearby Foxton
✓ Visit Lake Horowhenua and its surrounding wetlands
✓ More great bird watching on the Nature Coast Bird Trail
✓ Stroll along the beautiful beaches in the area

Now from Levin south to Wellington. This is one of our top areas to visit.

We usually go to **Otaki Beach**. One of the finest in the country to stroll along and enjoy. Worth the few minutes off the main highway to get there.

Leaving Otaki south just on the outskirts of town is one of our favourite cafes - **Brown Sugar**. Never miss a stop there for a Supreme coffee.

Just a few kilometres continuing toward Wellington one of the most eccentric collections of goodies made into a museum I have ever seen. Stop at Te Horo on the right and have a look. It is free and just mind boggling. Great fun. There are quite a few other shops and a cafe there also.

Through the town of Waikanai and just before the town of Paraparaumu on the right is **Southward Museum** a world class auto collection/museum - http://www.thecarmuseum.co.nz/ Anyone into old cars has to stop here. I really enjoyed the place and don't consider myself a car enthusiast at all. Tweaks the mind to think all these cars from all over were brought way out here to New Zealand. Have a look!

Next stop.......... Wellington!

So I have created the drive down the East Coast and the West Coast of the North Island and now the drive down the middle. Obviously at certain points there can be a diversification to be able to experience a bit of all of it with a bit of a back and forth but you can quickly see there are few roads to be able to cut across country readily.

NOTES:

Itinerary Three –North Island – Auckland to Wellington (through the middle of the island)

This is usually the itinerary trip I recommend for those who only have a short stay; as direct a route as possible to cover as much as possible in a few days when going on to the South Island.

Various itineraries can be adjusted using the information I have already provided in One and Two. Check you times and see what you are able to do.

What I recommend is on your way south no matter which way you plan be sure to stop and experience Rotorua. So let's take it from there on this itinerary to go down the middle of the North Island.

Basically from Auckland take route one to route 5 to Rotorua or if coming from the east coast I suggest route 29 from Tauranga.

Rotorua – http://www.rotoruanz.com/

This is the number one place anyone visiting New Zealand must visit. Highway 5 from Hamilton and access from Tauranga in the north is route 33. Rotorua enjoys a stable climate. The area is natures' cauldron of hot springs, boiling mud, geysers and the smell of hydrogen sulphide have made this thermal region world famous. This area is a basin-like structure 16km in diameter and 300metres deep that was formed 150,000 years ago.

At Whakarewarewa south of the city of Rotorua there are more than 500 hot springs. There are two types of hot springs - chloride and sulphate. A chloride spring runs clear that over time releases enough silica to form sinter terraces where as all geysers are chloride springs.

Ones to see in this area are Pohutu that has an eruption of over 18metres, the Prince of Wales Feathers and Waikorohihi. Be careful when exploring this area as much of the ground between the hot springs is warm and with steam coming from many small fissures. It is quite important one stays to the well marked paths provided. Some areas there is only a thin crust of ground over boiling mud. If you have never been around this type of terrain it will be one of your most exciting experiences.

The most violent and destructive volcanic eruption during European settlement time was by Mt Tarawera in 1886 destroying three settlements. It was this eruption that destroyed the then famous Pink and White Terraces and formed Lake Rotomahana. An interesting walk is to go to the isthmus between the Blue Lake and the Green Lake, created also by this eruption to see the actual colour difference.

One of the most interesting and most active thermal areas is at Hell's Gate. They offer a mud bath here you may enjoy. Also Kakahi Falls a major attraction where one can be splashed in a cascade of warm water.

Warbrick Terrace – Waimangu Volcanic Valley
The Waimangu Thermal Valley did not exist prior to the eruption when ten craters were formed with some filled from the overflow of Lake Rotomahana. The three most visited in the valley are the Inferno Crater, Echo Crater and Southern Crater. Echo Crater is filled by Frying Pan Lake, one of the world's largest "boiling" lakes. Several explosions have occurred over the years with the most recent in 1973 but no one was injured.

Cathedral Rocks – Waimangu Volcanic Valley

It is only 26kms from Rotorua to Waimangu and from there a track begins that can be followed through this crater area. A quick short walk of only an hour will get you to a good portion of it but if you continue along through the area and along the lake to circle back to where you begun it will take you to some very scenic sights and views of these thermal wonders.

The large Waiotapu Wonderland thermal area 25km southeast of Rotorua is open to visitors and has crater-like pits up to 20metres across with boiling pools of muddy water at the base of some. Southeast of the pits lies the spectacular Champagne Pool and at the south end of the pool is Bridal Veil Falls. Just outside the reserve are also some excellent mud pools and also the Lady Knox Geyser which was actually artificially created in 1906. It was discovered to erupt when soap powder was introduced by the local inmates of the prison in those days when they came to wash their clothes so the Chief Warden installed a cast-iron pipe and increased the height of the geyser....

After the hot pools or maybe before you check them out Rotorua is where you can get full immersion into the Maori culture. You have to visit the villages and you can't go to Rotorua without enjoying an evening meal or a hangi as it is known in Maori with its fantastic food and cultural show.

Rotorua itself as a town provides great accommodations cafes & restaurants and a good place to pick up some New Zealand souvenirs. Plan a couple of days here to really get full enjoyment of the area and what it has to offer.

Ron recommends one of his favourite places to stay at:

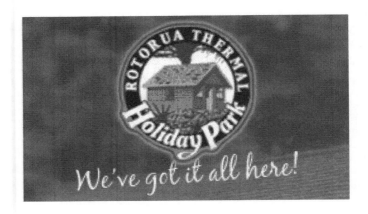

Contact:
Address: 463 Old Taupo Road (south end)
Phone/Fax: 07 346 3140
Email: info@rotoruathermal.co.nz
Website: www.rotoruathermal.co.nz

Sixty-eight kms from Rotorua is the Orakei Korako themal region. One way to reach the thermal valley is by jet boat across Lake Ohakuri and a walk of an hour or so around takes you by the Diamond Geyser, the Hochstetter Hot Pool, the Rainbow Terrace and the most spectacular Golden Fleece Terrace a gigantic deposit of white silica over 5 metre high cascading down the hill side. The best known is what is called Aladdin's Cave where in pre-European times it was used by the local Maori women to adorn themselves in the mirror pools. At night glow worms bring a strange glow to the cave.

The Rotorua area has vast forests of introduced pine for logging that covers over 111,000hectares. It is one of the largest in the world employing over 1500 people producing nearly 30 cubic metres of wood annually. The Park has been opened to recreation with many tracks and huts along with camping and picnic areas.

Lots of activities here and one of the most popular is rolling down a hill in a Zorb........

Plenty of adventure for the most hardy to the easy going for families and individuals.

Now we must go on south....................from Rotorua take either route 30 or route 5 south to **Lake Taupo -** http://www.greatlaketaupo.com/ .

A very popular holiday destination for Kiwi's and international visitors alike. Lake Taupo is the largest lake in Australasia. It is a very special place with Lake Taupo providing top quality water sports and just down the road the volcanoes of Ruapehu, Tongariro and Ngauruhoe to visit. Lots of adventure sports such as mountain biking, whitewater rafting, bungy jumping and sky diving. Taupo also provides top quality cafes and restaurants and funky bars along with arts and crafts of the region.

Five Top Things to Do in the Taupo Region
  ✓ Visit Huka Falls - NZ's most visited natural attraction

- ✓ Swim, waterski or cruise on the beautiful Lake Taupo
- ✓ Catch a trout in the world famous Tongariro River
- ✓ Enjoy a hike in the spectacular Tongariro National Park
- ✓ aVisit the Orakei Korako geo-thermal valley

Orakei Korako - http://www.orakeikorako.co.nz/

You haven't seen the best of our geothermal parks until you've visited the valley of Orakei Korako — hidden from the main highways, 25-minutes north of Taupo.

This geothermal park and natural treasure is considered one of the best attractions in the world by international travellers.

Your trip to this protected wonderland on the shores of Lake Ohakuri starts with a boat crossing from the park's entrance and café/observation area.

Whanganui National Park -

http://www.whanganuinationalpark.com/

The Whanganui National Park is based around New Zealand's longest navigable river, the Whanganui, which rises on Mt Tongariro and runs 329 km to the Tasman Sea

The 74,231 hectare park borders the Whanganui River. It incorporates areas of Crown land, former state forest and a number of former reserves. The river itself is not part of the park.

Tongariro National Park Village -

http://www.nationalpark.co.nz/ &

http://www.doc.govt.nz/parks-and-recreation/national-parks/tongariro/

National Park Village borders the World Heritage Tongariro National Park to the east and the Whanganui National Park to the West. National Park Village is located near the base of Mt Ruapehu, at the intersection of SH4 & SH47 on the volcanic plateau. The village has great views of Mt

Tongariro, Mt Ngauruhoe (Mt Doom in the Lord of the Rings filming locations) and Mt Ruapehu . To enjoy this scenic wonder it's not even necessary to leave the comfort of your car. The volcanic loop circles all three volcanoes — Mt Ruapehu, Mt Ngauruhoe and Mt Tongariro.

Tongariro Crossing -

http://www.tongarirocrossing.org.nz/?gclid=CKD9nu7VnqMCFSD3iAodznzMpw

The Tongariro National Park has dramatic scenery and unique land forms this combines to make the Tongariro Alpine Crossing a world-renowned trek. (Rated as the best one day trek in New Zealand and listed by many in the top 10 day treks in the world) Many who complete the 18.5 kilometre journey will tell you the climbs can be steep and the weather can be unpredictable. This is more then a gentle walk so be prepared.

The Bridge to Nowhere –

http://www.bridgetonowhere.co.nz/

Popular with trampers accessing the southern point of the Mangapurua Valley, The Bridge to Nowhere has had a film named after it and is now protected under an Historic Places Trust Category I listing.

You can access The Bridge to Nowhere by way of a gentle 40-minute walk from the Mangapurua Landing on the Whanganui River or, more vigorously, by a two-day tramp from Whakahoro Hut in the lower Retaruke Valley, via the Kaiwhakauka and Mangapurua Valleys.

Other towns to visit in the area south of Taupo:

Ohakune -

Situated at the base of Mount Ruapehu, Ohakune caters for visitors to the popular Whakapapa and Turoa ski fields.

Known as 'New Zealand's Carrot Capital', Ohakune's giant carrot monument has become a kiwi icon!

Taumarunui -
Taumarunui is the entry point of New Zealand's largest navigable waterway – the Whanganui River. Fishing, boating and swimming are popular in summer, with winter drawing visitors to nearby Whakapapa and Turoa ski fields. The Whanganui River Journey is one of the best in the world. For those driving through do the Forgotten Highway through to the Taranaki region. For those who enjoy trains vist the Raurimu Spiral known as a railway engineering marvel. Explore nearby Whanganui National Park.

Turangi -
Trout fishing capital of the world, Turangi lies alongside the Tongariro River and majestic Lake Taupo, and is also the gateway to New Zealand's best one-day walk – the awe-inspiring Tongariro Crossing. Check out the natural Tokannu Thermal Area

Whakapapa -
Located on New Zealand's largest active volcano, Whakapapa Village is an exciting ski resort with several accommodation options. Ski season runs from late-June to mid-November, but summer activities like scenic chairlift rides and hiking are also available. Visit the historic Chateau Tongariro. If a winter visitor ski or snowboard at NZ's largest ski area here. Play a round at New Zealand's highest golf course or explore the Tongariro National Park and its volcanos.

South of Lake Taupo at Turangi you can go around the west side of the Tongariro Park on route 47 or you can go straight ahead on route one. Going straight ahead you will go through the high desert country and the Waiouru Military Area. Both routes end up at **Waiouru** - http://en.wikipedia.org/wiki/Waiouru . Of interest there is the **National Army Museum** - http://www.armymuseum.co.nz/ and then on south on route one you come to Taihape.

For coffee lovers and those who enjoy good food I recommend the **Brown Sugar Café**
in Taihape on Huia Street, easy to find just off the main route one. We have always made sure our coffee schedule was set to get to Brown Sugar as we passed through this area.
Same owners for 18 years and they have not only maintained their high levels but have improved. They get rave reviews from locals as well as travelers. Always friendly and efficient and a real pleasure to stop and take advantage of the peaceful surroundings during our travels.

Taihape - The Gumboot capital of the World - So what is special about the town of Taihape? And what is a gumboot? It is known in the US as the Wellington and is the common rubber boot worn around the world. Here in New Zealand the farmer and the fishermen, a large part of our community, use the gumboot on a daily basis.
Tuesday 9 April 1985, the first GUMBOOT DAY was held at Gumboot Park at the northern entrance to the town.
There was gumboot throwing, gumboot races, decorated gumboots and shop window displays providing a day when both those from the farms and the town could get together and enjoy themselves while at the same time

promoting Taihape.

The next year in 1986 they developed the Taihape University theme. Degrees in "Gumboot Throwology" were awarded. The attempt on the gumboot throwing record has become a fixture for the event. the name 'Gumboot Country' now has become synonymous with the town and the event.

Now it has become the annual affair and enjoyed by local and visitor alike. Perhaps you might get lucky and be there for the big day.

From Taihape on south on route one you then get to **Bulls** and follow the same route as I have already shown or take route 54 into **Palmerston North** and on south to Wellington.

So now I have explained how to experience the North Island from the top at Cape Reinga to the bottom at Wellington. You should be able to create an itinerary to do exactly as you wish, find the right accommodations, the best cafes and restaurants, the top in activities that you wish to enjoy.

It may seem like a small country but it packs a lot into the area where it exists. You are never very far from a scenic vista or the ocean or a mountain, a lake or a trout filled stream. The cities and towns provide the culture and people to meet and enjoy. If you enjoy the outdoor world this is the real magic kingdom especially the next part – the South Island.............

So it is time to catch that ferry and spend the next 3 ½ hours cruising through Wellington harbour out into Cook Strait and over to the Marlborough Sounds to begin our adventure in the picturesque and pleasant town of Picton.

NOTES:

Part Two – South Island

One of the most enjoyable parts of the trip is the ferry crossing between the North and South Island. It is a 3 ½ hour trip between Wellington and Picton in the Marlborough Sounds. The trip is approximately 1/3rd cruising through the Wellington Harbour, 1/3rd crossing Cook Strait and the last 1/3rd in the Marlborough Sounds. I enjoy leaving through the Wellington Harbour standing on deck and then again upon entering the Marlborough Sounds into Tory Channel and the Queen Charlotte Sound. The entrance between East Head and West Head seems just wide enough for the ferry to enter. The ride down through the Sounds is one of the top scenic areas of New Zealand.

You have two choices for ferry crossing – the Bluebridge Cook Strait Ferry - http://www.bluebridge.co.nz/ and the Interislander - http://www.interislander.co.nz/

Picton arrival

The small town of Picton is a real gem and I advise stopping a few days and enjoying the many activities available from kayaking, walking the Queen Charlotte Track, swimming with dolphins, diving, fishing and much more plus Picton offers some great cafes, restaurants and shops.

I highly recommends <u>LeCafé</u> restaurant, bar and the top live music venue in Picton

The top of the South Island is a boater's paradise a water wonderland of submerged mountains with islands, coves and waterways to explore. A fabulous spot to go fishing, diving, swimming, exploring where seals and dolphins call home. Some of the greatest hiking and biking trails in the country.

From the North Island take one of the ferries across Cook Strait. A 3 ½ hour journey that is a scenic experience in itself especially as the ferry enters the Marlborough Sounds and cruises through Queen Charlotte Sound to the port of Picton a small village well worth stopping at to enjoy. There are a few roads that go back into the Marlborough Sounds to explore where isolated lodges and camp grounds are available.

Picton - http://www.picton.co.nz/_

The village of Picton offers one of the finest waterfronts in New Zealand to relax and stroll along. A beautiful lawn where families gather to picnic and the children play in the playground, ride the train while the adults play mini- golf. There is a museum and an aquarium to visit and a movie theatre on the waterfront plus the historic ship the Edwin Fox.

Find out the best spots for swimming, diving, kayaking, sailing or cruising the Sounds. Take one of the tours of the Sounds such as to Ship's Cove where captain Cook hung out when he visited or go swim with the dolphins. Great places for food and drink such as LeCafe on the waterfront and the Irish Pub for a great evening out. Several very good shops with local made products such as Latitude 41 and Evolve.

Check out the Echo Lodge B&B - http://www.echolodge.co.nz/ near the marina downtown.

I recommend the Broadway Motel when you stay in the Picton area:

Situated on the edge of town 700 metres from the Railway Station, BlueBridge and Interisland Ferry terminals. The Broadway Motel has fully self-contained units with laundry facilities and off street parking. The range of accommodation includes eighteen top of the range units (including two disabled-friendly rooms). This is one of Picton's newest motel facilities with contemporary guests in mind.

Contact:
Hosts Donna & Henry Kersten
Broadway Motel
113 High Street Picton
Phone +64-3-573-6563 Fax +64-3-573-8408
Freephone (within NZ) 0800-101-919
Email:stay@broadwaymotel.co.nz
Website: www.broadwaymotel.co.nz
==

Ron recommends staying here when in the Picton area...
Picton Campervan Park

We are a modern purpose built Campervan Park providing exclusive powered sites for both campervans and caravans (no tents). Our spacious powered sites are set out on flat gravel bays within the parks landscaped grounds and have their own power hook-up, switchable night light and fresh water supply for your convenience.

Why stay anywhere else, contact us today!

Contact
Address: 42 Kent Street, Picton
[GPS: 41° 17' 44.95" S   174° 00' 03.10" E]
Phone: +64-3-573- 8875
Fax: +64-3-573 - 8872
Email: picton.cvpark@xtra.co.nz
Website:
www.pictonholidaypark.co.nz

Ron highly recommends this B&B in the Marlborough region: the McCormick House:

Contact Carl & Jeanne:
21 Leicester Street, Picton 7220, Marlborough, New Zealand
Telephone: + 64(0)3 573 5253
 Mobile : 0212989106
 Fax : +64 (0)3 573 5263
E-mail: enquiries@mccormickhouse.co.nz
Website: http://www.mccormickhouse.co.nz/

History of McCormick House

Carl and Jeanne named McCormick House after Donald McCormick, who emigrated from Scotland in 1854. Most of his working life was spent farming at Whatamango Bay near Picton in the picturesque Marlborough Sounds, retiring to Picton in 1914, where he had this large architecturally designed house built on a prominent half acre site.

Jeanne and Carl purchased McCormick House in 2002 after searching throughout the country for a suitable property to start their bed and breakfast business. After 2 years of extensive renovation, McCormick House was opened.

A Real Hike – Queen Charlotte Track -
http://www.queencharlottetracknz.com/
For those interested in hiking the Queen Charlotte Track is one of the best in the country. You can do the whole 58-kilometre track from Ship Cove to Anakiwa in three to four days or you can simply do sections using boats to drop you off at starting points and pick you up at the end of the sections chosen. Great as you can make arrangments to stop overnight at one of the lodges scattered around the Sounds such as Lochmara Lodge that can only be accessed by boat or on foot…

Havelock - http://www.havelocknz.com/
From Picton take the Queen Charlotte road through the Marlborough Sounds so you can experience some of the more isolated areas. Be sure to stop at Cullen's Point on the right just before you leave the Sounds for an elevated look at the town of Havelock and the Sounds. You reach the town of Havelock, Greenshell Mussel Capital of the World.

Be sure to go down to the harbour to the Slip Inn and have a feed of the local mussels farmed in the Sounds while watching the locals get their boats in and out of the waterway.

Good place to join the local Mail Boat that takes the mail out to the many residents who live in the Sounds whare only a boat can reach them. If you are in a camper van the local holiday park right on the harbour is an excellent place to stay and the pub next door is one of the best in the country to enjoy.

Five+ Top Things to Do in the Marlborough Sounds

Greenshell™ Mussel Cruise – Havelock -
http://www.havelockinfocentre.co.nz/greenshell.html

Cruise the quietly gorgeous Kenepuru Sound while
listening to skipper and raconteur Chris Godsiff spiel his family's five-generation history in the area. Visit a mussel farm and taste the little morsels onboard fresh as fresh gets, slipped down with a glass of Marlborough Sauvignon Blanc.

Dophin Watch Ecotours – Picton -
http://www.naturetours.co.nz/
Visit the dusky dolphins, fur seals, King shags (native to Marlborough Sounds) and scads of shearwaters on one of marine biologists Amy and Dan Engelhaupt's ecotours. The sealife are friendly and plentiful – on a lucky day, endangered Hector's dolphins come out to play.

Queen Charlotte Track

It's all uphill from peaceful Ship Cove where Capt. Cook came ashore. Walk the 71km track, rent a mountain bike or do a guided 4-5 day walk or 3-day mountain bike trek or just dpo portions of it reaching the track by boat. Stop by the lodges along the way such as Lochmara Lodge out of Picton.

Kayak – Picton -

Oh to float upon the sea, just my kayak, paddle and me … rent kayaks by the day or explore the coves and critters of Queen Charlotte or Kenepuru Sounds on 1-3 day guided trips with camping or lodge accommodation options. You can also add a paddle track trek.

Cruise the Sounds

Take a closer look out into the water wonderland of the Sounds with the Beachcomber or the Endeavour Express out of Picton.

Time to move on after enjoying Picton and the fabulous Marlborough Sounds.

We are off to the Upper Northwest Corner of the South Island

The northwest region of the South Island is one of our most favourite areas to explore especially when you cross over the "Marble Mountain" to the Golden Bay area.

Two ways to get to this region from Picton -

You can take route one south to Spring Creek and turn right on Rapaura Road taking you through the fabulous Marlborough Wine region.

Or:

From Picton go through the Sounds on the Queen Charlotte Drive to Havelock, mussel capital of New Zealand. Two great eating spots here – on the waterfront is **Slip Inn** and for a tasty snack on the main road stop and see Lauri and Beht at the **Wakamarian** (a small place but Paula says they got the best quiche) Continuing on route 6 from Havelock toward the Nelson area and Golden Bay be sure to stop at Pelorus Bridge. You leave Havelock travelling along the Pelorus River. On the right you will see a sign to a picnic spot on the river. Be sure to drive down the short road to a very scenic location on the river. At Pelorus bridge there is a cafe plus several tracks to walk into the bush and along the river. Great place for trout fishing in this area.

After you cross the one way bridge a couple of kilometres on the right you will spot an unmarked dirt road on the right. Park on the road area and walk down this road to see one of the most beautiful river waterfalls and further on a large pool that is ideal for swimming. Of all the years I have visited this area I have never seen another person there.

If you continue along after Rai Valley you can delve deep into the Sounds visiting isolated areas such as Tennyson Inlet or Elaine Bay and on to French Pass and don't forget the Pinedale Camp at Canvastown.

This is real exploring but the roads are fine just hardly any people...places to park a camper though and several lodges, b&b's and farm stay accommodations.

Route 6 after Pelorus Bridge then enters into the Richmond Range of mountains until reaching Tasman Bay and the city of **Nelson** one of the most important small cities in New Zealand.

Nelson and Richmond's combined population of 54,500 ranks it as New Zealand's 10th most populous city. Their economy is based on seafood, horticulture, tourism and forestry. Port Nelson is the biggest fishing port in Australasia so you can see why seafood is high on the menus of local eating establishments.

Ron recommends when in the city of Nelson be sure to go to the Morrison Street Cafe
NZ's premier café, providing fresh food and superb beverages in a discerning and stylish setting

Contact:
244 Hardy Street, Nelson, New Zealand
Phone: (03) 548 8110
Fax: (03) 548 8113
Web: www.morrisonstreetcafe.co.nz
Email: mail@morrisonstreetcafe.co.nz

Nelson is widely known for its art studios, galleries and weekend markets. It shares the title of the sunniest place in New Zealand with Blenheim and offers to the visitor fabulous outdoor activities such as swimming and a fun park at Tahunanui Beach a great place for a picnic or enjoy the beach café there. A great spot for sailing and there is an abundance of fabulous wining and dining. A visit to Founders Historic Park – a 'living' museum with an adventure playground is well worth the time.

One of the most exciting places to visit I highly recommend is the **World of Wearable Art and Collectable Cars Museum** after Richmond at the turnoff to the airport. There is an abundance of festivals and events throughout the entire summer like the Nelson Arts Festival in October and the Sealord Summer Festival, Kite Festival plus the Opera in the Park in February. Winter is not overlooked as they offer several winter festival programs. It is an area of artists and craftspeople with many galleries, workshops and art studios to explore.

The "one ring" in the Lord of the Rings was created here in Nelson for the movie. If you are lucky you may get to visit the Saturday market in Nelson one of the best in the country. Not only all the fresh locally grown produce and products but many artists and craftspeople display their wares and crafts. Nelson is also home to New Zealand's only commercial rum distillery, which has a full range of grain spirits.

I highly recommend: Warwick House

Boutique Hotel, Bed & Breakfast – "Perfect house, lovely town" Lord Patten of Barnes
Elegant B&B accommodation in Nelson with self catering option

- 4 Large Luxurious Suites, 2 Standard double rooms with ensuite
- central location, 5-10 minutes riverside stroll into Nelson's attractive city center
- views over Nelson city to the Tasman sea
- located in Nelson's quiet dress circle of leafy lanes
- full cooked breakfasts are served to classical music in the Grand Ballroom
- free wireless internet, room only self catering options
- secure off street parking

Warwick House is located at:
64 Brougham Street
Nelson, New Zealand

Contact Nick & Jenny:

Ph: +64 3 548 3164
Freephone: 0800 022 233(NZ only)
email: enquiries@warwickhouse.co.nz

Website: http://www.warwickhouse.co.nz/

Five Top Things to do in Nelson -
http://www.nelsonnz.com/

- ✓ Visit the World of WearableArt™ and Classic Cars Museum - http://www.wowcars.co.nz/
- ✓ Go to one of the top restaurants for a meal and a local wine
- ✓ Visit the Saturday Market
- ✓ Go to Tahunanui Beach, the fun park and the Beach Cafe
- ✓ Check out the art and crafts shops

I also recommend staying at this Nelson B&B accommodation: An oasis of hospitality, relaxation and calm, where your hosts, Kees and Robyn Van Duyn, provide you with quality accommodation and "good old fashioned kiwi hospitality and according to guests **"five star service+"**

AMBLESIDE LUXURY BED & BREAKFAST
237 Annesbrook Drive, Wakatu, NELSON 7011
PH: +64 3 5485067
NZ FREEPH: 0800 306 555
CELL: 027 413 0876
EMAIL: ambleside@paradise.net.nz
WEB: www.amblesidenelson.co.nz

QUALMARK: FOUR STAR PLUS & ENVIRO SILVER
Affiliated Member of New Zealand Tourism Industry Association
Member of New Zealand Bed & Breakfast Association
Hosts: Robyn & Kees Van Duyn

Hiking, rafting and kayaking, fishing, caving, bird watching, photography are just some of the activities you can enjoy here. Along the region's highways are many stalls selling fresh produce. We really enjoyed finding blueberries and even one stall with fresh venison. Plenty of opportunity to visit and taste some of the fine wines produced here also.

New Zealand's hop crop thrives in ideal growing conditions here. The region is home to several world-class brewmasters producing boutique and organic brews. Brewery tours, sampling and sales are available.

How about the region's top rivers for trout fishing: the Motueka and Riwaka rivers, Wairau, Pelorus and Buller rivers. Lakes Rotoiti and Rotoroa near St Arnaud are also famous spots. The unrestricted season is from 1 October to 30 April. However in winter you can still gain access to the lower reaches of some rivers and fish year round!

The Nelson region covers five distinct geographic areas with the major urban centre being Nelson and its suburbs, the small communities of Mapua, Motueka and Moutere, the fantastic beauty of the Able Tasman Park with its magic coast, the Golden Bay area between the national parks of Kahurangi and Able Tasman and that portion dominated by alpine lakes and rivers in the Nelson Lakes area with the communities of St Arnaud and Murchison. Motueka, Takaka, Karamea, Tapawera and Murchison are National Park's gateway towns where roads lead into car parks within each park.

The Drive from Nelson to Golden Bay -

From Nelson follow route 6 through Richmond to turn onto route 60 to Motueka and Mapua for more exciting arts and crafts from art glass, dried flowers, candles, sculpture, painting, ceramics, cafes along the way and some 22 wineries en route.

Between Richmond and Motueka lies some of the region's most fertile land where export crops of apples, berries, hops and olives are grown. I found the hops growing in this area quite interesting.

Take the turnoff to the seaside community of **Mapua** - http://www.mapua.gen.nz/
to visit the cafes and shops on the waterfront. Motueka is a larger township (though smaller than Richmond) and provides the last opportunity to stock up on supplies and camping gear before you head into the Abel Tasman National Park. Maybe visit Rabbit Island sandy beaches or explore the Waimea Estuary by boat or kayak, fish the Motueka River.

Plenty of quality accommodation: motels, boutique bed and breakfasts, vineyard stays, backpackers, cabins, camping grounds throughout the region.

Motueka - http://www.motuekaisite.co.nz/
An hour's drive from Nelson is Motueka known for its orchards, hop crops and arts, Motueka is a pleasant town at the gateway to Abel Tasman National Park. With nearby golden beaches, green forests, and calm waters, Motueka encompasses the best of the Nelson region. They also have a great Saturday Market in the centre of town.

Abel Tasman National Park –

http://www.doc.govt.nz/parks-and-recreation/national-parks/abel-tasman/

North of Motueka it is New Zealand's smallest national park is 22,350ha and is internationally famous for golden beaches stretching from Marahau, near Motueka, to Wainui Bay, in Golden Bay.

There are two walking tracks: the beautiful coastal track, and the inland track through the hilly centre of the park. You must supply your own supplies and hiking gear. The inland track features the 178m-deep Harwood's Hole, the deepest sinkhole in the Southern Hemisphere. The Abel Tasman Coastal Track is one of New Zealand's Great Walks and it takes three to five days to walk the full length.

Near Marahau, and a short drive from Motueka, is Kaiteriteri Beach a favourite holiday spot for Abel Tasman accommodation, restaurants, camping, playgrounds and golden sands.

There are four main entrances to the park. Marahau and Kaiteriteri are at the southern end, reached by road from Motueka. The two northern entrances are at Totaranui and Wainui, reached by road from Takaka in Golden Bay. Regular and on-demand bus services provide access to both points. Commercial boat operators offer day excursions, drop-off and pick-up for hikers at various points throughout the park.

All levels of fitness can enjoy the coastal track with easy walking through native bush. Kayak the tranquil coastline past golden beaches, seals and dolphins.

Sea-kayaking operators based at Nelson, Marahau, Kaiteriteri and Golden Bay offer guided trips and rentals, plus gear and safety advice. Paddle a traditional Māori waka (carved canoe), skydive or take a water taxi.

Abel Tasman has excellent accommodation with lodges, holiday homes, b&b's and holiday parks. Designated Department of Conservation campsites and the eight huts (four per track) must be booked and paid for in advance during the summer. Campsites and Department of Conservation huts are all accessible from the track and sea. For more information on National Parks in the region go to the Department of Conservation website.

Over the Hill to Golden Bay -

http://www.goldenbaynz.co.nz/_

The winding road trip over the Takaka Hill is worth it with panoramic views along the way and of Golden Bay from the top. Takaka is the principal town with quality shops, cafes and restaurants. A lot of the residents are artists and craftspeople who have a close affinity to the natural world and as such it reminds me of the hippy and bohemian settlements in the US in the 60's. Many of New Zealand's top sculptors, painters, potters, jewellery-makers and bone carvers have made Golden Bay their home. You can visit most of their studios year round.

As you come up the hill over "Marble Mountain" stop at the **Ngarua Caves** -
http://www.showcaves.com/english/nz/showcaves/Ngarua.html where you can check out the prehistoric Moa bones. Then there is **Harwood's Hole** on the Takaka Hill - http://www.harlequin.co.nz/nelson_gallery/Harwoods.htm
The caves are just off the road but Harwoods Hole is several kilometres on a narrow dirt road so I don't recommend taking a large vehicle in there. Even a regular vehicle is hard but worth it to see the Southern hemisphere's deepest cave.
Just outside Takaka is **Te Waikoropupu (Pupu) Springs** -
http://www.goldenbaynz.co.nz/s_pupu_springs.html
one of the clearest fresh water springs in the world. This is a must to visit with paths and wooden walkways through

the area so you can enjoy the water and the surrounding area and it is free.

 Beaches abound - from Pohara and Tata to Wharariki Beach on the rugged west coast. Access the magnificent Kahurangi National Park from Collingwood or the Cobb Valley, south of Takaka, or try one of the short walks at Wainui Falls, the Grove or Payne's Ford.

I spend a lot of time at the **Pohara Beach Holiday Park** - http://www.poharabeach.com/ outside of Takaka. My favourite seafood comes from here - the **Golden Bay scallop**.....yum!!! http://www.seafoodindustry.co.nz/n1240,244.html .

Ron recommends the Pohara Beach Top 10 - Website: www.poharabeach.com/

One of my very favourite parks when after running around the country in our bus we would go to enjoy the Christmas holidays. Ah!!! Christmas brunch at Pohara.

It is a holiday park for everyone on the safe, sandy beach of Pohara, Golden Bay at the top of New Zealand's South Island. Check out their website to see the beachfront accommodation - campsites, cabins, motel units – something for everyone and explore Golden Bay and the Abel Tasman National Park.

Contact:
Pohara Beach Top 10 Holiday Park
right on the beachfront, Abel Tasman Drive,
Pohara Beach, Golden Bay, New Zealand
Phone (03) 525 9500 or 0800 764 272 or email
info@poharatop10.co.nz

Go mountain biking on the Rameka Track, kayak on the Aorere River. We like to drive off the normal path just north of Parapara (south of Collingwood) to wind through an isolated area on the opposite side of the point from Golden Bay to the settlements of Mangarakau and Paturau. There is a parking lot at the end you can stay on the ocean if you have a self-contained vehicle.

After **Collingwood** - http://www.fourcorners.co.nz/new-zealand/Collingwood/ drive all the way to Puponga Point to look out of the café at **Farewell Spit –**
http://www.doc.govt.nz/parks-and-recreation/places-to-visit/nelson-tasman/golden-bay/farewell-spit-and-puponga-farm-park/_
 in the distance or take a 4WD tour to Farewell Spit – a real bird sanctuary and wetland for wading birds such as godwits and curlews and beyond the lighthouse at Farewell Spit, is a gannet colony. For the rock climber Payne's Ford has the best limestone crag climbing in Australasia with cliff heights up to 30m.

The world famous Heaphy Track starts in Collingwood and goes through remote native forest to the West Coast near Karamea. Check out Onekaka Beach, explore the old goldfields in the Aorere Valley or enjoy the beauty of Golden Bay on horseback. A famous restaurant to stop at in the area is the **Mussel Inn**, 17kms for Takaka.

Motels, bed and breakfasts, backpackers, holiday houses and campsites are available throughout the Bay. Nearby Collingwood is the gateway to Farewell Spit and the place to get the tour bus. If you are not driving there is regular bus services to Golden Bay from Nelson and you can fly in by charter direct from Nelson or Wellington.

I recommend when in Golden Bay to stay at:

The Station House Motel
7 Elizabeth Street, Collingwood, Golden Bay
Phone: 03 524 8464
Website: www.accommodationcollingwood.co.nz

Enjoy a relaxing stay at this boutique motel, originally the Police Station villa and grounds, where you will find warm Kiwi hospitality and receive individual attention from your hosts, Darren & Sylvie Steel. Situated close to cafés, the beach, the Farewell Spit tour and many stunning walking tracks. Comfortable accommodation at very affordable rates.

It is a small quiet complex that offers you self contained motels in a garden setting with BBQ courtyard to enjoy.

All in all it is a laid back remote part of New Zealand loved and appreciated by the dynamic people who live there and visit it. If you have time I highly recommend it as most tourists do not get here in fact most Kiwis have never been here..............and do try the scallops....

Top Things to do in Golden Bay

- ✓ Visit Te Waikoropupu - the world's clearest freshwater springs
- ✓ Take a tour out to the tip of Farewell Spit
- ✓ Walk or hike in one of the National Parks
- ✓ Visit Pohara Beach
- ✓ Check out the salmon farm

Kahurangi National Park -

http://www.doc.govt.nz/parks-and-recreation/national-parks/kahurangi/

Reached from the Golden Bay area from the north at 400,000 hectares and with 570 kilometres of walking and tramping tracks, including the start of the Heaphy Track, Kahurangi is New Zealand's second largest national park.

There are both short walks and multi-day walking options. The park offers an enormous range of landscapes: alpine tussock downs, caves, natural arches, sinkholes and water-worn outcrops to the Nikau forests on the West Coast.

Wildlife includes the protected Blue Duck, giant land snail, largest cave spider, smallest giant weta, and the largest remaining population of Great Spotted Kiwi.

Walks and Trails
Kahurangi National Park encompasses 'The Heaphy Track' which is 82km- http://www.heaphytrack.com/
Longer hikes for several days or day trips include:
Wangapeka track 3-5 days,
Leslie/Karamea track 3-4 days,
Tablelands Circuit (track) 2 days.
Kahurangi - Short Day Trips
Mt Arthur Hut 1hr 15 mins
Flora Hut 30 mins

Now we move south.................

First we take the route is south from the Nelson region -

Now it is return from Golden Bay back to Motueka then at the clock tower turn right on College Street to the Motueka Valley Highway that follows the Motueka River. I used to love this route to park by the river and try my luck on the many trout that hang out in the river and also to stop by the blueberry farms that sell fresh blueberries at roadside stands with honesty boxes. One time I went through and a farmer had a cooler by his gate with frozen venison for sale with an honesty box. Got a package of venison, left the money and on we went. Can't do that often in the world today......You can get apples and other fruit in the region too the same way....

At Kohatu you catch back up with route 6 south. At the junction of route 6 then left to the **Nelson Lakes National Park** and St Arnaud with a population of 200.

St Arnaud is the gateway to Nelson Lakes National Park lying on the shores of Lake Rotoiti. Both Lakes Rotoroa and Rotoiti are each renowned for brown trout fishing. Take a leisurely day walk through native honeydew beech forests, fish or kayak or just enjoy the natural majesty and alpine surrounds of St Arnaud. There is a camp ground there on the lake. You may be there to see the annual antique & classic boat show on Lake Rotoiti in March.

Two ways to access this area one is route 63 out of Blenheim along the Wairau River and the other is the one above I mentioned. Bus services leave Nelson for Nelson Lakes and St Arnaud on a regular basis.

Scenic water taxis operate on both lakes. Several companies offer on-demand transport to Rotoroa from St Arnaud and Nelson.

Nelson Lakes National Park has 101,753ha of beech forests, valleys, isolated glacial lakes and craggy peaks. There is something for everyone at Nelson Lakes - boating, fishing, walking, mountaineering, bird watching, swimming. For more comprehensive information on Nelson's National Parks go to the Department of Conservation website - http://www.doc.govt.nz/parks-and-recreation/national-parks/nelson-lakes/

Lake Rotoiti – Nelson Lakes

It is home to the DOC Nature Recovery programme, which has increased the populations of native bellbirds and kaka. Other species earmarked for recovery are kiwi, kakariki, kakapo and bush robins.
There are a number of walks of varying lengths leading off from the campground, including a track around the lake.

Nelson Lakes National Park is centred on two beautiful alpine lakes: Rotoiti and Rotoroa. Craggy mountains, tranquil lakes, beech forest, clear streams and pebble 'beaches' are synonymous with Nelson Lakes.. Vegetation is predominantly red, silver and black beech.
The local birds are tomtits, robins and the tiny rifleman. The South Island kaka is less common, but can be spotted in Nelson Lakes.

Walks and Trails

There are both short tracks which highlight the forest, lakeshore and glacial features and longer hikes. In summer tracks are suitable for an average fitness level; in winter more experience is required.
The walk around the Nelson Lakes is spectacular and the terrain is suitable for most ages.

Be prepared if hiking -

While all three national parks are beautiful in all seasons, it's important to dress warmly in winter and, if staying overnight, be prepared as the weather can change quickly. Check at any of the local Department of Conservation offices for up-to-date information on weather and track conditions. Remember pack your food and water in, and take your rubbish out. Don't forget to check tides in the Abel Tasman National Park especially when crossing tidal inlets.

Basic Important Information - What to bring for hiking the parks

Warm clothes in winter
walking shoes or hiking boots
sleeping bags
towel
insect repellent
suntan lotion
cooking implements

bags to take rubbish out in and store wet clothes in
camera
torch

Staying overnight

Huts are available in all three national parks. There are also
designated campsites with water, toilets and fireplaces.
Lodges and Kiwi holiday homes are also an option in the
Abel Tasman National Park. PLEASE NOTE: All visitors
staying overnight in the Abel Tasman National Park are
required to book huts and campsites before entering the
park. To book contact the region's Information visitor
centres and/or the Dept of Conservation offices.

Continuing on south on route 6 –

From here you travel through some very scenic country
along the fabulous Buller River that has it start in the
Nelson lakes region. Kawatiri is at the crossroads of route
63 and route 6. Continuing along route 6 through
Gowanbridge and Owen River you reach the town of
Murchison   -
http://en.wikipedia.org/wiki/Murchison,_New_Zealand
– the whitewater capital of New Zealand.

The town of Murchison with a population of 700 and is the
southern gateway to Kahurangi National Park. It is a
farming community that lies beside the Buller River, which
flows from Lake Rotoiti to the West Coast.

Murchison is a capital for river-sports: with fifteen river runs located no more than 30 minutes out of town. Kayaking and whitewater rafting on the Buller River is for everyone. They provide lessons for novices.

Hiking and fishing are also popular activities, with a number of walking tracks located in the surrounding mountain ranges.
On the drive north of Murchison you will be driving along the Owen River that was immortalised in the film Lord of the Rings.

Explore a historic gold trail - or try your luck gold panning! Gold nuggets are still being found in the Buller River.

Learn about the local 1929 Murchison Earthquake at Murchison Museum. There is accommodation and café/restaurants available here along with a chance to fuel up.

If you plan to enjoy any river activities you have from the Buller Gorge Swing Bridge to white water rafting thrills. Good café s here and great accommodation for both the campervanner and the car traveller.

On south on route 6 and you really get a close look at the scenic Buller River. When you get to Inangahua Junction stop at the old building in town that has old photos and information on the 1968 7.1 earthquake that destroyed 70% of the town that we find really interesting - http://christchurchcitylibraries.com/kids/nzdisasters/inangahua.asp and well worth the stop.

Continuing on south we always stop at the Berlins Café on the left for a coffee. Great barista. The old photos on the wall are interesting. I like to stop just past to try my luck trout fishing on the Buller River where there is easy access.

Route 6 comes to a junction south of Westport. To the right is route 67 and Lower Buller Road that takes you to Cape Foulwind Road and to **Cape Foulwind** - http://en.wikipedia.org/wiki/Cape_Foulwind .

This is one of our favourite spots to park overnight in the parking lot overlooking the sea here and taking a walk to the lighthouse. Cheeky Weka families – http://en.wikipedia.org/wiki/Weka are always there to beg food.

I also recommend going to the seal colony - http://www.newzealand.com/travel/sights-activities/scenic-highlights/coastal-highlights/scenic-highlight-details.cfm/businessid/63692.html.

From here head north to cross the Buller River and into the town of Westport - http://www.westport.org.nz/westport . Great little town to poke around.

Have a look a the Coaltown Museum - http://www.nzmuseums.co.nz/account/3238 .
 Here are some attractions and crafts in Westport - http://www.westport.org.nz/attractionswestport . Never would have thought it but I found it really interesting. Coal mining is a big part of the West Coast life before and now.

This area is well known for their greenstone jewellery work. Check out the shops in town.
Hard to point out quality cafes or restaurants here. I usually top up here at the local supermarket before heading north or south…..

Now we will be going into an area not usually visited by the normal international visitor or even Kiwis. Quite a shame really but limited time this is a missed opportunity.

North from Westport to Karamea – 95km (1 ½ hours)

(If you come to Westport from any other route or direction you can pick up here to go north).

Head north on route 67 out of Westport to one of our favourite areas to spend time. First stop is the Denniston area - http://www.denniston.co.nz/ and http://www.denniston.org.nz/ .

At Waimangaroa take a right and go to the base of the Denniston incline - http://www.nzine.co.nz/features/dennistonincline.html - labeled as the eighth wonder in the world in its day. For one of the best books I have read it is by Jenny Pattrick – the *Denniston Rose* – a fictional piece based upon what happened in the early days of Denniston - http://www.thelostworld.co.nz/books/ but really provides an insight to the place.

There was talk about a movie at one time. Then after you have gone to the base of the incline take the road up to the top of the mountain. There wasn't any road up the mountain in the early days and everyone and everything had to be transported up and down on the incline. Most of the women who went up there never came back down until they died. After you visit the mountain and get back to route six just across the road is a road by the pub that goes to the ocean where there is a cemetery for all those who died up the mountain. You can see it when you are up there. Interesting inscriptions on the old gravestones.

Next stop north on route 6 is the town of **Granity** - http://en.wikipedia.org/wiki/Granity where we always stop at the **Drifter's Café** in the centre of town - http://www.menumania.co.nz/restaurants/drifters-cafe-restaurant-granity and perhaps a stop at the Big Fish pub on the north edge of town. Beautiful West Coast beach. Next you go through the towns of Hector and Ngakawan - http://en.wikipedia.org/wiki/Hector_and_Ngakawau . In Hector there is a country/western music museum worth stopping to see if that's your thing. There's an amazing collection of music and photos - http://www.bullerarts.org.nz/?q=node/31.

The next stop we recommend is on the north side of the Mokihinui River on the left. A narrow dirt road takes you to Gentle Annie's Campground. There's no electricity (showers are good though) to the campsites, but it's one of the best locations where river, ocean and bush join. They also have the Cowshed Cafe on site. It's definitely off the beaten path. You'll love it! - http://www.gentleannie.co.nz/ .

From here the road turns inland for 70kms until reaching Little Wanganui and finally coming to its end at Kohaihai Bluff north of Karamea - http://www.karameainfo.co.nz/ .

There is a DoC camp there and is the beginning or ending, depending, of the world famous Heaphy Track that goes through the Kahurangi National Park to end up on the Aorere River outside of Takaka in Golden Bay.

The drive to this point is worth it just to watch the Heaphy River empty into the ocean both fighting to keep their dominance during the tidal changes.
Be sure to take your repellent. One of the most exciting meetings of river and ocean punctuate the beauty of the DOC camp on the Karamea River.

If you enjoy tramping, you may wish to take the trip through the Kahurangi National Park to Golden Bay via the Heaphy Track or maybe take a short excursion along the path while you are there. There are some other major walks through the Kahurangi National Park such as the Wangapeka Track out of Little Wanganui on this side. This is wilderness made easy to access for those who are fit enough to do the hiking.
Now it is a turn around and back south to Westport and off down the West Coast of the South Island.

But first let's go back to Picton and take Route One south....................

This is the usual route for most people. So you understand the geography and road infrastructure of the South Island we have route one down the East Coast. Route Six from Blenheim south down the West Coast with both routes all the way south to Invercargill.
At the top of the South Island there is Lewis Pass (route7) from north of Christchurch to Greymouth and accessed from Kaikoura. Arthurs Pass or route 73 goes from Christchurch west to south of Greymouth and route 6 and that folks are the major routes. That giant area that basically divides the South Island known as the Southern Alps

doesn't allow any other roads criss-crossing. (more detailed information further on)

We do have access roads into the Mackenzie Country, Central Otago, the Catlins and Fiordland etc. So for those who have asked me if they can just go to one town and use it as a base to go everywhere else in the South Island it isn't that simple.

So off we go (again).........off the ferry after enjoying Picton and the Marlborough Sounds........

but this time it is.......

Picton south on Route One to Kaikoura – (157kms- 2 ½ hours)

It is on route one and within a half hour you will be in the number one wine region in New Zealand – **the Marlborough Wine region** - http://www.wine-marlborough.co.nz/. For the wine lovers this is the place. The wine makers here reached very high internationally with the wines from this region so it is a good idea to have a drive around or get a wine tour bus. Many of the wineries also provide top quality restaurants.

Before you get into Blenheim, a good size service town for the area where you can get what you may need for supplies, to begin your wine tour turn right at Spring Creek on Rapaura Road, the road marked as the turn off right to Nelson. If you like chocolate (and who doesn't) down the road on the left is the Makana Chocolate factory.......good start.....then I recommend stopping next on the right at Jane Hunter's winery. Taste her award winning offerings and pick up a vineyard map so you can begin your tour.

Some of my favourites are Allen Scott, Domain Georges Michel, Highfield Estate and Wither Hills. Doing the trip around the vineyards you end up in Blenheim from the south or if you are perhaps heading for the West Coast the turnoff of route 63 is at Renwick to route 6.

There is also a really exciting display of vintage aircraft - http://www.omaka.org.nz/ . I am not much of a history or airplane buff but I was astounded by what they have done here. The rare memorabilia is worthy of any national collection and ranges from beautifully crafted 'trench art' through to personal items belonging to the famous Red Baron himself. Right here in Blenheim!

The drive Blenheim south via route one...............

Be sure to stock up in Blenheim and for you who are missing McDonald's best get one here.

The drive from Blenheim to Kaikoura begins in the wine region then turns into barren hills before reaching the East Coast. Along the way you will pass New Zealand's salt works at Lake Grassmere. 1800 hectares of lakes where salt water is pumped in and evaporation takes place. Nearly 40,000 tons are treated. Visitors can stop by on Tuesdays and Fridays at 1:30pm for a guided tour but you can take the road out there to see the mountains of salt.

Marfells Beach, a Dept of Conservation camp, is just off the road 8kms past the salt flats. Great place to stop overnight. Not too many kms along is the small town of Ward. Continuing south on Route One you will find The Store (45 minutes south of Blenheim) judged the best cafe in Marlborough.

On to Kaikoura along one of the most spectacular coastal scenes on the East Coast. Stop just north of Kaikoura to have close encounter with the many seals lying about during the day such as at Opah Point but before getting there keep a sharp lookout for the DoC sign to the waterfall on the right with a large parking area on the left. Take a walk back to the waterfall and if the right time of year the pool will be full of young seals. Outrageous to experience.

The town of Kaikoura is on a peninsula overlooked by majestic mountains. Very deep and plankton rich sea at its doorstep provides the habitat for marine mammals and sea birds. The area is renowned for whale, dolphin and albatross watching. The town of Kaikoura offers great cafes and art galleries.

Just before getting into the main downtown area you can turn left toward the whale watch building where a large parking area is good for camper vans and easy access to the main town – **Whalewatch** – http://www.whalewatch.co.nz/ .

Next go on and turn left in the downtown area not too far on the left is also a large car park and the Information Centre.

Be sure to go on past the main segment of town and explore all the way to the turn around where a large colony of seals lay about. Last time I was there I had to drive around a big male that was using the road for his nap space. Don't get too close!

Kaikoura's early whaling history is featured at the Museum. One of the country's top festivals is held here: the Kaikoura Seafest. Have a look at one of the Kaikoura Information sites for the particulars. Don't miss going up the hill south of town to the Kaikoura Winery claimed to be the most scenic winery in New Zealand on the way south out of town on the right.

South of Kaikoura there are some of the greatest camping spots such as Peketa Beach and further south along the sea where there are four camps under the direction of John & Liz Mahoney at Goose Bay. Fabulous spots to enjoy the wild coast lines of this area. If you stay in the Kaikoura area these are the places I recommend without question. Just a few minutes from Kaikoura but you actually get to enjoy the area by being on the sea and out of all the noise and confusion of the town of Kaikoura.

If you would like to meet one great person and get a real personable insight to the long established world of the Maori in this area check in with Maurice at the Maori Tours. Maurice and Heather have created an experience that is truly enjoyable - http://www.maoritours.co.nz/ .

Plenty of things to do, places to stay, photos to take. This is a major attraction area for New Zealand. Be sure to mark this on your map and enjoy.....

Kaikoura to Christchurch – (181kms – 2 ½ hours)

Onward..... ever onward....... taking route one south. You may wish to stop at South Bay on the way on the south side of the Kaikoura Peninsula then on south stopping at the Kaikoura Winery - http://www.kaikourawinery.co.nz/ As mentioned it is located on a very scenic outlook on the limestone cliff. The Fyffe Country Lodge is on the right - www.fyffecountrylodge.com and then the airport where you can get the **Wings over Whales** flight then the Peketa Beach Holiday Park is next on the left.

On south to the town of Cheviot and than the road to the coast and Gore Bay for a pleasant spot to camp out of the way.

If you were to take the side road on the right (route 70) and head south you pass through the rural town of Culverden. Just south is the Balmoral Forest where you can stop overnight. Toilets are available there. Continuing south you next come to the historic pub the Hurunui Hotel. Route 7 meets up with route one again at Waipara. At Waikari there is the Rocking Frog Café a good place for coffee and/or lunch. There is a historic rural railway using both vintage steam and diesel-electric locomotives on 12.8 km of scenic line through the unique limestone beauty of the Weka Pass out of Waipara.

Next town is Amberley and there is a wonderful place to park overnight at Amberley Beach reached by a road out of Amberley. Town owned and run with limited facility but peaceful.

Now the next place I point out you must stop at – Pukeko Junction. Two very good reasons you will find one of the best cafes in the country and within the complex a fabulous wine shop.

The area north of Christchurch is New Zealand's fastest growing wine region. Waipara has produced around 80 vineyards in its 30 year history. I recommend stopping at the Mudhouse Winery on route 1 and to get a really good selection of the local wines at a decent price see Kevin at Pukeko Junction. On south is Woodend where you can stop at Prenzel of Canterbury in Woodend to sample a glass of creamy butterscotch liqueur and butterscotch schnapps.

A delicious stop on your travels, Pukeko Junction is a cheerful, buzzing, award-winning
destination café. The gourmet country food is all made in-house, from the bread to the tarts, cakes, sauces and fresh salads. Enjoy a hearty breakfast with local free-range eggs, generous lunches from the deli or afternoon tea. The café is bright and airy with great coffee, a log fire and lots of outdoor seating for sunny days.

Contact:
Celine Graham

458 Ashworths Road Leithfield
Phone: 64 3 314 8834 Fax: 64 3 314 8896
Email: pukekojunction@xtra.co.nz
Web: pukekojunction.co.nz

Before going on south to Christchurch and the East Coast......
One of the routes across to the West Coast I mentioned was Lewis Pass........................
I will take you this way now to the West Coast and on south to come back to Christchurch from the south but you can just keep going on route one to Christchurch.

But for now - Kaikoura to the West Coast via Lewis Pass -

If you are going to the West Coast from Kaikoura (or coming from that direction) just below South Bay you can take the Inland Kaikoura Road (route 70) that winds through the countryside coming to the alpine resort of **Mount Lyford Village** - http://www.mtlyford.co.nz/

Even though it is geared toward winter activities we enjoy stopping there in the summer for a bite to eat to a coffee. They do have accommodation along with a motor camp also.

Next you come to the town of Wairau. Just on the ridge overlooking the Wairau River is a great photo before you drop down into the river valley and the town. Instead of taking the inland road you can drive on south from Kaikoura on route one to south of Hawkeswood and take Leader Road to Waiau.

From there you continue along to route 7 take a right and then another right on route 7A to **Hanmer Springs Thermal Springs and Spa Village -** http://www.hanmersprings.co.nz/ Known as the finest thermal pools in the country Hanmer Springs is a year-round destination; if you're looking for a relaxing vacation this small alpine village is the right place.

I recommend the place to stay in Hanmer Springs

 CHARWELL ECO LODGE
82 Medway Road
Hanmer Springs, New Zealand
Phone: 64 3 315 5070
Fax: 64 3 315 5071
Website: http://www.charwell.co.nz/
Your hosts: Bill & Judy Clarkson

Hanmer Springs has lots of activities too with bungy jumping, jet boating, white water rafting available. Several good walks available along with horseback riding and quad biking. Excellent accommodation, restaurants and cafes add to the mix well. So even if you only have a few hours on your trip take the time to stop in the thermal pools for a relaxing dip.

If you happen to be coming from the south out of Christchurch take the turn off left onto route 7 at Waipara.

Five Top Things to do in Hanmer Springs

- ✓ Enjoy the famous thermal pools
- ✓ Have a lunch and coffee at one of the cafes
- ✓ Check out Thrillseekers Canyon
- ✓ Explore the back country on a quad bike or a 4WD tour
- ✓ Enjoy a nature park, local farm or a horse back ride

Driving to the West Coast - two roads from the east – Lewis Pass & Arthurs Pass

Due to the mountainous Southern Alps spine down through the middle of the South Island there is limited access from east to west. Route 6 that begins west of Blenheim curls through the northern portion of the island to Nelson then south to the West Coast south of Westport. Route 7 accessed from Kaikoura via route 70 and Christchurch by route 1 goes through some of the most beautiful countryside of black beech forests, stream valleys and over the Lewis Pass. The town of Reefton is along this route and the home to the Bearded Miner's who provide a welcome at their miner's hut in the middle of town.

The most famous route across the island is route 73, named Arthur's Pass, a scenic drive through the mountains that overlook the rivers and valleys that flow east and west from the peaks of the Southern Alps that spreads its foothills out in both directions.

From the south the only way to get to the West Coast by driving is route 6 through the Mount Aspiring National Park over Haast Pass.

Lewis Pass – Hanmer Springs to the West Coast – (216kms – 2 ½ hour drive)

Now for one of the most beautiful drives in New Zealand if you appreciate the natural world. Paula says it is as close to walking a wilderness track as you can come just driving along a major road. I enjoy stopping and teasing the trout with a fly. We enjoy driving from east to west it just seems to get better as we go along ending up in Reefton that is an 1 ½ drive from Hanmer Springs.

The Victoria Forest Park to the east, Paparoa National Park on the west of the road and Lake Sumner Forest Park to the South at the town of Reefton. This should give you an idea of the country you are in. There is very limited road access into all of this area. A lot of the black beech here something you won't see otherwise in the rest of the world.

You will pass by Maruia Springs Thermal Resort just after Lewis Pass where a Japanese theme is apparent with a Japanese bathhouses and traditional Utasyu massage. Ensuite rooms available also along with a fine dining experience with Japanese dishes at the restaurant,Shuzan. Bookings essential by the way.

.

There are several places along the way where you can park overnight and/or just take a rest. The DoC Camp at Marble Mountain is spacious plus is the starting point for a trek to Lake Daniels for the trampers/hikers. There is a place marker there for you. You will be right on the Alpine fault Line!!! Hope it doesn't shift when you are there!!

Next place along the road will be Springs Junction where you can stop at the cafe and fuel is available. It is at the junction of Route 7 and Route 65 that takes you north to meet up with route 6 just west of Murchison but to go west take Route 7 through the Victoria Forest Park. The road follows the Inangahuna River at this point. Lots of trout in the river if you would like to try your luck.

Next stop is **Reefton** - http://www.reefton.co.nz/ . When you get to Blacks Point (1.7k before Reefton) it is worth a stop to visit the Museum. This area was heavily mined for gold and coal. The Murray Creek Goldfield 12 km (five hours) track will take you to many of the old deserted mines.

A short 15 minute walk on the Golden Fleece walk by the museum for those in a hurry.

What I recommend is to go on into Reefton and stop by the **Information Centre**. One of the finest in New Zealand so don't miss it. There you can get all the information for the area before deciding what you may want to do. There is a fantastic presentation of the area and also a replica of an old gold mine to explore right in the Information Centre. Of course you must stop and say hello to the **Bearded Miners** in their shack in the middle of Reefton. They might even treat you to a yarn or two and a billy tea.

A stop at the where a real good cup of coffee should be considered.

A great time to visit Reefton is through December/January when they have their Summer Festival. .

Plenty of accommodation available. We were given a sneak preview of what had been what they named as the

Governor's Mansion and is being turned into a fabulous accommodation. It is a part of the Reefton Rover's Retreat complex that includes the Old Nurses Home Accommodation and Backpackers at 104 Sheil Street. What a building! A spacious lawn and garden along with plenty of space for sixty. Well maintained and done with style. You will enjoy.

An interesting side trip is to Waiuta, the town at the top of the South Island's richest gold mine now a ghost town but has plenty of caravan sites.

It is a 21km drive off Route 7 from Reefton about half sealed. Plenty of ruins and relics to see. Check with the Information Centre first.

The drive to Greymouth -

Leaving Reefton on Route 7 you now can head south to Greymouth on route 7 as one route. If you are real lucky and it is a weekend or a holiday you have the opportunity to visit Kopara **(website)**. Not on any tourist road map. Turn left at Ngahere to Nelson Creek and continue on the Nelson Creek Bell Hill Road. It's a long drive about 30 km mostly on an unsealed road. A group of South Islanders own the place and have black powder shoots with everyone dressed for the occasion. You are welcome to stay in a caravan. It is something worth seeing if you have the time and desire - http://tvnz.co.nz/view/page/411307/443475 .

The drive to Westport -

What I recommend is to take route 69 out of Reefton north to Inangahua Junction. When you get to Inangahua Junction stop at the old building in town that has old photos and information on the 1968 7.1 earthquake that destroyed 70% of the town that we find really interesting - http://christchurchcitylibraries.com/kids/nzdisasters/ina ngahua.asp and well worth the stop. Continuing on south we always stop at the Berlins Café on the left for a coffee.

Great barista. The old photos on the wall are interesting. I like to stop just past to try my luck trout fishing on the Buller River where there is easy access.

Route 6 comes to a junction south of Westport. To the right is route 67 and Lower Buller Road that takes you to Cape Foulwind Road and to **Cape Foulwind -** http://en.wikipedia.org/wiki/Cape_Foulwind . This is one of our favourite spots to park overnight in the parking lot overlooking the sea and taking a walk to the lighthouse. Cheeky Weka families – http://en.wikipedia.org/wiki/Weka - are always there to beg food. I also recommend going to the seal colony - http://www.newzealand.com/travel/sights- activities/scenic-highlights/coastal-highlights/scenic- highlight-details.cfm/businessid/63692.html

From here head north to cross the Buller River and into the town of Westport - http://www.westport.org.nz/westport . Great little town to poke around. Have a look at the Coaltown Museum - http://www.nzmuseums.co.nz/account/3238 . Here are some attractions and crafts in Westport - http://www.westport.org.nz/attractionswestport .

Here is where you begin your experience of the South Island's West Coast.
West Coast of the South Island –

The West Coast, a UNESCO World Heritage Site, is a fascinating length of 600kms of coastline providing a scenic wonderland of Southern Alps vistas, rugged coast and sandy beaches, natural wonders, swamp and rain forest, black beech forests, glaciers along with rough farm land lakes and streams bountiful with trout and wildlife throughout. It is a must on any visitor's travels and has been a constant place of return for us in our travels. We just can't get enough of the beauty of the land and the quality of the people who live here.

Westport south to Hokitika

After getting back to Westport it is on south through the bush country until past **Charleston** - http://en.wikipedia.org/wiki/Charleston,_New_Zealand home of the South Island caving - http://www.caverafting.com/ .

Then the road begins to come upon the magic of the scenic coastline in this area. The rugged coast interspersed with sandy and rocky beaches are a photographer's playground. One of the most startling natural scenic spots to make sure you stop and experience is the **Punakaiki Rocks** known as the Pancake Rocks as nature formed the ancient sea bottom now exposed into the shape of a stack of pancakes.

There are walkways through the area of the Pancake Rocks with good viewing points. **Punakaiki** lies on the edge of the Paparoa National Park and you can get information on walks and activities at the Visitor Centre here.

<u>Greymouth/Blackball -</u>

Next town of size is Greymouth but just before getting to town take the short side trip inland along the Grey River to the town of Blackball. Known as where the present day political New Zealand Labour Party was formed. Now it is a backwater community where the locals still find gold, make venison sausages and enjoy one of the best pubs in the country. **The infamous "Formerly" The Blackball Hilton Hotel**. So named after a legendary fight with Hilton International over its name. Make sure you stop and see the bar but even more check out the rooms that are all devoted to a theme each being absolutely unique and picturesque.

Might even decide to stay a day or two, we do when in the area.

So back out to route 6 next stop in **Greymouth -** http://www.greydistrict.co.nz/greymouth/ the largest town on the West Coast built on the Grey River. Good place to park the motor home is behind the Caltex station right downtown in easy walking distance to it all.

Be sure to stop and see the **Jade Boulder Gallery**, 1 Guinness Street, for the ultimate in jade work. A definite not to be missed place to go 10 km south of town is **Shantytown**, a restored 1800's pioneer town based upon the West Coast gold rushes of the mid 1800's. -http://www.shantytown.co.nz/ .

Greymouth is the home to **Monteith's -** a famous New Zealand beer established in the 1800s for 30,000 thirsty prospectors who arrived on the West Coast of the South Island in search of the elusive gold. New Zealanders' appreciation of Monteith's and other brews that fall under the 'craft beer' category has grown steadily over the past few decades. Its unique style has developed an almost cult following amongst certain beer drinkers. So much so, that when Monteith's owners, beer giant Dominion Breweries, announced the closure of the tiny Greymouth brewery in 2001, outraged customer reaction forced it to reopen. That same year, Monteith's won 23 medals at a range of international beers awards –proving that Kiwis aren't the only ones who appreciate Monteith's beer. Over the past years over 70 international beer awards have been received.

Lake Brunner - http://www.golakebrunner.co.nz/

I like Lake Brunner outside of town a few kms. One of the most beautiful places on the West Coast. You can reach it off route 7 by the Arnold Valley Road out of Stillwater or south of Greymouth on route 6 take Rutherglen Road inland south of Paroa.

There is a dirt road I take a lot on the south side of the lake and access off Arthurs Pass road (route73) either at Kumar on the west side or just west of Jacksons to Inchboddie.

Worth a trip for those who have the time…especially if you feel like trying for a trout… I have seen dozens

South on route 6 from Greymouth or Arthurs Pass –

You now will be going along the Tasman Sea south passing by South Beach below Greymouth and on to where Arthurs Pass, route 73, ends on the West Coast at Kumara Junction after crossing the Taramakau River and on south the next stop is Hokitika one of our favourite towns in the South Island. There is also one of our favourite camp grounds on the ocean on the north edge of Hokitika the Shining Star.

Hokitika - http://www.hokitika.org/

The South Island's number one arts and crafts centre, Hokitika. Be sure to take a stroll around this small town and walk to the beach that lies along its side streets. It is a real scenic picturesque West Coast beach full of driftwood and ocean bric-a-brac that has been thrown upon it as the wind and tides demonstrate their power. Great town to walk around and see all the crafts plus they have a great café (**Café de Paris**) plus a good supermarket for you folks in camper vans. If you are lucky you will be there during th Wild Food Festival (March)....

Personally I think this is one of the best in the country:

Shining Star *BEACHFRONT*
ACCOMMODATION
16 Richards Drive, Hokitika
Freephone 0800 744 646 or +64 3 7558921
Website: www.shiningstar.co.nz
Email: shining@xtra.co.nz

Just 50 metres from the beach, in four-acre grounds planted with natives there is a distinctive atmosphere in peaceful, rural, park like surroundings.

Amenities include a private spa room, available for hire with bi-fold doors opening on to a pleasant courtyard, covered barbeque area, a playground for the children, and a glow-worm dell to visit at night.

The pick of the bunch are the beachfront chalets. They'll sleep up to three, but they're just perfect for a couple – their sea views and privacy certainly add a little romance! Other options include executive apartments, and motel units suitable for families. Thoughtfully designed and showing off plenty of bare wood – both inside and out – all the accommodation feels light, natural and warm. The interiors are comfortable and stylish, with quality fittings and linens.

For the budget coconscious smaller cabins are available all with private ensuite bathrooms. You choose from self-contained to budget cabins with shared cooking facilities.

The central amenities block is similarly appealing, featuring top-notch appliances and hardwearing surfaces. It's attractive and homely, with the kitchen and patio particularly conducive to socialising. The tenting area and campervan pads are all close by, with plenty of grass and picnic benches. The four-acre grounds are attractively planted with natives throughout.

Direct access to the beach with dramatic crashing waves, sand piled high with driftwood and ocean sunsets to set your soul alight.

On south! One of the spots we like a lot to camp is not too far down the road on the right at the Dept of Conservation camp on **Lake Mahinapua**. Right across the road is also a great pub.

Ross - http://en.wikipedia.org/wiki/Ross,_New_Zealand_

Next place is the town of Ross with its Goldfields Heritage area 20 minutes drive from Hokitika. Ross was settled in 1865 as a gold mining town. The area was largely unexplored then. The area was gold-rich and the town thrived with about 2500 inhabitants, but the major Ross gold rush was over by the early 1870s. Stop by and pan for gold. It is a great place for the outdoor lovers. Take a drive up the scenic Totara Valley or climb Mt Greenland for some amazing views and discover the old quartz mine.

If you enjoy walking, tramping, hunting, fishing, mountain biking, kayaking then stop by Ross.

Pukekura - http://www.pukekura.co.nz/

Next, 35 minutes south of Hokitika, is one of our favourite stops on the West Coast, the town of Pukekura - population two - Pete & Justine. It was built in the clearing of the native Rimu forest beginning life as a stopping place on the stage coach trail south the a saw mill was built in the 1950's closing thirty years later with the Bushman's Centre being established in 1993. The centre offers a café, museum and shop. The café is open for breakfast and lunch specializing in possum pie with the Puke Pub Wild Food restaurant across the road serving a range of wild foods found in and around the West Coast specializing in serving such culinary delights as venison, rabbit, whitebait and wild pork plus much more. In the museum be sure to see the movie on the early beginning of the venison industry plus the resident live possums along with live eels, the resident wild pig, Tuku.

Outside you get to see the thar and their buddy the turkey.

At Pukekura they offer cabins, tents, campervan sites and a holiday house for accommodation. Lake Ianthe, renowned for its huge trout, lies 5 km down the highway. They have two Canadian canoes and fishing rods for hire. Needless to say it is more than worth a stop…………..

Now on south to:

Whataroa/Okarito   -

http://www.glaciercountry.co.nz/pages/38/okarito-&--whataroa.htm_

Mid way between Ross and Franz Josef is the town of **Whataroa**. From here you can take trips to the White Heron Sanctuary at the Waitangi Roto Nature Reserve this is the only breeding location of the rare white heron in New Zealand.

The only way to visit the White Heron Sanctuary is on a permitted guide tour from Whataroa, which includes a jet boat ride to the sanctuary, this is a wonderful way to observe these elegant birds look after their young. White Heron Sanctuary Tours are a family-owned company that has been in operation for 20 years, they are the only tour company approved into the Waitangi Roto Nature Reserve area under a special concession with the Department of Conservation.

The only access to this area is from Whataroa. Their tours occur during the summer months to coincide with the white heron breeding season and takes 2.5 hours. It consists of a short minibus ride to connect with their jet boat for a 20-minute scenic cruise on the Waitangi Taona river into the Waitangiroto Nature Reserve (the only way to access this area is by boat). For the nature/bird lovers it is a fabulous trip.

Route 6 continuing south along the West Coast the next place of interest is the **Okarito Lagoon**. A 13 kilometre sealed road takes you to the small community of 30 people once a thriving gold mining town in its heyday.

There you will discover the rugged coastline, tidal estuary, lagoon, sea cliffs, lush rainforest and the unsurpassed views of the Southern Alps. One of the local residents the Rowi, formerly known as Ōkārito brown kiwi, are New Zealand's rarest kiwi, with an estimated 350 surviving in just 11,000 hectares in South Ōkārito Forest. Thousands of native birds (more than 76 different species) visit the Ōkārito Lagoon and many make their home in the vicinity, including the famous white heron and royal spoonbills.

Now for the most exciting part of the West Coast adventure:

Glacier Country -
http://www.glaciercountry.co.nz/

Have you ever seen a glacier? How about walking on one? This is the place! Along with the Franz Josef and Fox Glaciers you can enjoy views of New Zealand's two highest mountains Mt. Cook and Mt. Tasman and explore the lowland rainforest of Westland National Park and Te Wahipounamu World Heritage Area.

Where else can you be where a glacier meets a rain forest by the sea?

Check out **Lake Matheson** - the most picturesque lake in New Zealand and take a walk on Gillespie's Beach just down the road. Watch the sunsets turn the snow covered mountains pink.

This is one of the most spectacular areas of the country and not to be missed.

All kinds of independent walks and hikes along with guided glacier hikes, ice climbing and mountaineering. How about a helicopter snow landing with one of the world class operators.
Something for everyone no matter your fitness and hot pools to ease your aching muscles afterwards.

Franz Josef –
The Franz Josef Glacier is a 12 km long glacier located close to the town of Franz Josef and together with the Fox Glacier 20 km to the south, forms part of a World Heritage Site. For those who have never experienced glaciers this area is fantastic. Franz Josef has numerous accommodation

options for every budget along with cafes/restaurants. Adventure activities include scenic flights over the glaciers, heli-hiking and guided glacier tours. There are also several good walking tracks around Franz Josef. Be sure to check out the Visitors Centre to see the video. One of my most memorable experiences is landing on the glaciers by helicopter and walking around throwing snow balls in the middle of the summer. You can also get close to the base of the glacier by driving the access road.

Fox Glacier -
23 kilometres south of Franz Josef is Fox Glacier. In addition take the Cook Flat Road to Lake Matheson and do the walk around the lake. If you can get there early in the morning you may get one of those spectacular photographs where there isn't a ripple on the water and the mountains are reflected in perfection. Continue past Lake Matheson to the Gillespies beach Road that is a 21 km drive to the beach. There is a seal colony out there too but it is over a three hour walk. The access road to the Fox Glacier is only a 10 minute drive and a short walk shorter than the one to Franz Josef. For the hikers Fox Glacier provides enjoyment for everyone who wants to do from a half hour walk to a 3 day hike.

To really get to be a part of the adventure I recommend Fox Glacier Guiding:

Enjoy a breathtaking guided glacier walk onto the world famous Fox Glacier with New Zealand's most experienced glacier guiding company; Alpine Guides Fox Glacier Ltd trading as **Fox Glacier Guiding**. They offer a full range of Fox Glacier tours and ice adventures to suit all fitness levels.

Fox Glacier is New Zealand's largest commercially guided glacier, situated in Glacier Country, on the West Coast of the South Island, only 21 km's south of Franz Josef.

The friendly and professional guides will take you on a glacier trip of a life time. Your guide will remain with you for the entire trip entertaining and educating you about the fascinating Fox Glacier, part of the Westland National Park, a World Heritage Area.

Drive south down State Highway 6 from Hokitika for approximately two hours. Driving north, we are the first of the Glacier towns you will reach, five hours from Queenstown, via Wanaka and Haast.

Contact Information: Fox Glacier Guiding

Street Address: State Highway 6, Fox Glacier

Postal Address: P.O. Box 38, Fox Glacier 7859

Telephone: +64 3 751 0825 or toll free 0800 111 600 (within NZ only)

Fax: +64 3 751 0857

Email: info@foxguides.co.nz

Website: http://www.foxguides.co.nz

Five Top Things to do in Glacier Country.

- ✓ Take a guided glacier hike
- ✓ View the glaciers via helicopter
- ✓ Enjoy the local hot pools
- ✓ Try indoor ice climbing!
- ✓ Visit and photograph Lake Matheson

Now on south again into more rain forest, swamps and lakes touching the coastline at Bruce Bay.

By the way be sure to stock up what you will need and fuel up in Glacier Country before this part of your journey begins and be sure to have your insect repellent on the West Coast. The sandflys will find you.

Driving inland then with the Southern Alps dominating the scenery but with Lake Paringa and Lake Moeraki providing stunning visuals along the way. Then the road comes back out to the coast at an elevated level at Knight's Point where you can pull over into large parking lot to experience the spectacular coastal view. It is on south until you finally reach the end of the South Island West Coast crossing the long one-way bridge over the Haast River.

Just past the bridge on route 6 is the UNESCO World Heritage building with very interesting information and displays.

The road to Jackson Bay -
There is a coastal road here that very few visitors ever take only because of time mostly but a really interesting stretch of area with the road winding along the coast with its small settlements of Haast Beach, Okuru, Carters Mill, Waiatoto, Arawhata, Neils Beach and finally to the end of the road at Jackson Bay.

One of the busiest times of the year is during the time the small whitebait, considered a delicacy, begins to travel from the ocean up the rivers. The West Coast and this area in particular provide some of the top whitebaiting and the areas along the rivers are jealously guarded and heavily used. Over the years the casual net that once was used has become a giant elaborate system along the rivers. For a lot of the locals this is their main income for the year with top dollar received for their catches.

So the West Coast of the South Island has been covered from Karamea in the very far north all the way south to Haast. One of the finest and most spectacular scenic areas of New Zealand with so much to do and all in only 600kms...............

NOTES:

......and now the exciting and scenic drive over the Alps to Wanaka and the Arrowtown/Queenstown area. Even when raining the mountains provide a world or waterfalls.

Haast to Mount Aspiring National Park –
http://www.doc.govt.nz/parks-and-recreation/national-parks/mount-aspiring/

From Haast Village now route 6 begins the beautiful route up the Haast River Valley inland to cross over the Southern Alps at Haast Pass. You will be entering the Mount Aspiring National Park. One of the most dramatic waterfalls is along this route not too far, Thunder Falls, just a short walk from a designated parking area on the road. Well worth the stop and the walk.

Just a very short drive past is another parking area that I recommend stopping at what is called the Gates Of Haast and at the bridge that crosses the rapids of the Haast River cascading down the Southern Alps mountain side. Very dramatic.

It is rather a steep drive up the mountain to cross over the Southern Alps but a spectacular drive to enjoy as you get to Haast Pass and down the other side surrounded by forest.

The Gates of Haast

Thunder Falls

From Haast Pass the road drops down to the Makarora River valley passing through the settlement of **Makarora -** http://www.makarora.co.nz/   where they have a good

Information Centre, fuel stop and café and a holiday park we enjoy staying at. From here route 6 goes along Lake Wanaka on the right...........

Great DoC camp right on Lake Wanaka

then over a saddle to Lake Hawea on the left and on to the town of Wanaka located on Lake Wanaka...

Wanaka region - http://www.lakewanaka.co.nz/new-zealand/

The next place you may want to visit on the left going into town is Puzzling World -
http://www.puzzlingworld.co.nz/ then on into the small but vibrant community of Wanaka snuggled along the beautiful Lake Wanaka. Plenty of fine cafes and restaurants such as Missy's Kitchen and the White House.

Park down on the lake and visit the Information Centre for complete information. Lots of air, water and land activities…and this is where you go skydiving!!

I highly recommend:

The only place to enjoy your sky diving thrills in New Zealand!

Adding a New Zealand skydive experience to your extreme activity resume is easy with Skydive Lake Wanaka. You don't need previous skydiving experience... the only thing a previous tandem skydive gives you is a better understanding of why people recommend Wanaka when asked where to skydive in NZ.

Beautiful Lake Wanaka is situated in the South Island of New Zealand, approximately one hour's drive north of Queenstown. Skydive Lake Wanaka operates from Wanaka Airport, which is situated 10km from the centre of Wanaka.

As the plane gains altitude for 15-20 minutes you will enjoy unrivalled and uninterrupted views of Wanaka's world-renowned lakes and mountains. Where else would you even think about sky diving.

Contact Sky Dive Wanaka:

Free Phone: 0800 786 877 (NZ ONLY)
Telephone: +64 (0)3 443 7207
Mobile: +64 (0)274 796 877

PO Box 322
Wanaka, New Zealand

E-mail: info@skydivewanaka.com

Website: http://www.skydivewanaka.com/

For the vintage airplane buff there is also the Fighter Pilots Museum- http://www.nzfpm.co.nz/
It is a beautiful area and the lake provides all kinds of activities such as fishing, sailing, cruises, jet boating, kayaking, rafting canyoning, whitewater sledging as a start.

For the winter visitor Wanaka has a reputation with four world-class ski areas – Cardrona Alpine Resort, Treble Cone, Snow Farm and Snow Peak.

Then you may wish to visit Rippon Vineyard the land owned by the Mills family since 1913 and the Wanaka Beerworks for a tasting of a Cardrona Gold or a Tall Black.

Plenty of artists and craftspeople here with class galleries and shops to poke around in.

Plenty of opportunity for walks with the fabulous Mt Aspiring National Park the third largest in the country or perhaps rent a bike to take advantage of the many trails available and there is golf courses and horseback riding. Then there is the Cardrona Adventure Park.

Wanaka is quite an exciting place in a beautiful setting. Good place to stock up also re-fuel.
It is a small community and easy to get around. Large parking areas along the waterfront on the main street where access to everything is in walking distance.
After the Wanaka visit it is back out to route 6 and on south or perhaps the alternative route (not recommended for camper vans) take the Cardrona Valley Road through the back country where Shania Twain had a farm. Stop at the historic Cardrona pub on the way through. At the end coming down off the mountain is quite a switchback descent down to route 6 again.

The alternative to me is one of the most exciting drives in the country taking route 6 from the Wanaka region turnoff where route 6 continues along the Clutha River and passes along **Lake Dunstan** a hydroelectric lake that submerged the original Cromwell town.

Looking across the lake as you get to the southern end is the present town of **Cromwell** built after the lake flooding. Cross the bridge and take a left through town you will come to the remnants of the **old Cromwell** you can stop and do a walk around.

Now back out across the bridge and to the left you drive along the Kawarau River coming to a fantastic drive through the Gibbston Valley and the Kawarau Gorge home to the local wine region - http://www.otagowine.com/cgi-bin/wineshop/perlshop.pl?thispage=gibbstonvalley.html&ACTION=ENTER&ORDER_ID=!ORDERID! .

Great place to stop and visit the wineries, their restaurants and even the cheese factory.

Now on down the road………..

After the wineries last place on the right is the **original bungy jump** you have to stop at to at
least see the place. Quite a spectacular job –
http://www.bungy.co.nz/kawarau-bungy-centre/kawarau-bungy . When I first came here in 1989
they operated out of an old bus.

1….2….3…and away we go………………

After the bungy jump next take the side road on the right to
the historic gold mining town of **Arrowtown** –
http://www.arrowtown.com/ .
If you get here in the fall the colours are outstanding and
they have a fantastic Autumn Festival.

A former gold mining town, Arrowtown is full of history and charm. Stroll along the quaint main street, sit and pass the time in a relaxed cafe, or enjoy the magnificent mountain surrounds from a resting place on the village green. Many craft and fashion stores, a boutique movie cinema, great dining and some fabulous accommodation make Arrowtown a must-do during your visit to this area.

Be sure to go down by the Arrow River and walk through the remnants of the historic Chinese mining village. Maybe even try you luck at gold panning.
They still find gold there you know. Take the 4WD tour to Macetown and learn how the early pioneers discovered gold and lived in those days.

From here it is a short drive to Queenstown. You can continue along route 6 to Lake Hayes cross the Lower Shotover River and on to Frankton and continue along Lake Wakitipu to Queenstown or from Arrowtown you can take Malagahans Road to Arthurs Point and on into Queenstown both drives worth it. Malagahans goes by the world famous Millbrook Resort and Gold Course and to Arthurs Point where a boat ride on the Shotover is a good thrill.

So you have made it to the fabulous world of **Queenstown**
- _http://www.queenstown-nz.co.nz/_
If you haven't heard of Queenstown you haven't heard of
New Zealand. Nestled in the mountains on the edge of the
deep blue waters of Lake Wakitipu Queenstown is the
major draw card for those who are looking for the adrenalin
thrills of life.

As the **Adventure Capital of the World** there seems to be
unlimited styles of derring-do from throwing yourself into
space with large rubber bands wrapped around your ankles,
jet boating rapids, whitewater rafting or jumping off a
mountain top with a hang glider strapped to your back.

We lived in Queenstown right downtown in a second floor
apartment where the picture window framed the lake with
the Remarkable Mountains towering over the far shore. I
took a photo and sent it back to my family in the US and
they thought I had copied a scenic post card. That's
Queenstown – a scenic post card.

The Earnslaw

Queenstown has more to offer than these thrills though with great shops, cafes and restaurants in just short walking distances of a few blocks of the village of Queenstown along with fabulous accommodations of every level. For those not into the action packed thrills how about taking a ride across the lake on the old steam ship the Earnslaw to Walter Peak, a beautiful active sheep farm for dinner or taking the slow ride on a gondola to the top of the mountain for a panoramic view 450 meters above the entire town and surrounding vista. (one of those WOW! places). A trip through the Lord of the Rings country is a must for fans. The fabulous golf course at Millbrook is available.

I think the drive along Lake Wakitipu out to **Glenorchy** is one of the most scenic drives in the country. Along the way is one of our favourite places to stay overnight at the Dept of Conservation camp at Moke Lake reached by a dirt road on the right a short way out of town past Sunshine Bay.

For the wine lovers there is a very special wine tasting shop in town we find fantastic - http://www.winetastes.co.nz/ Over 80 wines to choose from.

It is probably good to check into one of the Visitors Information Centres on Shotover Street to get yourself adjusted to what experiences you may wish to have. All bookings can be made there. You may want to also check in to the bus tours to the Fiordland National Park if you plan to go over to Te Anau a 2 ½ hour drive away.

Ski season
The ski season starts in June with the beginning of winter and may run through to October. At Coronet Peak, there is night skiing from 4pm to 8pm, usually from Thursday to Sunday. There are also opportunities for cross-country

skiing and heli-skiing around Queenstown. Ski clothing and equipment can be bought or rented in town. Maybe you will be lucky and be there for the Winter Festival.

Five Top Things to do in Queenstown
- ✓ Do any or all of the adrenalin adventures
- ✓ Take the gondola to the top of the mountain
- ✓ Walk the downtown area and stop at a cafe
- ✓ Do the drive along the lake to Glenorchy
- ✓ Take the steam boat Earnslaw out to Walter Peak

One of the best things about the Queenstown/Arrowtown region is the quality of the accommodations and restaurants.
For dining we find it hard to go by the Amisfield Bistro at the winery on Lake Hayes Road and Gantleys on Arthurs Point Road and love to go to Arrowtown to the Postmasters' House and Saffron. Bean Around the World is our coffee spot of choice.

NOTES:

And for the best in accommodation....................

TWIN PEAKS Bed & Breakfast
QUEENSTOWN NEW ZEALAND

Great start to any day, looking directly at the Remarkables and onto Lake Wakatipu.
Direct flights into Queenstown, and we are a five minute drive from the town centre.

Close to the town centre and central to the local ski fields. Ski season is late June to early October. Transport from reception is available to Coronet Peak, the Remarkables and Cardrona ski areas. Experience other activities on those warm sunny afternoons, we can arrange it all, combinations are even cheaper!

Your hosts –

Margaret and Derek Bulman
Enquire Today Ph +64-3-441-8442

Mobil phone +64-21-68-5520 - Fax + 64-3-441-8575

661 Frankton Road, Queenstown

Email: bulman@twinpeaks.co.nz

Website: http://www.twinpeaks.co.nz/

and...................... the fabulous award winning all-suite - in town - country

PENCARROW

Four acres of elegance with stunning views of Lake Wakatipu and the Remarkable Mountains.

- ✓ Trip Advisor Traveler's Choice Award and Certificate of Excellence Award

- ✓ Conde Nast Top 10 New Zealand Boutique Accommodation

- ✓ Fodor's Top 20 Worldwide Destination and a Fodor's Choice Hotel

- ✓ Frommer's Best in New Zealand B & B - Frommer's 3 star (maximum possible) rating, and a Frommer's *Value* rating

- ✓ Boutique Lodgings ranks Pencarrow guests suites 10 out of 10

Be sure to check this out for your Queenstown stay!

Your hosts: Bill and Kari Moers
678 Frankton Road, Queenstown 9300
Tel: 64-3-442-8938 Fax: 64-3-442-8974
Web: www.pencarrow.net
Email: info@pencarrow.net

After a superb time in the Queenstown region it is time to move on...........................

We now head south to the **Fiordland National Park**. Before you leave the area it is a good idea to stop at the large shopping centre after Frankton by the Queenstown airport. Take route 6 south out of Frankton across the one way bridge over the Kawarau River and a beautiful drive along Lake Wakitipu. There are many great pull off spots along the lake to stop. Route 6 continues south along the lake to its end at Kingston.

When you come to the Five Rivers café turn right on the side road there as a short cut to route 94 and Mossburn then on to the town of **Te Anau** and the world famous **Fiordland National Park**. If you have never experienced a fiord you will be most impressed. http://www.fiordland.org.nz/

Fiordland's West Coast is deeply indented by 14 fiords spanning 215 km of coastline. Established in 1952, Fiordland National Park is now over 1.2 million hectares in size, and encompasses mountain, lake, fiord and rainforest environments and is administered by the Department of Conservation.

The town of Te Anau lies on the edge of Lake Te Anau, with a backdrop of Mt Luxmore and the Murchison mountains.

The Fiordland National Park is the ultimate goal of most visitors whether it be to walk the tracks, visit the area by vehicle or explore the fiords by boat for a day visit or overnight. Be sure to have this marked on your "must do" list. The area is listed as a World heritage site.

Important! Remember - In the Peak period between October and April it is very important to book your accommodation and activities in advance to ensure you secure these.

For the bird watcher and nature lover you are likely to see common forest birds like Tomtits, Brown Creepers, Grey Warblers, Fantails, Tui, Bellbirds and Woodpigeons. The cheeky mountain parrot, the Kea, will be in the parking lot at Milford Sound looking to tear off the windshield wipers of your car. Brown Teal, Blue Duck and Southern Crested Grebes are found on Fiordland lakes and streams. In and around the water are Bottlenose dolphins, New Zealand fur seals, Fiordland Crested Penguins and little penguins.

Te Anau –

Te Anau rates as a top outdoor and adventure destination with multi-day walks and jetboating, kayaking, mountain biking, diving and fishing along with quality accommodation and restaurants. It is the focal point of the area to see all the fiords have to offer. Good place to stay while in the area to discover all Fiordland has to offer. All the required services are here plus seven day shopping. Te Anau Glowworm Caves should be visited for one.

I recommend when staying in the area:

BIRCHWOOD COTTAGES

BIRCHWOOD COTTAGES IS ACCOMMODATION
IN TRUE NEW ZEALAND STYLE

Te Anau Accommodation –

Make Birchwood Cottages your base for your Milford Sound or Doubtful Sound tours.

If you are looking for the perfect Te Anau/Milford Sound accommodation, we will make you very comfortable in one of our self contained cottages.

Contact:
Address: 208 Milford Road, Te Anau
Freephone: 0800 BIRCHWOOD(0800 247 249)
Phone: +64 3 249 9368
Fax: +64 3 249 9367
Email: birchwoodcottages@xtra.co.nz
Website: www.birchwoodcottages.co.nz

Manapouri –

Lake Manapouri is a beautiful lake with bush clad edges, sandy beaches and coves and 33 small islands with a backdrop of the Cathedral Mountain range. The small settlement of Manapouri lies on its border. It is known as the departure point for Doubtful Sound excursions and trips to the West Arm Power Station, the largest underground power generation in the southern hemisphere.
There are several tracks around the lake that
include 'The Monument', 'Waterfall Walk' at Stockyard Cove, Gorgeburn Falls Track, the Kepler Track, Cone Peak, Percy's Pass, and Dusky Track and all are accessible by water taxi.

Milford Sound -

The road to Milford Sound is one of the world's finest drives. The road is fully sealed, but the 240 kilometre return journey between Te Anau to Milford takes a minimum of two hours driving (in each direction) without allowing for stops such as Mirror Lake to have a closer look at and Homer Tunnel. After going through the tunnel be sure to stop for a photo of the twisting road down the next few kilometres.

Among the Sounds most striking features are Mitre Peak, rising 1,692m above the sound. Milford Sound is a popular and scenically stunning place to visit. The drive into Milford is a journey in itself in terms of the beautiful scenery you will view en route. Milford's abruptly carved peaks are majestic. I absolutely recommend taking the boat ride out through the Sounds past all the waterfalls and when having reached the ocean look back and wonder how Captain Cook and crew ever found the entrance while in their sailing ship.

Doubtful Sound -

Doubtful Sound does not have the dramatic scenery as Milford but the scenery is still awe inspiring. The difficulty of accessing Doubtful Sound creates a limitation to the number of people who go there, so you are more likely to have a more "remote" experience. Wildlife is slightly more abundant here so you have a higher chance of seeing the resident pod of dolphins or penguins and seals.

The Fiordland National Park is the most visited in all New Zealand by international visitors plus a lot of Kiwis so be sure to get all your bookings completed as soon as possible for this area and actually that goes for everything if coming during the busy months from Christmas through February.

Also remember this is the wettest area in the country so be prepared. One of the dramas of the area though is when it rains with waterfalls cascading off the tall peaks of the fiords.

I really recommend a boat ride out through the Sounds so you get to actually experience the fabulous area that is there. For the camper vanners and others looking for a good place to stay :

Fiordland Great Views Holiday Park

Contact:

Website: www.fiordlandgreatviewsholidaypark.co.nz

phone: (from inside NZ) - 0508 34673

Email: fiordland.holiday.park@xtra.co.nz

Fiordland Walks – http://www.fiordland.org.nz/
Fiordland has earned its reputation as the "walking capital of the world", with many excellent walking tracks throughout its dramatic landscape.

Coach and boat transfers access the major tracks, including the Great Walks: the Milford, Routeburn and Kepler Tracks.

The Hollyford Track, the Tuatapere Hump Ridge and Dusky Tracks, can be explored independently or as part of a guided group.

In addition to the multi-day tracks, there is a range of short walks providing walking options for people of all ages and ability. These walks enable access to the rainforest, lake and alpine vistas for those with limited time or fitness. If you plan to walk anywhere while here this is the area.

Dusky Track – http://www.duskytrack.co.nz/
This track links Lake Hauroko with Lake Manapouri plus a two-day detour to Supper Cove in Dusky Sound. The track traverses three major valley systems and crosses two mountain ranges. Another walk - Greenstone/Caples Walk - http://www.doc.govt.nz/

Milford Sovereign, Milford Sound –
realJOURNEYS - www.realjourneys.co.nz/

So you hopefully have learned a bit about the world of the Fiordland National Park and all it has to offer and now must move on. Two routes out of here to continue on south and it really depends upon how much time you have.

By the way I suppose you understand this route information does not dictate the direction you take from Christchurch as you can go either way down the east coast to Dunedin or cross over to the West Coast and south.

Routes through Southland
Two ways to go through Southland from Te Anau

✓ **First route** is route 94 through the town of Gore, internationally renowned as the World Capital of Brown Trout Fishing -http://www.gorenz.com/ and on to route one taking you to Balclutha on the East Coast then north.

Gore has the Hokonui Moonshine Festival and Museum and the Croydon Aviation Museum. One of our favourite places to park overnight is at Dolamore Park about ten kilometres out of Gore off route 94 by Croyden Bush for great walks and the park itself has over 500 mature Rhododendrons that make a spectacular show in spring.
Gore has several great cafes and a big plus for the best lamb racks we have ever got at the supermarket.

From Gore you can take route one south to Invercargill or take it east to Balclutha and then north all the way through Dunedin to Christchurch. This is the quickest route if you do not have the time to take going around the southern tip of the South Island.

✓ **Second route** is to go south on route 95 and route 99 skirting along the National Park and take **the Southern Scenic Route** -
http://www.southernscenicroute.co.nz/ to Invercargill, Bluff, Stewart Island and on through what is called the Catlins.

Southland - http://www.southlandnz.com/

The Southern Scenic Route is located from Dunedin through the Catlins, Invercargill and on to Fiordland. The road takes you along white sand beaches, rugged coastlines, ancient forests, historic cities and towns, lakes and rivers. Get off the main road in the Catlins to discover the many beaches with seals and penguins as the residents.

So let's leave the Te Anau region on route 95 and head south on then Southern Scenic route. There are two lakes you can visit via roads into the park, Lake Monowai and Lake Hauroko, and you will be by the Wairaki River on the way to the town of **Tuatapere**, the iconic sausage town. When you get to Tuatapere at the sharp left bend go straight ahead on the Papatotara Road to the beach and the end of the Wairaki River.

Not too many people know about this spot but we find it quite striking. The world famous Hump Ridge Track also starts in this area - http://www.humpridgetrack.co.nz Route 95 has also become route 99.

This actually is one of our favourite drives and most visitors do not have or take the time to go this route which is a shame as it is the wild south of New Zealand with nothing between here and the Antarctic. It is a three hour drive from Te Anau to Invercargill.

After Tuatapere you will be driving along the ocean a portion of the way to Orepuke and then to Colec Bay and on to what we have called our southern home when on the road, Riverton.

For a real out of the way unique spot south of Pahia take the Mullet Bay Road to where it ends on the ocean at a place called **Cozy Nook**. Some hard core fishermen and families tucked into small shacks and houses in the bay. Beautiful spot but I bet it is harsh in the winter wind.

Stop at **Gemstone Beach** on the way through. Gemstone Beach is accessed directly off the Southern Scenic Route just West of Orepuki .

I have found numerous semi-precious stones here especially after a storm. The following have commonly been found: garnet, jasper, rodinguite quartz, simi nephrite, fossil worm casts, oil shale and sapphire.

Be sure to go into **Colec Bay** for a brief look and perhaps as top at the cafe then on to the town of **Riverton**. As you get into the centre there is a one way bridge to cross to the left over the Aparima River but continue on and go out to the end of the road at what is known as the Riverton Rocks for a good look across the Foveaux Strait with Steward Island in the distance.

Riverton - http://www.riverton-aparima.co.nz/ - is small town of less than 2000 residents it once was a major whaling station and now its major occupation is fishing. The paua shell from this area is some of the most beautiful in the world.

What I recommend to do in Riverton:
- ✓ Take a ride out to the Riverton Rocks
- ✓ Get your photo taken at the world's largest paua shell!
- ✓ Make your own paua shell jewellery
- ✓ Get a pizza at the Globe Hotel
- ✓ Visit the Early Settler's Museum

Riverton Rocks
It is a short drive on route 99 to the major city in the South –

Invercargill - http://www.invercargill.org.nz/
Invercargill is known for its wide streets, quirky Mayor - Tim Shadbolt, weather blowing in from the Antarctic, the Southland Museum and the home to Burt Monroe, who won the world's speed record with his Indian motorcycle. (movie – "World's Fastest Indian"starring Anthony Hopkins). Go out to Oreti Beach where Burt put his motorcycle through its paces.

The large pyramid style building in Queens Park is the **Southland Museum** that is home to fifty live tuatara, the world's oldest living reptiles known as "living fossils" the tuatara.
And the "Beyond the Roaring Forties" is a gallery dedicated to the Antarctic Islands south of New Zealand.

Awarua Wetlands -. Many species of wading birds can also be observed at Awarua Bay. Altogether, Awarua Wetlands Scientific Reserve and the adjoining Seaward Moss and Toetoes conservation areas cover 14,000 hectares. This is the largest protected wetlands in southern New Zealand.

Take route one out of Invercargill and to the end of the road at **Bluff** - http://www.bluff.co.nz/_ Bluff is the oldest European settled town in New Zealand and home of the Bluff oyster plus where you catch the ferry over to Stewart Island.

The end of route one is at Stirling Point well worth going to and also up to the top of Bluff Hill for the panoramic views of the area.

Foveaux Walkway – Bluff

Foveaux Walkway is a walk along rugged coastline below the Bluff. A circular track just over 7km in length starts out on the Foveaux Walkway. It continues on from Lookout Point, over Bluff Hill and back to Stirling Point

The major event of the year is the annual Bluff Oyster Festival held usually in May.

.

Stewart Island - http://www.stewartisland.co.nz/_

For those of you having the opportunity to go to Stewart Island here is where you can catch the boat or the plane over. Ferry and helicopter services depart from Bluff and fixed-wing aircraft depart from Invercargill Airport. The ferry crossing takes approximately one hour; flights take approximately 15-20 minutes.

In 2002 the very qualities that make this a great place were recognised in the formation of the Rakiura National Park, comprising 85% of the Island.

At latitude 47 degrees south (the "Roaring Forties") the weather is often unpredictable, but the climate is surprisingly temperate with summer temperatures climbing to the mid-20's. Sunshine hours are equal to the national average, and while it may be true that it rains on a higher number of days, our annual rainfall is less than that of Auckland.

Accommodation from backpackers to lodge. For the bird watcher/nature lover the island has an overwhelming population including the day roaming Kiwi and the cheeky South Island Kaka. Ulva Island - Since the eradication of rats, Ulva Island has become the 'Jewel in the Crown', offering a predator-free environment for rare and endangered birds including South Island Saddleback, Yellowhead, Rifleman, Stewart Island Robin, Stewart Island Brown Kiwi. The Marine Reserve in Paterson Inlet, which was established in 2004 and covers 1075 hectares, is the ultimate diver's paradise.

There are walks for all different fitness levels and ability ranges where one can enjoy the diverse bush, birds, scenery and landforms. There are several guided walks and easy walking tracks within the vicinity of Oban, the main community, varying from 10 minutes to 3 hours. One of New Zealand's "Great Walks" is the Rakiura Track - a moderate 3 day, 36km track. For the hard core enthusiast they offer: The North West Circuit - a 10-12 day, 125km challenging hike and can be quite demanding due to the often wet and muddy surfaces.
Side trips to Mount Anglem and Rocky Mountain provide views across the Island and The Southern Circuit a hike of 6-9 days covering 105kms.
Side trips to Mount Rakeahua and Rocky Mountain again offer amazing views. Both these walks are challenging and they suggest are only suitable for experienced and well equipped trampers.

Several cruises and boat charters available along with kayak rentals along with car rental, bikes and scooters.

After Steward Island, Bluff and Invercargill it is time now to head back north up the East Coast. Off the Bluff Road (Route One) take Kew Road by the hospital to Ells Road and a dogleg left to turn right on McQuarrie Street that becomes Scott Street that becomes the Gorge Road-Invercargill Highway.

Catlins - http://www.catlins.org.nz/

Here it is best you get off the main road and go down the side roads to the ocean and visit places like **Niagara** (good café) and Curio Bay in order to see fur seals, sea lions and penguins along the Catlins coast........ **visit the Jurassic fossilized forest at Curio Bay**

Go to Purakaunui Falls - NZ's most photographed waterfall!

Visit the Lost Gypsy Gallery Caravan

The Catlins is an isolated and interesting spot in New Zealand well worth the time to drive through. Here you will see what the strong winds have done to the trees that have bent to the severity and are almost horizontal to the land.

Here is a great map provided by the Whistling Frog Café - http://www.catlinsnz.com/images/Whistling_Frog_Touri st_Map.pdf

A side road out of **Pounewea** takes you to one of our favourite camps and owners at **Newhaven** where just a short walk along the beach is a seal colony you can get close to (but not too close as they are fast). I love to walk down the beach to the seal colony and watch their antics.

Newhaven Holiday Park offers a range of new, modern accommodation on the Catlins Coast at beautiful Surat Bay.

Just 5km from Owaka, Surat Bay is the home to many sea lions, sea birds and native birds all of which can be viewed in their natural environment.
Newhaven Holiday Park provides beach access to Surat Bay where an excellent beach walk can be made to adjoining Cannibal Bay.
Other tourist attractions on the Catlins Coast such as spectacular waterfalls, Cathedral Caves,Jack's Blowhole, bush walks, penguin viewing, horse treks, golf course and canoeing are just a short drive away.
Newhaven Holiday Park has beautiful sea views and is set amongst inspiring scenery in a quiet, peaceful environment.
Self contained Tourist Flat
Comfortable Chalet Cabins
Powered sites
Tent sites

The modern home-style amenity block has many well appointed features for all camping needs including guest lounge, kitchen, bathrooms and laundry.

Contact Lyndon & Jacqui Clark
324 Newhaven Road
RD1, Owaka, The Catlins,
South Otago, New Zealand

Phone:+64 3 415 8834

Email: newhaven@ihug.co.nz

Website: www.newhavenholiday.com

The road out of the Catlins swings north and ends up in Balclutha and route one - http://en.wikipedia.org/wiki/Balclutha,_New_Zeala nd on the Clutha River and so you have been through the Southland.

On North on Route One from Southland..................Central

This area is known as the **Otago Goldfields Heritage Trail** - http://www.nzsouth.co.nz/goldfields/roxburgh.html .

After Balclutha take route one north to the turn off on route 8 inland to one of the least visited for most tourists but to me one of the most starkly beautiful parts of the South Island. For those on limited time this area is usually left out which is a shame but with so much to see and do and limited time something has to go but do try to schedule this part.

Turning inland on route 8 you come to the town of **Lawrence** - http://www.lawrence.co.nz/ the place known as the area's first gold mining town and **where the first gold was discovered at Gabriel's Gully** - http://www.doc.govt.nz/conservation/historic/by-region/otago/gabriels-gully/ and the world rushed in a frenzy in 1861 bringing a population of 11,000 to the area and the beginning the development of New Zealand.

Now it is a sleepy little town that can boast several good cafés. For those of you going directly to Queenstown from this area this is the quickest route taking route 8 at Milton south of Dunedin. I would like to see more visitors go into this area as it is special by overlooked a lot.

Gabriel's Gully

Next continuing along route 8 inland you come to
Roxburgh – I suggest you stop here awhile .
http://en.wikipedia.org/wiki/Roxburgh,_New_Zealand

The area is known for its apples and cherries and you can
always find roadside fruit stands to enjoy their bounty. For
a gee-whizzy fact they still have an operating theatre that
opened in 1898.

Be sure to stop in **Fruitlands** to visit the old cottage where
its construction was begun in the 1880's finishing in 1904.
Ten children of the Mitchell family were raised there in
those early days.

This is a great place to stop and visit and stay for awhile.
Here is a place I recommend:

This is a great place to stop and visit and stay for awhile. Here is a place I recommend:

Roxburgh's Clutha Gold Cottages

Just over the bridge of the mighty Clutha River is the Roxburgh's Clutha Gold Cottages. Find peace and quiet with excellent family value accommodation and personal hospitality at your 'home away from home'. Clutha Gold Cottages has the perfect setting for the whole family.

Offering a range of accommodation available to suit everyone's needs.

All accommodation offers laundry facilities, cot & highchair use, DVDs, Indoor Games and BBQ to use at your leisure. All linen is fully supplied.

Off street parking for all cars and large truck / trailer units.Backpackers - Fully equipped kitchen, large living / dining area, internet access, diesel fire, bathroom with shower & toilet / separate toilet.

 Cottages – Four separate Cottages for your choice of accommodation.

Cottages 1 & 4 - 1 Bedroom Double Bed & Single Bed

Cottages 2 & 3 - 2 bedrooms Double Bed & 2 Single Beds

All cottages have double fold out couch in lounge.

Caravan / Motorhome / Tent – Quiet area with plenty of space to park available for all caravans, Motorhomes and 5th wheelers. For those looking for the more "back to nature" holiday there is plenty of room to pitch a tent with the same facilities available as caravans.

Contact:
Christine Bennenbroek
141 Roxburgh East Road
Roxburgh, Central Otago
Mob: 027 203 7061
Tel: 03 446 8364
Email: cluthagoldcottages@extra.co.nz
Website: www.cluthagoldcottages.co.nz

Five Top Things to enjoy while in the area:
- ✓ Visit and sample wine from award-winning vineyards Three Miners & Black Ridge (Earnsleugh) & Wooing Tree (Cromwell).
- ✓ Catch the Central Otago Tours and Wildflower Walks
- ✓ Explore the Otago Goldfields Heritage Trail
- ✓ Walk or ride the famous Central Otago Rail Trail
- ✓ Or challenge yourself on some of the other exciting mountain bike rides on offer, take a four-wheel drive trip on the Old Man Range and picnic on "top of the world."

For more info about Central Otago, click on the website: Tourism Central Otago .

The next spot is **Alexandra** known for its warm temperatures in the summer time. What a great town. http://www.nzsouth.co.nz/centralotago/alex.html

and nearby is the town of **Clyde** –
http://www.clyde.co.nz/ that is also fun to stop and walk
around. This is a town we really enjoy stopping at with a
couple of pleasant cafes and pubs to enjoy and for those
interested the hydro-electric Clyde dam is just north of
town.

One of the top places in the world to enjoy your bicycle is
the 150km of the Rail Trail
http://www.otagocentralrailtrail.co.nz/ and also for the
keen hiker. The year-round cycling and walking **Otago
Central Rail Trail** is a public reserve owned by the people
of New Zealand so there's no cost for using it. Because the
Otago Central Rail Trail follows an old railway line, hills
are not steep, thus making it accessible to most ages and
those with a reasonable degree of fitness.

From Alexandra we go deeper into the Otago region on
route 85. The surrounding landscape to me is a
photographer's dream as you go through the small towns of
Omakau, Lauder and on to Naseby and Ranfurly but take
the time to go off the main highway to the communities of
Ophir and Ida Valley.

The best, where we always make a point to go, is **Saint
Bathans** to visit the pub. Beautiful small historical town
and also just across the road visit the Blue Lake created by
the early gold mining. It is rumoured the pub is haunted by
the way.

The favourite town to visit in this area for us is **Naseby** and
the Royal Hotel - http://www.naseby.co.nz/ Naseby had
its early beginnings by the discovery of gold in 1863 and
became a large thriving community. One of the most
thrilling experiences

I find fascinating is the curling rink - http://www.curling.co.nz/ having never seen anything like it in my travels before. You just got to stop and give it a go!

From Naseby you can take the back road, Dansy's Pass Road, that actually cuts across to Duntroon and route 83 but not recommended for camper vans but you can go out to the **Dansy's Pass Coach Inn**..............what a magic spot - http://www.danseyspass.co.nz/ . Not too many international visitors ever get out here.....or kiwis for that matter.....

From Naseby back to route 85 and continue along the the art deco town of **Ranfurly** - http://www.visit-centralotago.co.nz/html/ranfurly_central_otago.html . If you are here in February you will get to enjoy the **Art Deco Festival** - http://www.maniototo.co.nz/events-central-otago/ranfurly-art-deco/ well worth planning for if you can. It is a return to the 1930's - Ranfurly style...

One of the greatest events that occurs in this area to me is the **Goldfields Cavalcade** – http://cavalcade.co.nz/ We would make sure we were there for many years during our travels.

Some are on foot, others in wagons and ones on horseback. At the end they all come together to have a parade and a party and you are invited. Each year it follows different trails.

It is like stepping back into the past. You can also be a part of it if you are sturdy enough.

After Ranfurly the curve back to the East Coast on route 85 or you might want to explore a bit further into this country and take route 87 to Dunedin. Two route one further in, route 87 takes you to the town of Middlemarch and on to Mosgiel south of Dunedin.

If you stay on route 85 it takes you to route one at Palmerston about 45 minutes north of Dunedin (54km).

Dunedin -

http://www.dunedinnz.com/visit/home.aspx_

So let's go to one of the most important towns in New Zealand. With a population of around 124,000 Dunedin is the seventh largest urban area in New Zealand and is the largest by land area. It is 362 kilometres south of Christchurch on the east coast of the South Island.

Due to Dunedin being the home of the University of Otago and the Otago Polytechnic almost 20% of the population are students.   Scottish migrants established the town in 1848 as New Edinburgh. When gold was discovered in Central Otago Dunedin became New Zealand's largest city and prospered as the commercial centre of the country until the end of the gold rush.

I like what Mark Twain remarked upon his visit here: "The people here are Scots. They stopped on their way to heaven thinking they had arrived."

In the heart of the city is the city square but it is actually octagonal. Beautiful Edwardian architecture from the early days is seen in St Paul's Cathedral, the Railway Station and Olveston House.

In addition on the Otago Peninsula is the Larnach Castle re-built to all its glory. Several gardens such as the Botanic Gardens and the Glenfalloch Woodland Garden adorn the area.

Of importance is the Royal Albatross Colony at Taiaroa Heads at the end of the Otago Peninsula along with other wildlife such as the yellow-eyed penguin and others. Great place to take a harbour cruise to see the wildlife.

The Guinness Book of Records lists Dunedin's Baldwin Street as the steepest street in the world.

For the train enthusiast one of the most exciting train trips starts in Dunedin and goes into the isolated and scenic Taieri Gorge - http://www.taieri.co.nz/

For the person enjoying riding bicycles this is a good starting spot to do the Otago Rail Trail via Dunedin - http://www.otagorailtrail.co.nz/ .

Five Top things to do in Dunedin
- ✓ Visit the Albatross Colony - http://www.albatross.org.nz/
- ✓ Explore historic Larnach Castle - http://www.larnachcastle.co.nz/index.pasp
- ✓ Tour the Cadbury Chocolate factory - http://www.cadburyworld.co.nz/home.html
- ✓ Ride the Taieri Gorge Railway - http://www.taieri.co.nz/
- ✓ Check out the Speights Brewery - http://www.speights.co.nz/Home.aspx

Larnach Castle – Otago Peninsula

So now on north on route one from Dunedin. Just past Palmerston keep an eye open for the road to **Shag Point** on the right. Go to the end of the road to discover a seal colony of young male fur seals (waiting their turn to challenge the adult males in other colonies). You can walk right out on the overhanging rocks to be just close above them and not bother them and they can't come after you.

Great seal photographic opportunities.

Now back out to route one and north. The next interesting stop next is the **Moeraki Boulders** on Koekohe Beach. Either follow the road to the top of the cliff where the shop/restaurant is located or drive straight down to the beach parking lot and walk along the beach to get a closer look and touch of these giant round rock balls lying about with easy access at low tide formed over 60 million years ago. They weigh several tons and some are over 3 metres in diameter. The complex charges you to go down to the beach while it is free at the parking lot but it provides a good outlook overall especially if the tide is in.

Moeraki Boulders

Now on to the small fishing village of **Moeraki** next just down the road on the right to my favourite restaurant in New Zealand. **Fleur's Place -**
http://www.fleursplace.com/ - a restaurant, cafe and bar right on the waterfront at the old jetty.

Her specialty is fresh fish straight from local Moeraki Bay fishing boats. The restaurant is established on an early whaling station site in 2002 and is built from gathered collectables and demolition materials from all over New Zealand. Funky spot with wonderful food that Fleur has won all kinds of awards for. Be sure to tell her I said hi when you stop by.

Also while there go visit the lighthouse area. The yellow eye and blue penguin colonies, sea birds and seals can bee seen resting on the rocks alongside the Moeraki Lighthouse built in 1878.

When British television chef and restaurateur Rick Stein was told he could choose to go anywhere in the world to write a travel article for English newspaper, the Daily Mail, he chose Fleur's Place in Moeraki, New Zealand. Good choice!

The restaurant, run by the inimitable Fleur Sullivan, was 'Just one of those places that keeps cropping up in conversations' whenever there was a gathering of 'foodies', he said. Set in the sleepy little fishing village of Moeraki on the Otago coast, Fleurs Place has an unbeatable setting.

There's water on three sides, fishing boats bobbing in the harbour, the famous Moeraki Boulders across the bay and, to the north, the open sea. Fleur uses only the freshest of local ingredients - indeed, fishing boats land their catches right into her restaurant.

I have been there when I went with Fleur outside to a fisherman who had just came in where she quickly grabbed a grouper to rush back into the restaurant for a man sitting at a table who had just ordered grouper for dinner. She means it when she says fresh!!!! ......

Fleur is one of the nicest kindest people I have met in New Zealand....no make that the world!

Contact:

Phone: +64 3 439 4480
Fax: +64 3 439 4481
E-mail: mail@fleursplace.com
Web: www.fleursplace.com \

318

**and between Moeraki and Oamaru there is a great
place to stay: Olive Grove
It is a Lodge, Backpackers and Camping Area -
Website:** www.olivebranch.co.nz

Olive Grove is a unique Kiwi family run eco-friendly
lodge of 27 organic acres.
Our warm country retreat is within a natural river setting
(swimming) with spacious riverside camping.
You can choose your own tent site or powered site
(campervans) which
are amongst our manicured grounds with mature trees.
Enjoy our beautiful gardens, spacious colourful bedrooms
with Lyn's artwork and relaxing living areas with log fire,
internet, library, no TV.
Enjoy our own range of organic Herb teas.
Hammocks, outdoor fire place with seating to enjoy the
night sky or relax in
the outdoor hot tub/spa or sauna. BBQs avaliable for guests
to use.
Nature lovers/bird watchers, photographers paradise.

We offer our guests small private penguin and wildlife
tours!!

Close to beaches, fishing charters available and Moeraki
Boulders a must to see.
(25km south of Oamaru and 12 km north of Moeraki)
Contact:
Kim and Lyn Simpson
2328 Herbert/Hampden Road, (SH1)
Waianakarua, Oamaru
Tel: (0)3 4395830
Email: info@olivebranch.co.nz

And now to one of my favourite small towns in the South Island. Several good cafes and a host of interesting shops plus we really enjoy walking around in the old Historic Precinct. Don't forget the cheese factory! And they even have a whiskey distillery & pub.

Oamaru - http://www.visitoamaru.co.nz/

The next place of interest is the town of **Oamaru**. Be sure to check out the 19th century Historic Precinct of the town being revitalized with period shops. Let Oamaru Steam and rail take you on a journey back in time with a trip on their "vintage train" from the Historic Precinct to Oamaru's Harbour. Stop and visit Michael the book binder and the other great shops.

Be sure to stop and pick up some absolutely wonderful **Whitestone cheese** at the factory on town. I can't go by this place...
http://en.wikipedia.org/wiki/Whitestone_cheese .

Be sure to check out my website for the Festivals in town
www.ronlaughlin.net

If you are here at night for the penguins perhaps you might enjoy strange and slightly scary stories of Colonial Oamaru by master storyteller, Annette Knowler, and how about riding a penny farthing - The Oamaru Cycle Works building is located on the corner of Harbour and Tyne streets where you will find a unique 1880's Penny Farthing Manufacturing Facility, and Antique Bicycle restoration and repair workshop.

A Shop with Cycling Memorabilia and a Bicycle Museum housing a fascinating collection of Veteran and Antique

Bicycles. The Bicycle Museum has the largest collection of Penny Farthings in New Zealand on display and also includes a replica of the **very First Bicycle built in the World,** the Draisine or Hobby Horse from 1816.

How about a tour of the beautiful historic estates. Visit the famous **Totara Estate** where you'll drink billy tea and share stories with historic swaggers. Then to Burnside Homestead whose décor, fabrics, and furnishings are little changed from yesteryear, as the butler will point out. A lunch of traditional Victorian fare will be served from recipes handed down through the decades.

The adjoining **Elderslie Estate**, whose grounds were designed by Sir Joseph Paxton, is next. Here you will be met by the gardener and taken on a walk around the grounds before enjoying home-made lemonade on the lawn. Finally to Parkside where we visit the home of Oamaru Stone - the purest limestone in the world and a mere forty million years in the making! Your costumed guide and hosts will make this an experience to remember.

The most exciting experience for the nature lover is the **Little Blue Penguin Colony -** http://www.penguins.co.nz/ on the edge of town. Be sure to stop by and see the penguins. I recommend taking the time to stay for the night in the area so you can watch the adults that have been out fishing all day return to their babies who are anxiously waiting for their feed. I recommend you can also take the behind the scenes tour.

Just down the road south is the beach where the yellow-eyed penguins come in. Go there first at dusk as they come in earlier than the Little Blue. There is a hide (blind) there where you can watch as they come ashore and climb to their perch for the night then after there is plenty of time to go to the Little Blue Colony for the "return of the penguins".

Now on north on route one turning off to the town of **Waimate** - http://www.waimate.com/_ ,home to the wallaby, a small to medium-sized kangaroos , and the strawberry capital of New Zealand.

Perhaps you will be here in mid-December to enjoy the annual Strawberry Festival. The Whitehorse monument, on the Hunter Hills, commemorates the Clydesdale horses which were originally used to break in the land. Waimate boasts several short walks including the Waimate Walkway which leads to the Whitehorse Lookout providing hikers breathtaking views over the district.

This is the only place in New Zealand where the Bennett's Wallaby were released in 1875 and they still roam free in the area surrounding Kelceys Bush.

Kelceys Bush Farmyard Holiday Park is a wonderful place http://kelceysbush.co.nz/ and a great environment for children (and adults) where you can enjoy the bush walks, feeding farm animals, BBQs and camping. This is where you can get up close and personal with a wallaby and many other friendly animals.

Here is a place that has it all. I highly recommend staying at the:

Glenmac Farmstay

A TYPICAL NEW ZEALAND HIGH COUNTRY FARM

Waitaki Valley

Glenmac is a high country merino sheep and beef cattle farm spread over 1583 hectares. Nestled in the quiet Waitaki Valley, the family farm is 60km's from Oamaru and 15km's from Kurow township.

Your hosts Kaye and Keith welcome you and guarantee an enjoyable and relaxing holiday experience for all visitors to their friendly high country farm accommodation. Glenmac provide information on local activities including horse treks, tramping, mountain biking, local winery, fossil trail, hot tubs and much more to help you plan a great holiday.

An affordable range of farm style accommodation is available to suit the budget and requirements of independent travellers and families to our rural South Island destination.

The Dinner, Bed and Breakfast accommodation option is a great way to experience the fun of farm life without any of the hard work involved! Dinner is a time when guests join the hosts for a home cooked meal, country hospitality and a relaxing chat. Guestrooms are either ensuite or shared bathroom. All beds have electric blankets, duvets, blankets and wool rest underlays. Each room has a heater provided. Tea and coffee facilities available at all times and home cooked baking provided.

The Backpackers Cottage has beds for nine guests and provides clean, warm and comfortable budget farm style accommodation. All linen is supplied and the shared TV lounge and full kitchen facilities provide wonderful opportunities to meet other interesting people from all around New Zealand and the world!

Our Campervan Park campground is designed for travellers and holidaymakers who prefer to avoid crowded camping sites and noisy motorhome parks.

Situated in a picturesque rural setting, our boutique campervan and camping area has shower, toilet, laundry and full kitchen facilities. However if you don't feel like cooking don't despair! For a minimal cost you can join the family for a hearty evening farm meal!

Contact:

Ph: +64 3 436 0200
Fax: +64 3 436 0202
Mobile: 027 222 1119
Email: glenmac@farmstaynewzealand.co.nz
Internet Address: www.farmstaynewzealand.co.nz
Postal: Glenmac Farmstay, Gards Rd, 7K RD, Kurow

Off to the Mackenzie Country and Mt. Cook –

Now we are off to one of my favourite areas in New Zealand, the Mackenzie Country - http://en.wikipedia.org/wiki/Mackenzie_Basin. From Waimate take route 82 inland to cross the Waitaki River at Kurow and then continue on route 83 to the hydro-electric lakes area. If you come off route one north of Oamaru you take the route 83 turn-off.

This is a very special area around the town of **Duntroon** - http://www.duntroon.org.nz/. If you come from Waimate to Kurow then turn back to the east on route 83 to a fascinating place I really enjoy exploring in the town of Duntroon -

Vanished World - http://www.vanishedworld.co.nz/ .

The Vanished World Fossil Centre is an amazing place that introduces a range of fossils that have been discovered in the region. Fossils like whale, penguins, dolphins and many more. They have on display a 25 million year old shark-toothed dolphin uncovered here and having been a living part of the area when it was underwater all those many years ago.

Vanished World is run by local volunteers who live here and all have interesting stories of the area to relate. Pick up the map and take the time to explore the whole area. This is where parts of the movie "Narnia" were shot. Be sure to see Elephant Rocks on the self-drive tour. Just outside of Duntroon about five miles are early Maori rock drawings along the road of interest.

While here have a look at the old gaol (jail), Nichol's blacksmith shop and maybe get a coffee and muffin at the Flying Pig restaurant.

Take a guided tour of the fabulous **Tokarahi Homestead** - built with locally quarried limestone in 1878 by Alexander McMaster. The homestead was at the centre of the Tokarahi Estate consisting of 13,500 acres and has been faithfully restored to its full grandeur. It boasts its original Japanese embossed wallpaper, one of a handful of examples still in existence in the world today. They also provide accommodation - http://www.homestead.co.nz/ .

For the campers one of our favourite camp grounds is near here at Dansey's Pass 15kms south of Duntroon. Swim in the river pools and also pan for gold while there. http://www.danseyspass.com/index2.html .

On to the Mackenzie Country passing Lake Aviemore and Lake Benmore to the glider capital of the world – **Omarama** - http://www.glideomarama.com/.

If you come from Queenstown you would take route 8 through the **Lindis Pass** to Omarama a little over a two hour fantastic scenic drive.

Catch a salmon and have it prepared for your meal in less than an hour at the Ladybird Winery - http://www.ladybirdhill.co.nz/

Take route 8 north to the town of **Twizal** - http://www.twizelnz.com/ and on to the turn off, route 80, to Mt Cook - http://www.mtcooknz.com/ .

The drive along Lake Pukaki to the base of Mt Cook is one of the most spectacular drives in the country. It is a very special place.

At 3764 metres, Mt Cook in New Zealand is the highest of the country's 27 mountains over 3000 metres. The surrounding Mt Cook National Park offers spectacular flight-seeing, hiking and skiing. Visit the Sir Edmund Hillary Museum or get up close to a giant iceberg by boat on the Tasman Glacier terminal lake- http://www.glacierexplorers.co.nz

Mt Cook is a World Heritage area. Mt Cook National Park is 700 square kilometres in size, more than one third of which is perpetually under snow or ice.

Turnoffs to the Hooker Glacier and the Tasman Glacier are at the far end of the Mt Cook road with a good Dept of Conservation camp to stay for the campers or the Glentanner Holiday Park - http://www.glentanner.co.nz/

For those looking for top accommodation be sure to stay at the world famous Hermitage Lodge - http://www.hermitage.co.nz/ . It is a 45-minute drive from Twizel at the end of SH80.

Mt Cook was first climbed in 1894 by New Zealanders Jack Clarke, Tom Fyfe and George Graham. It has been climbed by New Zealand explorer and mountaineer Sir Edmund Hillary who scaled Mt Everest in 1953.

The village
The National Park Visitor Centre is in Mt Cook Village, close to The Hermitage, which is one of New Zealand's more famous hotels, with its close-up view of the snow-clad peak.
Also in the village is the Mt Cook YHA Hostel which provides lower-cost accommodation.
Accommodation at Mt Cook should be booked in advance to be sure of a place to stay.

Skiing the glacier slopes
The Tasman Glacier, roughly north-northeast of the Mt Cook Village in the Mt Cook National Park. At 27 kilometres, it is one of the world's longest glaciers outside the polar regions. Take a helicopter to the Tasman Glacier and feel that wind whistle by as you glide down the magical landscape. Skiing won't ever feel quite the same again after skiing at Mt Cook. You can organise your helicopter flight to the Tasman Glacier from Queenstown or Christchurch or stay here and enjoy the area.

After skiing at Mt Cook, you can claim having conquered New Zealand's highest mountain.

Back out to route 8 and continue through the Mackenzie Country next stop at the Information Centre on Lake Pukaki if to do nothing more than to take a photograph from the parking area.

It is about 30 minutes to Lake Tekapo but first just before the lake take the road to the left to the top of Mt John for the best scenic outlook - http://www.newzealandsky.com/earthandsky/ . Have a coffee at the Astro Café at the very top.

Lake Tekapo from the top of Mt John & the Observatory

Now on to **Lake Tekapo** next -
http://www.laketekapountouched.co.nz/
Lake Tekapo, with its milky blue lake and majestic surrounding peaks, is sure to make you have your camera out and active. Right on the lake is the historic stone Church of the Good Shepherd and the statue to the faithful sheep dog.
Popular in summer for boating, waterskiing, swimming, fishing and walking, Lake Tekapo is also a winter destination with hot pools, ice skating and skiing.
There is a new pool complex you would enjoy on the lake - Alpine Springs - http://www.alpinesprings.co.nz/ .

Time to move on out of the high country lake region taking route 8 east through Burkes Pass and on to the town of Fairlie.

One route from here is
If you continue on route 8 you go through Pleasant Point - http://www.pleasantpointrail.org.nz/ - and travel by steam train or one of the world's only Model T Ford Railcars. We have parked overnight out of town on the Opihi River in order to see the little brown bats in the area. These bats are the only native land mammal to New Zealand. Great river for trout fishing too.
On the way out to the river is the Opihi Winery with a good café worth stopping at for a coffee.

Route 8 comes out just north of the town of **Timaru** - http://www.southisland.org.nz/Timaru .
Timaru is the urban hub of this region that has all conveniences. They have a really nice park to enjoy as you enter the main part of town at Caroline Bay.

People have been flocking to this stretch of sandy, safe beach for more than 100 years. It still retains some its traditional flavour with promenades, playground and picnic areas and adds real excitement with its long-running annual Christmas -New Year Carnival .

Be sure to visit the Trevor Griffiths Rose Garden on Caroline Bay.

The Aigantighe Art Gallery has a well-deserved reputation as having one of the best collections of New Zealand art to be found in any provincial city.

Next route:
If you take route 79 out of Fairlie you go through the town of Geraldine -
http://www.gogeraldine.co.nz/
This is one of our favourite communities with its many local gardens.

Just a few blocks in the main area of the town it has several places of interest to explore such as **the world's largest sweater at 'The Giant Jersey' and the mosaic Bayeux Tapestry replica**, a medieval mosaic that depicts the Battle of Hastings (1066) and is supported by a complete analysis of the events, culture and history concerning the Norman Conquest. This re-creation is a stunning 42 meters; painted onto a canvas of steel chips.

For those interested in history there is the **only surviving 1929 Spartan Biplane** in the world at the Geraldine Vintage Car and Machinery Museum.

A very convenient place to stop and enjoy the several small shops is the Barker Berry Complex (some of the best jams and jellies in New Zealand) on the edge of town on route 79 the road that goes on into or comes from the Mackenzie Country.

A top quality restaurant is Verde, 45 Talbot Street, located by the river before the junction and the turn off to the Berry Complex.

We always make sure we stop here for the excellent service, coffee and food they serve.

The town also has an excellent super market to stock up the camper van.

Peel Forest nearby offers several short walks, tramps, and one longer route that leads to the summit of Little Mt Peel.

The Rangitata River Valley was used by Peter Jackson and crew in the filming of Edoras, the city of Rohan, in the Lord of the Rings.

This is one of our favourite parks to stay at. What a magnificent setting in a perfect location. Either coming from or going to Christchurch it is ideal.

Geraldine KIWI Holiday Park

Geraldine is just one and a half easy hours of travel south from Christchurch and the airport and is a great location for the night, weekend or for a full week of holiday. It is in the centre of the South Island of New Zealand and a short and spectacularly scenic trip from the lakes and New Zealand's tallest mountain- Mount Cook. Geraldine Holiday Park caters for all styles and budgets of travellers and is a great place to stay.

Tranquil park setting among huge specimen tree. Enjoy the peaceful sound of the native birds yet only a two minute stroll to shops, cafes, galleries. Close to the heritage cinema and museums.

Community outdoor swimming pool(Seasonal) Bush/river walks . Great fishing spots, 4x4 trips, skiing, white water rafting.

It is the perfect place to stop and experience the best a holiday park has to offer and the town of Geraldine is fabulous to visit.

Contact Information:

Hosts - Brian and Kathryn Horrell

39 Hislop Street

GERALDINE 7930

Ph/Fax 0064 03 6938147

Freephone: 0800 – 393693 (NZ only)

Email: info@geraldineholidaypark.co.nz

Website - www.geraldineholidaypark.co.nz

From Geraldine it is out to route one and north to the south **Canterbury region** south of the city of Christchurch. From Christchurch in any direction there is plenty to see and experience for the visitor. To the north there is the world of the whales, seals and sea birds to be visited at Kaikoura the area I have already covered earlier in the book.

If your trip is just starting from Christchurch or coming down from the top of the South Island quite obviously all you have to do is reverse how I have written it down. It is the same either way. We only have a few roads to travel to everywhere in the country.

You may wish to go to **Akaroa** first, with its beauty, charm and fine restaurants. It is a town sitting in the middle of four extinct volcanoes on Banks Peninsula. I have provided more detailed information ahead. If you are at the Christchurch airport take route 1 to route 73 to route 75.

I will also cover taking Arthurs Pass to the West Coast in this next portion.

<u>Now back to </u>coming north from Geraldine to Christchurch.................
or reverse it and go south from Christchurch...

Look west over the Canterbury Plains and enjoy the tallest mountains in Australasia, the Southern Alps. You will drive through the vast farming region of the area across rivers known for their salmon runs and the Mt Hutt ski region. All through the region is fantastic scenery from mountain to coast along with all the attractions to go with it.

This area south from Christchurch on route 1 has many very fascinating locations. Route one goes through the Canterbury Plains that has been created over geological time by the erosion of the Southern Alps that dominate the skyline to the west. The Plains are heavily farmed mostly dairy. You will see giant watering devices stretching for miles bringing water to the farming district.

As you go north from the Geraldine turn off the next large community is Ashburton - http://www.ashburtondistrict.co.nz/ .

New Zealand is known world wide for its quality salmon fishing and the centre of attention is the Rakaia River. The Rakaia bridge, at 1.8km, is the southern hemisphere's longest bridge. The town's centre has a large salmon statue as its defining marker.

In late February you might want to get involved in the annual salmon fishing competition or maybe just go salmon fishing.The New Zealand salmon season runs from early October (spring) through to late April (autumn). This area offers superb angling conditions and good fishing for New Zealand chinook or quinnat, a species of Pacific salmon originally introduced from that area of the world 100 years ago. While the chinnook is now scarce along the Californian Pacific coast, it has thrived in New Zealand waters. A group of people from that area came to New Zealand recently to see the stock and were discussing the possibility of taking some back to rejuvenate the diminishing US population.

Here is where you stay in this part of the South Island whether fishing or not......Rakaia River Holiday Park – south of Christchurch

Robyn, Ross and Sam (our Border collie) welcome you to Rakaia River Holiday Park, located beside the Rakaia River, one of the best salmon fishing rivers in New Zealand.

We are sure to have something to fit your requirements and budget with our range of Accommodation facilities that include - Park Motels, Fisherman's Cottage, Backpacker Cabins, Onsite Caravans and Powered & Tent Sites. You will enjoy our sheltered powered sites and tent sites set amongst the trees.

You will find us only 40 minutes drive South of Christchurch, 20 minutes to Ashburton and 35 minutes to the Mt Hutt Ski area. In only 30 minutes you can drive to 5 beautiful and challenging golf courses. There is also a number of interesting nature walks in the area.

If its fishing you are after - there are salmon and trout in the river and Kawhai, Cod and other sea fishing only 10 minutes drive away. Our central location is an ideal base from which to explore the wonderful and varied Ashburton District, and our friendly relaxed environment assures you of a restful holiday in our sheltered riverside location.

Main South Road, Rakaia, South Island
Contact:
Phone: 0800 226772
Fax: + 64 3 302 7257
E-Mail: rrjackson@xtra.co.nz
Website: http://www.rakaiariverholidaypark.co.nz

A drive to the interior from Rakaia takes you to the **Mt Hutt/Methven** area -
http://www.destination.co.nz/methven/ Renowned for its winter recreation with skiing at Mt Hutt on what is considered the best lift and terrain mix in the South Island located on 472 hectares. All levels of skiers are provided for. Mt Hutt is a 90-minute drive from Christchurch and 35-minutes from Methven. Ski shuttles offer daily services to and from Methven and Mt Hutt is open seven days from 9am to 4pm.

The area also has a lot to offer the summer visitor such as one of the finest golf courses in New Zealand: Methven Golf Club. Just 40km northwest of Ashburton is Mt Somers surrounded by lakes and mountains. Mt Somers is a nature lover's and hiker's paradise with one of the top walks created by the Mt Somers Walkways Society.

And how about a ride on a **Aoraki Balloon Safari -** http://www.nzballooning.com/

They are recognized as a principle leader in the New Zealand tourism industry for innovation and an excellent record in Hot Air Ballooning adventures. The balloons are actually constructed at the Aerostar Factory in Sioux Falls, South Dakota.

Website: www.nzballooning.com

The central Canterbury Plains is the finest place in New Zealand for Hot Air Ballooning.

See the full 300km panorama of the entire Canterbury Plains including pristine views of Aoraki/Mt Cook and the Mt Cook National Park mountains by Mt Hutt ski field.

A unique way to enjoy New Zealand's rural heartland and the spectacular Southern Alps

Let our experienced pilots and ground crew take care of you on a fantastic skyward adventure. We are passionate about both hot air ballooning and the central Canterbury region and we look forward to sharing our knowledge and time with you ensuring a personal experience you will never forget.

Celebrate your time in a magical way, aboard a hot air balloon! Aoraki Balloon Safaris has been a part of many weddings with couples coming from all over the world to be married aboard a hot air balloon in Methven.

Contact:
Aoraki Balloon Safaris
Address: PO Box 75, Methven
 Phone: 03 302 8172
Email: aoraki@nzballooning.com

Off to Akaroa –

From the south direction first - Heading north on route one toward Christchurch at Burnham take the Ellsmere Junction Road to the right to the town of Lincoln and on to Tai Tapu turning right on route 75 to visit Akaroa & Banks Peninsula-

http://www.akaroa.com/fpnew/fastpage/fpengine.php/templateid/204

Akaroa is the historic French settlement formed following the violent eruptions of two volcanoes and is nestled in the heart of an ancient volcano. Akaroa remains unique as the only attempted settlement in 1840 by the French in New Zealand. Many streets have French names, and there are descendants of the original French families still living in Akaroa.

Explore the village with its colonial architecture, galleries, craft stores, and cafés. Relax or take part in the many activities that are on offer. Explore the dramatic outer bays and take your time to soak in the magic of this area. Here is where you can go visit the rare Hectors dolphin.

The Top Five Things to do in Akaroa
- ✓ Swim with the rare Hector's Dolphin
- ✓ Visit the Giant's House
- ✓ Taste Akaroa's French inspired cuisine
- ✓ Do one of the harbour cruises
- ✓ Visit the unique shops and galleries

Akaroa Harbour's Bays:

Scattered around Akaroa Harbour is a collection of tiny settlements: Barry's Bay, home to the famous Barry's Bay cheese factory; Duvauchelle with its historic hotel; and Takamatua, perfect for boating, fishing and swimming.

Eastern Bays

Banks Peninsula's Eastern Bays are popular summer retreats. French-settled Le Bons Bay has secluded accommodation and rare wildlife. Okains Bay is known for its museum, while Hickory Bay offers excellent surf.

Eastern Bays Information:

THE MAJORITY OF LAND IN THIS AREA IS PRIVATE FARMING LAND. IF YOU ENCOUNTER LIVESTOCK, LEAVE IT BE; IF YOU ENCOUNTER A GATE, LEAVE IT AS YOU FIND IT. DO NOT LIGHT FIRES AND DO NOT LITTER. FIND OUT BEFOREHAND WHETHER DOGS ARE PERMITTED IN THE AREA YOU ARE GOING. THE ROADS ARE NARROW, ROUGH AND HIGH. PLEASE KEEP YOUR SPEED DOWN, STAY TO THE LEFT WHERE POSSIBLE AND DRIVE CAUTIOUSLY.

South East Bays

Best accessed by walking the Banks Peninsula Track, Pohatu/Flea Bay, Stony Bay and Otanerito Bay offer a variety of natural attractions including excellent wildlife spotting and the spectacular Hinewai native bush reserve.

Southern Bays

Accessed by rough, narrow roads (recommended for 4WD vehicles only), Banks Peninsula's Southern Bays are secluded and tranquil. Peraki Bay is said to have been the first permanent European settlement in Canterbury. A great place to enjoy the isolation.

On to Christchurch from Akaroa -

From Akaroa you take route 75 to Christchurch. You drive by Lake Elsmere that has a very large population of waterfowl including a great many black swans.

It is 85 kilometres from Akaroa to Christchurch -
http://www.christchurch.org.nz/

On 22 February 2011, Christchurch was hit by a magnitude 6.3 earthquake followed by another on June 13 that sent the city to its knees. In spite of the earthquake, Christchurch is still the gateway to the South Island but much of the inner city has been laid bare. It is unknown how long it will be before the areas destroyed will be back open to tourism but still the majority of the city and area are functioning quite well but a lot of this listed will be gone or not been repaired or replaced but I will list them anyhow and when getting ready to visit you can check on the internet.

The English style city of Christchurch is the third largest in the country known for its parks and beautiful gardens having been given the award of the "Garden City of the World" winning over 620 international entries in an international competition. Central to the city is Hagley Park with almost 400 acres and the fabulous Botanic Gardens. If you visit here in February you will be able to see the annual Floral Festival in all its glory.

Cathedral Square, in the heart of the city, is where the majestic neogothic designed cathedral focuses the centre of attention. The cathedral has suffered greatly but all hopes are it will be restored. You will enjoy the more laid back lifestyle than other cities of this size. The river Avon provides the opportunity to sit and enjoy its grassy river banks and maybe a slow quiet boat ride through the area. My favourite is to take the tram through the city as an introduction to all it has to offer.

Christchurch History

Maori history has it that people first arrived over a thousand years ago. The first European landed in Canterbury in 1815 with whaling ships operating from the area by 1850.

The first English settlers, the founders of Christchurch, arrived in 1850-51 on the first ships into Lyttelton Harbour. Christchurch is the oldest established city in New Zealand with the Royal Charter granted in 1856. In 1893 New Zealand women achieved a first in the world when they won the right to vote. Seattle is a sister city to Christchurch.

What to See and Do in Christchurch

The Cultural Precinct – (make sure you check to see what is up and running by now after the earthquake devastation.)

Christchurch's Cultural Precinct where areas of culture and learning, entertainment, shopping, leisure, history and heritage can all be reached easily on foot or by historic tram.

Sites include: Art Gallery, Botanic Gardens, Provincial Chambers, Arts Centre, Canterbury Museum, i-site Visitor Centre, Christchurch Central Library, Christ's College, Cathedral.

The Precinct is easy to walk around, or you can travel by tram and hear stories about the area's history and personalities from a friendly tram driver.

Most Cultural Precinct activities are free.
Website: www.culturalprecinct.co.nz

-

The Arts Centre – www.artscentre.org.nz

Christchurch's hub of arts and crafts, featuring art galleries, craft studios and shops, theatres, cinemas, a selection of cafes, restaurants and bars and an exciting colourful weekend market and ethnic food fair. Lunchtime concerts feature every Friday and live music every weekend in summer.

This historic site was originally home to Canterbury University College, first established in 1873.

It includes many wonderful places of historic note, including the oldest lecture theatre in New Zealand and the centres latest attraction, "Father of the Atom", Ernest Lord Rutherford's Den. Open every day.

Cathedral Square Market

The Cathedral Square Market is located in the heart of the city, Cathedral Square. An outdoor market with stalls offering handcrafted and imported goods such as New Zealand wood-ware, handknitting, jewellery, pounamu, paua, bone carvings, possum fashions, sheepskins, clothing, healthcare products, sunglasses, t-shirts and much more. Grab something to eat at one of the food vendors and enjoy the atmosphere which makes the Square unique.

Open Wednesday to Saturday, 10am-4pm (with extra days for visiting Cruise Ships)

Centre of Contemporary Art – www.coca.org.nz

The largest selection and display of contemporary art can be found at 66 Gloucester Street in downtown Christchurch. Five galleries and over 60 exhibitions per annum will enable you to gain an in-depth understanding of both New Zealand and Cantabrian Contemporary Art.

Besides providing numerous specialised art services for members, the centre also hosts an extensive Open Gallery where hundreds of art works are on display and for sale by renowned New Zealand artists.

The Centre, established in 1880, is the oldest art institution in the Canterbury region.

Open Tuesday to Friday, 10am-5pm

Saturday and Sunday, 12pm-4pm (telephone for information about the Centre's lunch hour and city weekend tours)

Christchurch Art Gallery -
www.christchurchartgallery.org.nz

Located in the heart of the City's cultural precinct The Christchurch Art Gallery is the city's public art museum and is the home of Christchurch's public art collection, including international and New Zealand historical and contemporary pieces.

Christchurch Casino - www.chchcasino.co.nz

Christchurch Casino offers twenty four hour gaming entertainment to visitors to Christchurch. The casino has 428 gaming machines and a wide variety of Table Games including Blackjack, American Roulette, Mini Baccarat, Midi Baccarat, Tai Sai, Money Wheel and Caribbean Stud Poker as well as The Racing Game and Live Keno.

Christchurch Casino is centrally located and is easily accessible from all inner city hotels and motels. and is open 24 hours a day. You must be 20 years or over to enter Christchurch Casino, Restaurants or Bars. The Dress Code requires smart casual attire, no blue or black jeans. Free Shuttles operate to and from local hotels and motels each evening.

Christchurch Gondola - www.gondola.co.nz
Unique 360-degree panoramic views of Christchurch, the Canterbury Plains and Lyttelton Harbour unfold as you rise to the summit of Christchurch's famous extinct volcano. Visit the Heritage Time Tunnel Experience. The Christchurch Gondola Base Station is located 15 minutes drive from central Christchurch. Open daily, from 10am

Punting the Avon - www.christchurchnz.com
Sit back, relax and just drift along through parks and gardens, under shady trees and enjoy the tranquillity of your own punting journey on the Avon River. Each punt is custom-built, fully upholstered and comes complete with its own boatperson to do all the work. All you have to do is enjoy the ride.

Willowbank Wildlife Reserve - www.willowbank.co.nz
New Zealand's premiere wildlife park showing one of the most complete selections of native and introduced wildlife in their natural environment, as well as a wonderful farmyard and exotic display.
You can also enjoy the rare experience of New Zealand's largest and most unique daytime Kiwi viewing area. Willowbank places special emphasis on spacious surroundings and animal contact. Experience Wildlife by Night. See many of New Zealand's rare nocturnal animals and birds, including kiwis in their natural environment. Buffet dinner and BBQ lunches available. See the Maori experience at the Tamaki Heritage Village.
The park is open from 10am until 10pm daily

Orana Wildlife Park - www.oranawildlifepark.co.nz
Orana Wildlife Park is New Zealand's only open range zoo. The Park specialises in offering close up, exciting animal encounters: you can hand feed Giraffe, meet Rhino 'face-to-face'.

See the Cheetah sprint and experience the awesome Lion Encounter, which enables visitors to travel through the Lion Reserve.

Animal feeds occur throughout the day and a range of animals are displayed, including Monkeys, Meerkats, Otters, Porcupines and more. An extensive native collection features New Zealand's national icon, the Kiwi, Tuatara and a wide range of stunning birds and reptiles. Visitors can pet friendly domestic animals in the Farmyard.

Guided tours operate daily. Orana Wildlife Park is open every day of the week (except Christmas Day) from 10am - 5.00pm (last entry is 4.30pm).

Air Force Museum – www.airforcemuseum.co.nz

Discover one of the world's premier military aviation collections at the Air Force Museum of New Zealand; from aircraft, engines and assorted displays to medals, pin-ups and parachute-silk wedding dresses.

Check out the collection of classic aircraft, fly a simulator, take a guided tour and step back in time in a replica 1940's home. Your journey through the Air Force Museum of New Zealand will be something very special. Free admission by the way on your own or take one of the guided tours.

Christchurch Central City Lanes Walk: Lichfield Street

Christchurch's central city lanes and alleys, once home to many of Christchurch's early warehouses and factories, is now a thriving entertainment and retail precinct.

Stroll through the lanes and take in the variety of rich architecture, while enjoying some of Christchurch's best boutique shopping, restaurants and bars. (Let's hope it will be restored).

Clearwater Golf - www.clearwaternz.com

Home of the ING NZPGA Championship is the international resort standard, 18-hole golf course designed by John Darby in consultation with New Zealand golfing legend Sir Bob Charles. With a choice of five tee positions the course can be both challenging and enjoyable for players of all levels. Playable year-round, it is set amongst extensive lakes and clear-flowing streams, native fauna, grassland and native trees.

Clearwater is situated 15 minutes from the city centre and 7 minutes from Christchurch International Airport.

Ferrymead Heritage Park - www.ferrymead.org.nz

A bygone era come alive at Ferrymead Heritage Park. Ferrymead marks the site of the first New Zealand railway, which operated between the park and the city from 1863. Today the park comprises an Edwardian township and an exhibition area. Step back in time to experience the streets, buildings, fashions and transportation of colonial Christchurch.

Open daily, 10am-4.30pm.

Southern Encounter Aquarium and Kiwi House - www.southernencounter.co.nz

Located in the heart of Christchurch's Cathedral Square, Southern Encounter Aquarium & Kiwi House will take you on a journey of discovery to explore the splendour of the South Island's unique aquatic wildlife as well as lively NZ Kiwi, Tuatara and native Geckos.

Over 120 different species are displayed including Sharks, Rays, massive Eels, Seahorses, Octopus, Blue Freshwater Crayfish and much more. Visitors can view native freshwater fish set in a simulated glow worm grotto, stroll across the swing bridge for views over the facility and enjoy a range of short wildlife films in the theatre.

Scheduled feeds enable visitors to either feed the fish or observe aquarists interacting with marine creatures.

Southern Encounter is open daily (except Christmas Day) from 9.00am until 5.00pm. Kiwi are on display from 10.30am until 4.30pm.

Yaldhurst Museum of Transport and Science -
www.yaldhurstmuseum.co.nz

Set in the grounds of the original homestead of 1876, the museum is just 20 minutes from the city centre. View over 100 vehicles, from horse and buggy to classic cars, printing presses to fire engines, racing cars to military displays. First turn right past Yaldhurst Hotel on Main West Road Christchurch (close to Christchurch International Airport). The Museum is open every day (except Christmas Day) 10am to 5pm

Tranz Scenic Unique Train Journeys -
www.tranzscenic.co.nz

Travelling around New Zealand by train is enjoyable. From the Overlander to the world famous TranzAlpine you get to experience a new dimension than usual. One of my favourite trips in the country.

Two spectacular South Island unique train rides including the TranzAlpine, rated one of the top six journeys in the world. Travels daily from Christchurch to Greymouth on the West Coast through the massive Southern Alps.

The TranzCoastal travels daily between Christchurch to the port of Picton where it connects with the InterIslander. The journey travels along the rugged Pacific Ocean on one side and the steep mountains on the other.

Black Cat Cruises - www.blackcat.co.nz
Christchurch Wildlife Cruises: Discover one of the world's rarest and smallest dolphins - the Hector's Dolphin just 15 minutes from central Christchurch. You will see significant Lyttelton sites including those of the early Maori and European settlers as well as Little Blue Penguins, coastal marine birdlife and other natural wildlife.
Island Adventures: Lyttelton Harbour is home to two islands: Ripapa Island Historic Reserve and Quail Island – both of which have an incredible link to Canterbury's past.

International Antarctic Centre – www.iceberg.co.nz
This is a must see!!!!!!
The World's Best Antarctic Attraction – Quite a unique experience not to be missed. Christchurch is the world's gateway to the Antarctic and has been proudly associated with the Antarctic since the early heroic era and has twice **been voted the best attraction in NZ.** It is a fun interactive and hands on experience the whole family will enjoy. The outdoor Antarctic Hägglund Ride is a "must do" and a visit to the penguins. Right by the Christchurch airport the attraction is open seven days a week.
So let's hope the city of Christchurch comes back stronger than ever from the disaster that has occurred.....and by the time you are reading this book you will be able to plan time to enjoy the city.

Now let's do the Arthurs Pass from Christchurch to the West Coast:

This is considered one of the most scenic drives is the country. Several choices as to how best be able to do this route such as from the north you may come down on either the East Coast or the West Coast and then across or you may wish to continue along the East Coast after Christchurch and go on around to the West Coast from the south and come up to Arthurs. It really all depends upon your time and schedule to be able to fit it in. Then you have the choice of getting to Christchurch and taking the train ride across and back so you can begin your vehicle holiday after that.

Arthur's Pass National Park –
http://www.newzealand.com/travel/destinations/nationa l-parks/arthurs-pass/arthurs-pass.cfm

The drive in the middle of the South Island through the Arthur's Pass National Park is one of the best in the world. The road is good so don't worry about that rental camper van making it. We have crossed it numerous times in our 7 metre bus with no dramas. Make sure you stop at the lookout of the Otira Gorge where the view is spectacular along with the cheeky Kea's that hang out there vying for your attention. take the detour to **Lake Brunner** for a visit if you got time....... this is one top trout lake.

Arthur's Pass is a real get-away destination in any season. Close to a selection of top ski areas, tiny Arthur's Pass Village is also the base for a range of walks in the Arthur's Pass National Park, and offers spectacular alpine isolation for anyone wanting to really get away from it all!

Top Five Things to do along the Arthur's Pass Highway, New Zealand
- ✓ Check out the Otira Gorge bridge
- ✓ Take one of the short walks available in the park
- ✓ Visit the historic Jackson's Pub
- ✓ Catch the TranzScenic - one of the world's top train journeys
- ✓ Visit Lake Brunner and maybe go trout fishing

Top Ten Short & Half-Day Walks in Arthur's Pass, New Zealand

1. Millenium Walk
2. Devil'sPunchbowl Waterfall
3. Bealey Valley (half-day)
4. Dobson Nature Walk
5. Bridal Veil
6. Otira Valley (half-day)
7. Village Historic Walk
8. Temple Basin (half-day)
9. Cockayne Nature Walk
10. Old Coach Road

Visit the Department of Conservation website more information on Arthur's Pass walks>>

Otira Gorge

So I have taken you on all the primary roads and some secondary ones that will provide you with the best in the scenic wonders of New Zealand, the tops in accommodation, the exciting activities for the most adventuresome to the laid back. We have visited cafes and restaurants and sipped exquisite wines at their sources and eaten the fresh food on offer.

We have seen the historic elements of what made New Zealand what it is and immersed into the world of the Maori culture. For the animal lovers I have pointed out where to find everything from whales to kiwis to a plethora of animals that enjoy the woods and streams of this country. You have been introduced to isolated beaches and walks into pristine wilderness, wild rivers and lakes and the majestic Southern Alps.

I have provided you the opportunity to meet and enjoy the people and explore the cities and villages of New Zealand. It is a magic world of beauty and spectacular wonder. Please enjoy.

End of the Journey

Now I am going to list **important websites and information** you can use to further enhance your knowledge of traveling around New Zealand.

Major Points of Interest in New Zealand

Everybody has an opinion but what I have tried to do is point out the places that I think are uniquely New Zealand. Unless you have a long time don't expect to get to all of them.

From the Far North to Wellington:

Cape Reinga Lighthouse at the very top
Ninety Mile Beach
The Dunes in the Far North
Waitangi Treaty Grounds
Bay of Islands
Tane Mahuta(God of the Forest)
Auckland – Sky Tower, Kelly Tarlton Underwater World
Coromandel Peninsula
Waitomo Caves
Billy Black's Woodland Park
Rotorua
White Island
Mt Taranaki
Wellington – Cuba Street

South Island:

Marlborough Sounds
West Coast (from top to bottom)**
Punakaiki Pancake Rocks
Glaciers**
Kaikoura Whale Watch**
Lewis Pass
Hanmer Springs
Akaroa
Arthurs Pass
Mount Cook*
Mackenzie Country
Oamaru Blue Penguins*
Moeraki Boulders
Dunedin
Milford Sound**
Queenstown*

List of useful New Zealand websites:
http://www.newzealand.com/travel/sights-activities/events-calendar/new-zealand-events-calendar-home.cfm - Festivals
http://www.nztourmaps.com/ - the best map site
http://www.leadingattractions.co.nz - free map and attractions
http://www.pricewatch.co.nz/ - petrol prices in New Zealand
www.bluebridge.co.nz - Bluebridge ferry
http://www.tourism.net.nz/tours/bus-and-coach-tours/index.html - bus tours
Theme parks (children) -
http://www.nzs.com/travel/attractions/theme-and-leisure-parks/region.html

Motorcycles/bicycles –
http://www.nzs.com/travel/attractions/theme-and-leisure-parks/region.html
http://www.dropbears.com/bikelinks/Clubs/NZ_Clubs/
http://www.naturalhigh.co.nz/index.html (bicycles)
http://www.eventfinder.co.nz/festivals/events/new-zealand - Festivals
Rugby Museum -
http://www.rugbymuseum.co.nz/default.asp?level1=Home
NZ Rugby - http://www.rugby.co.nz/
www.truenz.co.nz/horsetrekking/
www.travelsuperlink.com/airtravel
http://www.truenz.co.nz/farmstays/

Here is a list of restaurant websites:
http://www.menumania.co.nz/
http://www.eatout.co.nz/
http://www.dineout.co.nz/
http://www.menus.co.nz/
http://www.experiencenz.com/New-Zealand-Restaurants/
http://www.reservecuisine.co.nz/
http://www.entertainmentnz.com/
http://www.queenstown-nz.co.nz/information/WineandDine/
http://forum.time2dine.co.nz/christchurch-restaurants/

<u>Accommodation websites:</u>
www.aatravel.co.nz
www.bnbnz.com
http://www.nzcamping.co.nz/

North Island towns websites:
Auckland - http://www.aucklandnz.com/
Whangarei - http://www.whangareinz.org.nz/
Warkworth - http://www.warkworth-information.co.nz/
Orewa - http://www.orewa-beach.co.nz/
Dargaville - http://communities.co.nz/Dargaville/Index.cfm
Whangaparaoa - http://www.whangaparaoanz.com/index.html
Hamilton - http://www.hamiltoninfo.co.nz/
Tauranga - http://www.tauranga.co.nz /

Coromandel Peninsula - http://www.thecoromandel.com/
Rotorua - http://www.rotoruanz.com/

Taupo - www.laketauponz.com/
Gisborne - www.gisbornenz.com/

Napier - www.napier.nz.com/

Hastings - http://www.hawkesbaynz.com/hastings_new_zealand.htm

Masterton - http://www.cityofmasterton.co.nz/
New Plymouth - www.windwand.co.nz/
Wanganui - www.wanganui.com/

Wellington - www.wellingtonnz.com/

Hokianga area -
Hokianga - http://www.hokianga.co.nz/
Waipoua Forest - http://www.doc.govt.nz/templates/PlaceProfile.aspx?id=34423
Kauri Museum - http://www.kauri-museum.com/

South Island:

Picton/Blenheim/Marlborough:
http://www.marlboroughsounds.co.nz/
http://www.marlborough.co.nz/
http://www.picton.co.nz/
http://www.cityofblenheim.co.nz/
http://www.wine-marlborough.co.nz/home.htm
http://www.winesofmarlborough.co.nz/
http://www.kaikourawhalewatching.com/
http://www.naturetours.co.nz
http://www.cougarlinecruises.co.nz
http://www.mail-boat.co.nz
http://www.mailboat.co.nz

Nelson/Able Tasman/Golden Bay:
The Buller Gorge Swing Bridge -
http://www.bullergorge.co.nz/
http://www.nelsonnz.com/
http://www.abeltasman.co.nz/
http://www.nelsonnz.com/nelson/golden.bay

West Coast:
http://www.west-coast.co.nz/
www.glaciercountry.co.nz
http://www.hokitika.com/
http://www.westport.org.nz/
http://www.adventuretours.co.nz/rafting/index.html
rafting
http://www.geocities.com/dropmeoff/Greymouth/
http://www.discover-new-zealand.co.uk/haast/
www.pukekura.co.nz - sandfly town of two

Kaikoura
www.kaikoura.co.nz
www.whalewatch.co.nz

Lake Tekapo -
http://www.winterpark.co.nz/pages/33/hot-pools.htm

Wanaka -
http://www.lakewanaka.co.nz/index.cfm/Home
http://www.warbirds.co.nz/shows.htm (Warbirds Show)

Queenstown:
www.glenorchy.co.nz
www.queenstown.co.nz
http://www.everythingqueenstown.com/
www.dartstables.com/

Te Anau/Southern Route:
www.fiordland.co.nz
http://www.realjourneys.co.nz/Main/Doubtful/
http://www.mitrepeak.com/ (Mitre Peak Cruises - Milford)
http://www.redboats.co.nz/home/
http://homepages.ihug.co.nz/~bobm/manapouri/Manapouri.html
www.riverton-aparima.co.nz
http://www.southernscenicroute.co.nz/
http://www.doubtful-sound.com/ (Deep Cove Charters)

Invercargill:
www.invercargill.org.nz/

Bluff/Stewart Island:
http://www.bluff.co.nz/
http://www.stewartisland.co.nz/
http://www.bluffoysterfest.co.nz/?menu=home.about

The Catlins:
http://www.catlins-nz.com/

Dunedin:
www.dunedinnz.com/
www.albatross.org.nz
www.wildlife.co.nz - Monarch Cruises
www.arthurstours.co.nz

Oamaru:
http://www.visitoamaru.co.nz/
www.penguins.co.nz
http://www.moerakiboulders.com/ (Moeraki Boulders)

Timaru:
http://www.southisland.org.nz/timaru.asp

Central Otago:
http://www.centralotago.net.nz/
http://www.otagocentralrailtrail.co.nz/ (Biking Rail Trail)
http://www.cavalcade.co.nz/ (Gold Trail cavalcade)
http://www.maniototo.co.nz/ranfurly.htm (Art Deco Town)
http://www.maniototo.co.nz/naseby.htm (town of Naseby)
http://www.nzsouth.co.nz/centralotago/curling.html (New Zealand Curling)
http://www.dreamofkiwi.com/alexandra/index.php (town of Alexandra)

Mt Cook/Mckenzie Country:
www.mtcooknz.com
http://www.tourism.org.nz/regions/mt-cook.html
http://www.hermitage.co.nz/
www.aorakialpinelodge.co.nz/accommodation.htm

Christchurch:
www.christchurch.org.nz/
www.tranzalpine.com   (8:15am -6:05pm Britmart
Railway Station $130)
www.iceberg.co.nz - Antarctic Centre
www.tram.co.nz - Chch tram
www.artscentre.org.nz - Chch arts centre
www.christchurchartgallery.org.nz
www.festivalofflowers.co.nz - (Chch Festival 22 Feb-
1March)
www.akaroa.com

Hanmer Springs :
www.hanmersprings.co.nz
www.thrillseekerscanyon.co.nz
www.hanmerhorses.co.nz

Murchison:
http://www.tourism.net.nz/region/nelson/nelson---
murchison-and-maruia/

The Five Great Walking Tracks:
North Island
1. Tongariro Alpine Crossing -
This walk will take around 7-9 hours. It is a 18.5 km walk the
length of Mt. Tongariro starting from the Mangeteopo Valley.
This is a great North Island walk.
http://www.nationalpark.co.nz

2. Lake Waikaremoana Track -
Do you like to fish or swim? This is the place. The Te Urewera
National Park has over 650 species of native plants along with
native birds. It is 46km, around a 4 to 6 day tramp of moderate
level following the lake shore mostly.
http://lakelodge.co.nz/walkingtracks.html

South Island

3. Heaphy Track -

For those quite fit this is the longest DOC walk. It is in the Kahurangi National Park and is 82km long taking around 4 to 6 days to complete. Home to the great spotted Kiwi and a host of other wildlife. You can enjoy views of the rugged West Coast, forest and tussocks and a couple of ancient settlements dating from the 13th 14th century.

http://www.heaphytrack.com

4. Routeburn Track -

From Lake Wakitipu (Queenstown area) it is a moderately easy walk 32km about 3 days through the Mt Aspiring and Fiordland National Parks.

http://www.ultimatehikes.co.nz

5. Milford Track -

An impressive 53.5km for 4 days this walk features waterfalls, scenic mountains. It is for moderately fit walkers.

http://www.milfordtrack.co.nz

New Zealand Camping Grounds

Numerous campgrounds of a very high standard are found throughout the country. Almost all campgrounds offer full kitchen facilities, BBQ areas, TV lounges, Internet connection as well as washing machines and dryers.

Visitors are impressed by the cleanliness of shower and toilet blocks and the comprehensive facilities on offer. Campgrounds are often in scenic locations and the management is always happy to assist with information on local attractions and sightseeing.

It is recommended to book ahead during the New Zealand school holidays in December and January to ensure a powered site.

The majority all provide cabin and motel facilities for those seeking quality accommodation at a decent price.

Rainforest Retreat – Franz Josef

Camper vans/car rental.....which one do I choose?

Here are the ones I have provided for hundreds of visitors now for years and feel very confident in saying you will get top quality camper vans without hidden costs and value for money.

My major comment to everyone is you are about to spend a lot of hard earned dollars to come a very long way to be able to experience and appreciate one of the finest natural places on earth. The one place where you should not try to save is on the camper van you plan to use. The heartache, hardships and time lost is always attributed to the failure of the vehicle one uses to go around the country.

New Zealand has extremely well maintained roads but it is a country where 80-90% of the travel is on mountainous terrain with twists and turns everywhere. Hardly a flat straight road anywhere especially where the traveler wishes to go. The roads in the mountainous regions that twist and turn are also have very steep valleys along side. One does not need to be told how it feels to have a safe vehicle when moving along these areas.

Most of it is quite remote also and a breakdown can be a long time consuming problem.

For instance I had brakes go out in Milford Sound. It was two days of harassment getting back out of there...........not to mention the 2 weeks it took to get back on the road (but this was my own bus so the time of delay wouldn't be the same).

Here is the list of the top ones I have culled out after years booking vehicles for visitors:

Don't forget I create you a personal itinerary _free_ when you book your rental vehicle through me.

1. KEA - http://nz.campers.com

2. Wendekreisen -
http://www.wendekreisen.co.nz/default.aspx

3. Jucy - www.jucy.co.nz

4.Backpacker - www.backpackercampervans.co.nz
5. Britz – www.britz.co.nz
6. Maui - www.maui.co.nz
7. Walkabout - www.walkaboutrentals.co.nz
8. Abuzzy – http://www.abuzzy.com/
9. Pacific Horizon – http://www.pacifichorizon.co.nz/
10. Freedom/Tui - http://www.freedomcampers.co.nz/

The following car rental companies:

1. Ace – http://www.acerentalcars.co.nz/
2. Pegasus – http://www.rentalcars.co.nz/
3. Apex - http://www.nzrentalcar.co.nz/

Ron's Rave Restaurant Reviews

South Island –

Christchurch
Pescatore (at the George)*
Annies Wine Bar
Hay's Restaurant* (for lamb)
Canterbury Tales

Akaroa
Cest la Vie
Harbour 71

Oamaru
Bean
Hotel Brydon

Dunedin
Bell Pepper Blues*
Plato
Bacchus

Te Anau
Redcliff

Queenstown
Amisfield*
Gantleys

Arrowtown
Saffron
The Stables

Gibbston Valley
Winehouse
Gibbston Valley Wines

Wanaka
Missy's Kitchen

Kaikoura
Hislops

North Island -

Rotorua
Bistro 1284

Taupo
Pimentos
The Bach

Napier
Provedore
Pacifica

Martinborough
French Bistro

Wellington
Matterhorn
Logan Brown
Maria Pia's
The White House
Monsoon Poon

Some food and drink winter festivals

Manawatu Wine & Food Festival – www.mwff.co.nz
Matariki Gourmet Hangi & Concert– www.rmtyc.org
Cadbury Chocolate Carnival–
www.chocolatecarnival.co.nz
The Food Show Auckland– www.foodshow.co.nz
Wellington on a Plate– www.wellingtononaplate.com
BrewNZ & Beer Awards–
www.brewersguild.org.nz/beervana

Upcoming Festivals for Jan/February –

World Buskers Festival (Christchurch) –
www.worldbuskersfestival.com
Adam Chamber Music Festival (Nelson) –
www.music.org.nz
Sculpture on the Gulf (Waiheke Island) –
www.sculptureonthegulf.co.nz
Auckland Seafood Festival – www.aucklandseafood-
festival.co.nz
Positively Pasifica Festival (Wellington) –
www.niufm.com
22nd Annual Crankup (vintage machinery) Invercargill –
www.edendalevmc.com
New Zealand Fringe Festival (Wellington) –
www.wellingtonnz.com
Waiheke Wine Festival – www.waihekewinefestival.co.nz
Festivals continued:

Kawhia Kai Festival – top Maori experience(King Country)
– www.kawiakaifestival.co.nz
Harvest Hawke's Bay – www.harvesthawkesbay.co.nz
Marlborough Wine Festival – (Blenheim)- www.wine-
marlborough-festival.co.nz
Te Matatini National Haka Festival – (Tauranga) –
www.festival.tematatini.co.nz
Art Deco Weekend (Napier) – www.artdeconapier.com
Festival of Flowers – (Christchurch) –
www.festivalofflowers.co.nz
Devonport Wine And Food Festival (Auckland) –
www.devonportwinefestival.co.nz
Cuba Street Carnival – (Wellington) –
www.cubacarnival.org.nz

Winter Events:

Arts/Music –

Te Papa – www.tepapa.govt.nz
Sky City Theatre Auckland – www.skycityauckland.co.nz
Auckland International Film Festival —
www.aucklandnz.com
Wellington Film Festival –www.WellingtonNZ.com
  Taranaki International Festival of Arts –
www.artsfest.co.nz
Christchurch Art Festival –www.artsfestival.co.nz
Bay of Islands Jazz and Blues Festival –www.jazz-
blues.co.nz
Hastings Blossom Festival –www.hastings.co.nz
World of Wearable Art (Wellington) –
www.WellingtonNZ.com

Food and Wine Festivals –

Bluff Oyster Festival –www.bluffoysterfest.co.nz
Hot Red Hawke's Bay Wine Expo –
www.winehawkesbay.co.nz
Cadbury Chocolate Carnival –
www.chocolatecarnival.co.nz
Whitianga Scallop Festival – www.scallopfestival.co.nz
Hawke's Bay Olive Festival –www.telegraphhill.co.nz
Havelock Mussel Festival –
www.havelockmusselfestival.co.nz/

Mussel Eating Contest – Havelock Festival

<u>**Sports Events –**</u>
<u>**Rugby**</u> — www.allblacks.com
<u>**Netball**</u> – www.netballnz.co.nz
<u>**Basketball**</u>– www.basketball.org.nz
<u>**Horse Racing**</u> – www.nzracing.co.nz
<u>**Catlins Great Escape**</u> – www.catlins.org.nz

check also on http://www.eventfinder.co.nz/
and my website – www.ronlaughlin.net
So I have tried to get as much information to you as I can based upon my personal knowledge I picked up travelling my adopted country and one I truly love and respect.

I suppose I could just keep spouting on about a lot of areas I have not really covered well and much more about the ones I have but maybe later.
If you get to discover and appreciate what I have given you to check out it will fill a lifetime of pure pleasure for you as it has mine.

I have over 10,000 photographs I took on my sojourn through this world of New Zealand and had a hard time not adding hundreds to these pages. It is a photographer's heaven if you love nature.

So I guess all I can say now is _do_ take the time in your life to come here and experience one of nature's wonderland. The place and the people are special and I want to help everyone share this in their life....

Don't forget if you want a personal itinerary and help with your trip please get in touch.

With love and respect to all who visit our shores and those who are already here,

Ron Laughlin
New Zealand Travel Guide
www.ronlaughlin.net

So.................as an ancient American TV game show I remember from the past the host always said.......................

Come on down!!!!!

Be sure to check out the travel videos I have on YouTube – All 22 videos - http://www.youtube.com/profile?user=newzealandtraveler#g/u

List of book's Information

South Island

8465345R00208

Printed in Great Britain
by Amazon.co.uk, Ltd.,
Marston Gate.